THE MAN WITH HIS HEAD IN THE CLOUDS

Also by Richard O. Smith

Oxford Student Pranks: A History of Mischief and Mayhem

Britain's Most Eccentric Sports

As Thick As Thieves: Foolish Felons and Loopy Laws

THE MAN WITH HIS HEAD IN THE CLOUDS

JAMES SADLER:
The First Englishman to Fly

Richard O. Smith

Signal Books
Oxford

First published in 2014 by
Signal Books Limited
36 Minster Road
Oxford OX4 1LY
www.signalbooks.co.uk

A catalogue record for this book is available from the British Library

ISBN 978-1-909930-01-8 Cloth

Cover Design: Baseline Arts, Oxford
Typesetting: Tora Kelly
Cover Images: Baseline Arts, Oxford; Wikimedia Commons
Half Title Image: Sadler flies in Nottingham, 8 November 1813

Printed and bound in Great Britain by TJ International Ltd, Cornwall

CONTENTS

PROLOGUE: THE END?

They say being on death row clarifies the mind. They also say that the footsteps of a dead man walking emit no sound - although that could be because they've just had death row carpeted.

60 seconds and counting...

I am facing death in public and no one is offering me a blindfold, cigarette or last meal. Usually when a firing squad ties you to a pole, it is probably a good time to start thinking about life insurance. I haven't got life insurance. Maybe I should ring a call centre and spend my last few seconds on earth listening to someone with a Geordie accent read through the small print of an insurance policy that I - or rather my widow - will be able to claim on within sixty seconds of taking out the cover.

50 seconds...

This is the most terrifying thing I have ever encountered. Forget screeching dentists' drills or imagined monsters stalking my childhood bedroom or that time I gave a bus driver a £50 note.

40 seconds...

I am a cliché whirling into life. My whole existence is flashing before me. I never thought this literally happens when you are about to die. Yet there I am, the only cinema-goer in a big screen multiplex watching an edited compilation package of my own, admittedly rather average it transpires, life. That time I wet myself at Amanda Jones' fifth birthday party. (Why did that scene make the cut? Who edited this?) I can see myself, asking my mother for a pound in order to buy her a birthday present - and then spending it on an action man accessory. There is a parade of characters and suddenly recalled experiences competing for airtime. All represent the cluttered colours of my life.

30 seconds...

Hang on, my life has actually been alright, pretty good even, on this quickly flicked highlights package. What an inconvenient time to make that discovery, when I'm just about to die pointlessly in an Oxfordshire field. The worst possible time to make that breakthrough, I can tell you - as it's all too late now.

20 seconds...

Admittedly, I may have worried about a lot of stuff that never happened, carried the imagined weight of irrelevant burdens. Why did I worry so much? Waste such precious time-on-earth anxious about petty imagined dangers, ruminated fears, when I could have saved it up for this? A situation that really needs worrying about.

15 seconds...

Look, I know I have been quite rude about the world in the past. But I've just discovered that I really, really do want to live now. Please can I live? I promise to be good.

10 seconds…

Hi God. Yes, I'm aware it's been several decades since we last spoke. I have been busy though - well, you'd probably know that, what with the omnipotence. No, don't make that face. Anyway, in the statistically unlikely occurrence that a supernatural deity exists outside human comprehension, rather than an inevitable artificial construct of a guilt-induced afterlife expectation to offset nihilism, please save me from my upcoming certain death. Amen. Cheers.

9 seconds…

It was worth praying. After all, that's the potent appeal of religion. Join most organisations or societies and they'll present you with an introductory free pen, windscreen de-icer or Amazon gift voucher. Join a religion and you're offered everlasting eternal life. That's a hard sell to compete with.

8 seconds…

Just in case you didn't catch that last sentiment, God: I REALLY WANT TO LIVE NOW, OK?

7 seconds…

Memories. There's space on my hard drive to download a lot more from life. So stop the countdown. Please stop. It seems to have stopped. Flooded with relief, I feel like a soldier surviving a war. They'll be no more…

6 seconds…

Oh B*^&*%$*&! How could I think that? The countdown is appearing slower as an illusion. Like a car crash, everything appears to slow down before the moment of impact.

5 seconds…

Of course there were girls I kissed whom I shouldn't have, and girls I didn't kiss whom I definitely should have. Emotion rises within, swelling up like the hot air inflating a balloon, causing a geezer burst of tears. I try and shape words out of these emotions, wanting to reveal my love for my partner. Without a blindfold I am able to see my wife is playing with her phone, smirking at a text message from a friend. I call out my wife's name with honest affection. "Er… can it wait a minute… texting," she replies. Insensitively.

4 seconds…

Time for some profound words. Final words, simply by an accident of time, can become gilded with an undeserved poignancy. Rendered significant merely by being the last words you ever drew breath to orate. There is also that tense expectancy to make one's final words profound. And then, once you've uttered them, you are forced to remain silent. There's no point in superseding profound grandiloquence as your chosen final utterance, only to remark ten minutes later: "Could I have another glass of water?"

3 seconds...

I wish I hadn't got so attached to the world as I'm not ready to leave it yet. The world is like a pet that dies too young. Oh God, I'm actually leaving the world. So long, world - thanks for the good times, and frankly your bad times weren't that bad. I know that now. It's my sort of world, the earth, and I'm sure I can be happy here. If I'm given another chance, I promise to be reformed, better with my time. I won't leave toilet rolls unchanged or expect someone else to clear up the crumbs near the toaster. I won't stare at my wife's younger sister anymore, even if we go on holiday again and she insists on wearing that tiny bikini (which, you have to admit, was odd for a Helsinki city break). I'll get a direct debit done for Oxfam. No, I will.

2 seconds...

Allow me to share, as my final words, a thought on humanity. My observation is a positive one. Being this close to death has provided me with some good news to share: the compulsion to tell someone in your final moments that you love them is far stronger than the instinct to tell someone you hate them. That's why passengers on doomed hijacked planes leave messages of love on answer phones. No one rings up that bloke they work with in HR called Dave to inform him: "I just called to say I always thought you were a twat."

1 second...

Trying to compose myself now in order to step out of the world and disappear for ever. We're all admitted into the world with that same pre-determined plot ending hanging over us. The agreement is, that by accepting life you simultaneously hereby accept to one day leave it, to disappear for ever, as the waters close quickly about you. Well, I never signed anything agreeing to that.

0 seconds... Countdown completed. We have lift-off.

I hear a terrifying loud noise.

BANG!

And with that sound, my soul starts to drift upwards to heaven.

"Basket-case!" says my wife. And then everyone's faces fold into laughter.

You see, that's funny. Perhaps cruel, but undeniably funny, because I'm standing in a basket. And having a breakdown - a breakdown that is entirely justified in my view.

We have lift-off. I am taking my first ever balloon flight and suffer from crippling acrophobia - that's a fear of heights to you and me. I've never seen, nor imagined, anything this terrifying before.

And yet I am trusting my continued existence to a fifty-foot plastic inverted teardrop. As we inch above the ground I am in a full-on state of fight or flight emotional arousal - my brain ordering my heart to palpitate like someone's kicking a bass drum pedal inside my chest cavity. My palms trickle sweat. Fear fibrillates throughout my body

I want one of the last things I see to be my wife's face. She's smiling. An image I frame in my memory. She's come to watch me take-off with Sofia - a friend's five-year-old daughter, not the capital of Bulgaria. I feel a sense of handing over to the younger generation. Her smile is to be the last thing I ever see, like those heart-scarring final messages left on answer phones from doomed victims. Then, although you never really want an enjoyable book or movie to end any more than you wish a fulfilling life to end, at least that would make a satisfactory final scene: my wife's smile before the final fade to permanent terminal blackness.

Also I want her to be happy and meet someone else. Judging by her reactions to the texts, she probably already has.

Right, I'm off to die now. And it only cost me £125.

INTRODUCTION: SADLER AND ME

James Sadler was born in Oxford some time in February 1753. It was a dark (obviously) though not necessarily stormy night. And they say historical biographies never start with opening lines like that anymore.

This attempt at historical biography does not even try to escape convention as it tells Sadler's story via a chronological narrative. Also, in common with historical biographies, the subject dies at the end - I know, spoiler alert! Why do all historical biographies insist on the same sad ending? This conventional narrative approach to structuring a life is perhaps particularly necessary in the case of the category-defying, amorphous and highly unconventional existence that James Sadler lived.

Sadler has become undeservedly forgotten. This was not someone joyriding on the back of the age's discovered advancements, then merely popularising them. Sadler's legacy is that he showed scientific progress could be hacked for the masses. Throughout his lifetime, Britain was the opposite of a meritocracy; he was often dismissed in accounts of the period as "that pastry cook from Oxford". His name became extinguished, uncommemorated by history, perhaps because he was outcast by both the military (Royal Navy) and the establishment (Oxford University). No one else got to write the history at the time.

My achievements compared to Sadler are on a 1:100,000 scale. But I am determined to give back to Sadler the reputation that somehow went missing in the nineteenth and twentieth centuries, gleaming and polished for the twenty-first century. Frankly, no definitive list of Great Britons is complete without James Sadler's name. Moreover, that immodest "Great" prefix in Britain's name would hardly have been justified without practical visionaries like Sadler - although countries that insist on having an adjective in their nation's name are usually deluded (see anywhere misleadingly clinging to the word "Democratic").

The *Oxford Dictionary of National Biography* issues a clear warning to anyone contemplating writing a biography of James Sadler; here's how his entry ends: "Sadler's life was of deeds, not words, and left great problems for any biographer." In other words: "Expect to encounter huge problems due to lack of research sources." Or to précis that sentiment down to one word: "Don't!"

Perhaps Sadler's is a life destined to be captured in silhouette rather than a full-on portrait. Some of the unvarnished truths of this life are hard to discover - newspaper articles of the age provide most of the testimony that establishes his achievements, but these are from unchecked sources, and they always ensure he is the hero of any reported adventures. Bordering on hagiography, reports of the time ensured Sadler's name always appeared attached to superlatives.

Yet Sadler, son of another Oxford pastry cook also confusingly called James Sadler (1718-1791), achieved undeniable greatness. And it is possible to call character witnesses from the age who are prepared to testify as much. John Southern confirms in his *Treatise upon Aerostatic Globes*, published in 1785, that Sadler invented the gas cistern, preferring to use his own reciprocals instead of casks. In his (also) 1785 book *The History and Practice of Aerostation*, written within a year of Sadler's first historical flight, author Tiberius Cavallo credits Sadler as "the sole projector, architect, workman and chemist in this experiment".

Sadler was the first Englishman to do what I am attempting to do: fly in a balloon. In fact, he was the first Englishman to fly by any method (falling doesn't count). Thus it is difficult to comprehend why a once ubiquitous household name such as his should become so little known today - given that his accomplishments still resonate with a contemporary interest in aviation. Even the brightest stars one day collapse, and Sadler's name emits virtually no light today.

Balloon enthusiast and publicity addict Richard Branson authored a surprisingly readable 350-page love letter to the pioneers of flight, *Reach for the Skies*. A quick index consultation will confirm that James Sadler, who invented the whole concept in Branson's home nation, gains exactly zero mentions. Author Richard Holmes' fine and mighty bookshelf-buckling 2013 tome *Falling Upwards: How We Took to the Air*, specifically about eighteenth-century aeronauts, does not include a single reference in the index to James Sadler on any of its fact-filled 416 pages. This is akin to writing a book about the Second World War without mentioning Germany.

I have a particular reason why I want to tell James Sadler's story. In an age when celebrity status is awarded to people who enter televised talent contests or reality shows, it can be reassuring to retreat to an era when people had to accomplish something worthwhile to be garlanded with such status. Socrates defined celebrity as "the perfume of heroic deeds", which is worth remembering, the next time someone from a scripted reality TV show achieves vast media coverage by strategically offering waiting photographers a willing knickers-flash when getting out of a car. Much of our modern media's attention is focused on the famous, with especial relish reserved for those broken by fame.

And yet Sadler earned his celebrity status at a time when society rewarded individuals with its attention for genuine acts of derring-do. Not many people would be known by their face in the late eighteenth century, except perhaps the King. Yet engravings of Sadler were big-selling, mass-produced items. Even rarer for a celebrity of the age were his origins. To become a household name without education or breeding was exceptionally uncommon, and undeniably added to his appeal with the masses. The "it could be you too" appeal is a probable explanation for the otherwise mystifying obsession with today's sad parade of celebrated vacuous non-entities. Sadler's origins were humble, but his achievements were the opposite.

He soared upwards into what were then wholly mysterious and uncharted skies, rumoured to be inhabited by roaming sky dragons. Try persuading a hot air balloon pilot today to take off in a gale and then reach 13,000 feet. Yet that is something Sadler fearlessly accomplished by himself. John Hodgson observed in his 1924 book *History of Aeronautics in Great Britain*: "It may in justice be added that Sadler's many severe experiences in landing were due in some measure to his courage in ascending in high winds." He was a risk taker of pathological proportions, yet also a man with an honest affection for science and a desire to expand our knowledge of the skies. He was one of the first to collect air samples, as it was widely believed that "sky air" contained different properties to "earth air". Sadler was also probably aware that the Montgolfiers' explanation for airborne propulsion, their so called "electric smoke", was nonsense - and that it was the properties of hot air alone, not smoke, that caused a balloon to rise.

Often, when someone leads a life of fragmented disciplines, tangled interests, cross-discipline accomplishments and competing enthusiasms, we are encouraged to sneer - selecting pejorative phrases such as "jack of all trades" ahead of "polymath". Indeed, "polymath" is a modern word - well, for us English-speakers, who have yet to completely clean it of its stained disapproval, but Greeks have been using both the word and concept happily for just a few thousand years now. Still, it took us Britons two thousand years to accept olive oil, so maybe there is hope ahead.

Sadler achieved such a ridiculous amount of cross-discipline successes that it is hard to place them into any meaningful compartmentalised categorisation. One eminent engineer in 1928 accused his colleague J.E. Hodgson, after he had addressed an engineering society with a well-researched paper on Sadler's life, of refusing to acknowledge that there were different James Sadlers sharing the same name. Such a long list of accomplishments across different disciplines could thus not possibly belong to the same person.

In reality just the one James Sadler improved the Royal Navy's firepower - radically redesigning both cannons and rifles - and likely affecting the outcome of the war with the French. Lord Nelson certainly thought so, and expressed such thoughts in preserved letters requesting all the inventions Sadler could design for the Navy. Nelson declared: "I would take on board the *Victory* as many guns as

Mr Sadler could send alongside." It was estimated, then empirically proven by Sadler, that a third of all British guns missed their target before the modifications he devised.

Sadler also invented mobile steam engines. Perhaps even before James Watt - although this is too clouded by controversy to ever permit a clear image of what happened. Only one patent was filed by Sadler due to Watt's somewhat more litigious approach. Yet Sadler was unquestionably the very first Englishman in history to literally soar above his homeland and look down at his country from the skies above. He also started a carbonated water business, crucially using a balloon motif on the label - an early celebrity endorsement of a drinks product. There Sadler designed and built a steam engine to use at the bottling factory.

But above all, he did something no Englishman had ever done before: fly. And he did everything himself, designing and building his own balloon and basket, manufacturing his hydrogen and piloting his own creation.

Undoubtedly Sadler was an old-fashioned daredevil too - to an extent this

Pilâtre de Rozier, first to fly and first to die (Library of Congress, Washington DC)

man of science also doubled as the eighteenth century's Evel Knievel. Taking off in gales, crashing into hills, plopping into the Irish Sea and Bristol Channel, Sadler lived like a prototype version of *Jackass the Movie*. He once ascended in a severe gale. Aiming for Birmingham, he landed near Boston, Lincolnshire. This probably constitutes close enough for most budget airlines (after all, Sadler's home town now genuinely boasts an airport officially named "London Oxford").

Yet perhaps Sadler's greatest achievement was in possessing the necessary scientific wisdom to survive, in an era when most of his fellow pioneering aeronauts perished. Jean-François Pilâtre de Rozier may have been the first person in human history to fly - ascending in the Montgolfiers' famous balloon in France in 1783 - yet by June 1785 he had also become the first person to die in an aviation accident when his balloon exploded into a fireball.

The Man with his Head in the Clouds is James Sadler. He is also me. I am attempting to overcome a life-long aversion to heights in order to replicate Sadler's first flight. I am terrified of heights, really terrified. Actually, best make that really, really, really (…one more "really" should suffice) terrified. I cannot imagine anyone braver than Sadler.

Hence, I have to conquer my deepest - or, more accurately, highest - fears in order to tell Sadler's story. Inspired by Sadler's determination to be the first Englishman to see his own nation from above, I wanted to replicate his experience. Like Sadler, I am used to living in Oxford beneath the shadows cast by the University's Dreaming Spires.

Somehow he attained these achievements with little if no formal education. Mirroring Sadler, I have virtually no academic qualifications either. Like Sadler, I'm from Oxford's Town not Gown. Like Sadler, after feeling that Oxford has spent a long time looking down on me, I crave my turn to look down at Oxford. Unlike Sadler, I am an idiot.

Not least because I booked a balloon flight despite my acute acrophobia. And here's a tip for you: should you want to acquire more respect for an irrational fear, make sure you medicalise the condition and refer to the phobia's correct clinical name. Announcing "I've led a life-long struggle with astihophobia" guarantees more immediate respect than "I'm scared of rubber bands."

My fear of heights is extreme. Acute acrophobia forbids me from standing on a stool, yet alone dangling at 3,000 feet from the strings of an oversized party balloon.

The first piece of info for any potential nervous aeronauts is that balloons never land - technically they only ever crash. This is because balloons do not contain an engine, or steering mechanism.

Hence I needed to recruit some pre-flight counselling quickly. Plus discover what Oxford University psychiatry experts can tell me about their latest research into phobias. After all, it transpires I have harboured not one, but two phobias for most of my life. This revelation occurs during my first visit to a counselling practice. Here I discover that I am not only acrophobic but also suffer from bathmophobia. I complain that their counselling practice is like the MRSA equivalent for phobias. I entered their consulting room as a patient requiring treatment for one phobia, where I picked up a second phobia during my stay.

No, bathmophobia is not the fear of baths - a condition more commonly known, as "being French". Nor is bathmophobia an irrational fear of quaint Georgian towns selling over-priced Jane Austen tea towels.

Bathmophobia is a condition I have genuinely been diagnosed with by a mental health practitioner. It is an irrational fear of stairs. That's right. I am a functioning adult man who is terrified of heights and stairs. I appear to be suffering from the complete set of height anxieties - a full house (or full bungalow, as I prefer) of height phobias.

This explains why I have never been a high-octave high-flyer, high-achiever or high anything. I don't even like legal highs, especially ladders. My life has mainly been conducted on the ground floor, both literally and metaphorically.

I may not have a head for heights, but I do have a body for falling.

Prodding memories best left marooned in the past, I confront a past entirely spent travelling on the bottom deck of buses and living on the ground floor - by deciding to seek professional counselling. Here I am diagnosed by mental health practitioners as doubly phobic. I also discover that most acrophobics have actively done something about their condition: they've stubbornly ignored it.

And yet everyone I meet without exception who suffers from height anxiety is adamant that they suffer from vertigo. In fact, I am about to make a startlingly discovery about vertigo, once I embark on a programme to educate myself about the condition - a breakthrough that immediately changes my outlook on life.

Hence this book is about the twin dreamt ambitions of one man's journey to become the first to fly above the earth, and another man's decision to finally go upstairs.

You see, I am rarely comfortable on stairs. Occasionally I am forced to concede why I am behaving irrationally, suspiciously even, on a staircase. If stairs are steep and what I call "unfinished" (i.e. the designers have not added a back to each step), I like to negotiate them slowly. Not necessarily holding the handrail, but within sufficiently close proximity should I need to clutch it to feel less anxious. After explaining my predicament, people nod and say "that's OK" - even though it clearly isn't OK. Although I will avoid admitting my predicament whenever possible I will occasionally have to concede that I am frightened of heights, and yes, this single-flight staircase does constitute a height. And that I am uncomfortable being here. For this immense bravery, I receive looks of pitying bewilderment.

Normally I am more likely to tell a woman of my shameful predicament and hide it from men, fearing such an admission would erode masculinity - although to be fair, men have often been as empathetic as women.

With a significant birthday approaching (no, not the Big Six-O, thanks for asking) I decide a change has to occur. At this point I need to admit to my phobias, especially if I harbour any truthful ambitions of overcoming them. It's time to address this thing, and get it sorted. Starting with addressing vertigo. Which turns out to be completely the wrong place to start.

1 AT DAWN'S FIRST FLIGHT: JAMES SADLER AND OXFORD

James Sadler was born in Oxford and baptised there soon afterwards on 27 February 1753 at St. Peter-in-the-East Church in Queen's Lane. Thereafter we know almost nothing about him until some thirty years later. In fact, there is frustratingly little known about Sadler's formative years. Apart from popping up in the parish register for a baptism and a marriage, we don't hear from him again until his proclivity for flying test balloons makes the news in 1784. In the interim Sadler worked at his father's business the Lemon Hall Refreshment House in Oxford's High Street, while his older brother John was employed at the café's second branch located in St. Clement's.

Notably, Sadler's story will become hazy again when he curtails his aeronautical activities in 1785 - disappearing into the clouds like one of his ill-advised ascents in an overcast sky. Brief glimpses through the mist during these so-called "Missing Years" show his polymath's diversity before he returns to ballooning in July 1810. Sadler accomplishes an array of different achievements across different disciplines during this period. We know the headlines, if not always the complete story.

In 1784, when Sadler's story comes into view, he was working in the kitchen at the back of the Lemon Hall Refreshment House, which he inherited from his father. *Rowlandson's Oxford*, a compendium of Oxford life produced by the eponymous Georgian satirist and cartoonist notes, "I dined in the High Street at Sadler's", thus indicating that the café was more readily known by its owner's name. Located where the Examination Schools now stand in Oxford's High Street, Sadler's refreshment rooms were demolished for the University's expansion. The Schools were finished in 1882 by Thomas Jackson, the architect who also designed Oxford's most photographed icon, the Bridge of Sighs, and who spent his entire honeymoon period in Italy visiting quarries to source marble for the building that replaced Sadler's café. Presumably he read in the evenings by the light of his new wife's fury.

Oxford University, as is its aggressive wont, has long since colonised most of central Oxford, and Sadler's historic pastry shop was simply another building whose destiny was an inevitable, incontrovertible property transfer from Town to Gown.

Sadler had started to construct airworthy balloons by February 1784, even exhibiting at Oxford Town Hall in St. Aldates a sizeable 63-foot diameter hot air balloon constructed "with great labour and expense". This was a marketing exercise, used to garner publicity and gather admission fees as vital funds were raised this way in order to build a new vessel that he christened "a large Aerial Machine".

19 FEBRUARY 1784: THE FIRST UNMANNED FLIGHT

In common with human gestation periods, James Sadler took nine months from conceiving his unmanned test flight to launching himself skywards and becoming the first Englishman to fly.

He tested both hot air and hydrogen balloons on an unsuspecting nation. Quite how unsuspecting a nation Britain was as regards balloons in 1784 was proved a few months after Sadler's debut historic manned ascent, when Scottish scientist James Dinwiddle launched an unmanned test balloon from Bath. Recorded in his journal, the hemisphere measured 27 feet in diameter. Its landing in Dorset five miles south of Shaftesbury in the hamlet of Farrington prompted considerable trouble.

A farmer summoned a posse of labourers and entered the field where the fallen balloon wobbled in the breeze like an oversized green jelly. Stalking their prey like primitive Neanderthal hunters, they cautiously approached it downwind with pikes primed, and then charged, hacking the balloon into silken strips. To their relieved surprise, the balloon offered little resistance. The farmer was steadfast in his conviction that it could only be one thing: an alien monster originating from overseas intent on abducting his cows.

Wisely, Sadler decided to steer clear of Dorset, and had earlier launched a test flight from Oxford. He launched his relatively small test balloon, constructed from silk, from a field situated just to the west of where The Plain intersection at St. Clement's currently lies permanently surrounded by the constant deep roar of traffic. The field was then managed by John Sibthorp of Lincoln College. Sibthorp, who had studied medicine in Edinburgh and France, had been appointed the University's Professor of Botany in 1784 and so would have been a useful and influential ally for Sadler when attempting to cross the high-fenced Town and Gown division.

Although Oxford University seemingly helped fund Sadler's pioneering aerostation work, and Sibthorp supported his endeavours, it appears that the Sherardian Professor of Botany may not have witnessed Sadler's later manned flights as he was away in the Far East plant collecting. He was certainly better in this post than his nepotistic appointment would imply, since his predecessor was his father Dr. Humphry Sibthorp of Magdalen College, who "gave not very successful lectures and every scientific object slept during the 40 years he held the post," according to John Pointer writing in *Oxoniensis Academia* in 1749.

It was probably during Sibthorp's protracted absences that one of the first balloon ascents in England was made, launching from near the Botanic Garden, then known as the Physic Garden in Oxford, though the actual spot is more likely to have been where St. Hilda's College has stood since 1893 as this was the field then under the control of Sibthorp. It is equally likely that Sadler returned to this location in the autumn of the same year for his first manned flight.

It is clear from the larger scales of successfully unmanned test flights that Sadler was envisaging a more spacious design eventually carrying him into the skies. His balloons, or "envelopes" in technical aeronautical language, were increasing incrementally with each unmanned flight. For the details of Sadler's early experiments, we are indebted to an anonymous letter writer.

On 25 February 1784 the *Daily Chronicle* newspaper received a letter dated 21 February. This was the primary news source for newspapers of the age, since communication networks were barely in their infancy. The paper's correspondent had been walking through a field in Wrotham, Kent, when he discovered "a large Air Balloon, which from the label prefixed to it, appears to have been made by Mr Sadler of Oxford".

It was indeed Sadler's creation. This represented one of his largest balloons; its smaller-scaled predecessors would have probably been launched near the same site in Oxford. One uncollaborated report implies that Sadler's unmanned test balloons were launched from near the Queen's College on the High Street - the same street where Sadler's pastry shop was located almost directly across the road at no.84. Although possible, this would imply an unproven partnership with a Mr. Rudge of Queen's. In fact, how much the project belonged to Rudge is unclear - certainly Sadler was not a University man, and at this stage of his career would have done well to have overcome the strict Town and Gown sectarianism as a mere kitchen worker and pastry cook. His invitation to connect with the University would most likely have been provided by his later fame.

Rudge was an intriguing aeronautical pioneer in his own right, and appears to have motivated Sadler in an arms race to be the first Englishman to reach the skies. Rudge launched his own unmanned balloon from Queen's in February 1784. A vicar visiting the Dreaming Spires from Honiton in Devon, the Rev. W. Tucker records meticulously that Rudge's balloon was fifteen feet in diameter and made from alternative strips of red and white material. Rudge himself later confirmed that his balloon's colour scheme was intended "to appear like meridional lines on a terrestrial globe".

Taking-off at 1.15pm, the balloon flew until 3pm when it landed in a field just outside Wallington, midway between Sutton and Croydon in Surrey.

Although including information on the balloon's construction, the scientific integrity of his report is boldly compromised when the Rev. Tucker includes in his same account an assured cure for the plague which involves simply mixing asses' milk with homemade raspberry wine - a product he was hoping to sell. A visit from Trading Standards may have been imminent.

Crucially, the balloon was filled with the so called "inflammable gas", later to be known as hydrogen. Astoundingly insensitive to the cardiac health of any modern day college Health and Safety executive, Rudge was manufacturing huge quantities of his own hydrogen inside the prestigious walls of the Queen's College. This involved pouring buckets of neat sulphuric acid over large quantities of shaved iron or zinc filings and attempting to catch the ensuing gas in a silk duvet.

This practice inevitably risked permanently separating the Dreamers from their Spires. If this super-inflammable gas had ever caught light, the resultant bang may have been heard in Cambridge.

Perhaps surprisingly, Rudge was content to share his technology, even writing to newspapers to inform them of the process. His self-described recipe for producing the lifting gas: "19 pounds of iron filings and 40 pounds of the concentrated vitriolic acid and a quantity of water in proportion to the latter as five to one. Produces a sufficient quantity of gas to fill it to such a degree as to float, which it did when about two-thirds full." Rudge also confirmed that his balloon was capable of containing upwards of 65 cubic feet of air, and added equally detailed instructions on how he manufactured his unique sealant varnish for the balloon envelope, using gum to ensure it stuck.

However, one connection that Queen's does not seem to possess is a direct link to Sadler. That rightly prized British asset *The Oxford Dictionary of National Biography* appears to have miscredited a Rudge test flight at Queen's to Sadler. Oxford historian Mark Davies was the first to discover this anomaly.

It is then announced in the press, without making any economical cuts in the fanfare department, that James Sadler is already contemplating his next bigger, bolder balloon project, and has already began construction on a balloon (with suspiciously exact measurements provided by the newspapers of the day) 54 feet in circumference, containing 22,842 gallons of "exhuberated air extracted from burnt wood, a method entirely new, and which has hitherto not been attempted in this Kingdom". This was a brand new concept - as was the word "exhuberated".

People were certainly keen to help Sadler, often writing him letters no more fully addressed than: "Balloon man of Oxford University". One of the correspondents providing published testimonies in newspapers (they were nearly always nameless, anonymity hardly the best guarantee of journalistic accuracy) enticingly revealed that 20,000 spectators were present in Oxford for Sadler's next unmanned test launch, each watching "the magnificent scene with admiration and astonishment. The air took only 20 minutes to fill, although

Sadler had intended 30 minutes would be required." This does appear to be a suspiciously short-timed estimate.

Dead on the hour, the University Church of St. Mary in Oxford's High Street struck one o'clock - the timing was important for subsequent calculations. Sadler's balloon ascended almost directly vertically. Fortunately its trajectory was recorded. At a height "of about 100 yards it was amidst the clouds". The day must have offered good visibility, as the balloon was later reported as being "perfectly visible for 7 miles" from the Oxford launch site once it had passed through broken cloud.

Speculation abounded that the globe fell in Lincolnshire. The newspaper correspondent concludes by enthusing: "The singular and wonderful experiment is allowed to be the most complete of the kind ever exhibited in this kingdom, if not in Europe, and was executed by the ingenious Mr James Sadler of this city, who received the warmest congratulations from the whole University to whom, in general, he gave the utmost satisfaction."

Regrettably this warm relationship with the University would later cool, as both sides returned to their encamped Town and Gown trenches.

Sadler's test balloon landed at 4pm that same afternoon at Stansted in Essex. It had travelled an impressive 79 miles. Only eight minutes after the recorded take-off time, the balloon had been sighted over Wootton, in Buckinghamshire. Far-sightedly, the observer had the presence of mind to record the exact time, realising that this might be significant for subsequent calculations. Thus, by plotting the co-ordinates of both the take-off and observer's position eight minutes after the launch, calculating speed at the distance of sixteen miles distance is er, er, I can do this... just a bit longer... around 100mph. Which is an astonishing twenty-first century speed attained in the eighteenth century, when the fastest people could reasonably have expected to travel was probably limited by how fast a horse could gallop.

Spotted in several parts of Northamptonshire, it was possible to chart the balloon's progress heading in a north-easterly direction: "and upon a moderate computation [it] travelled upwards of 200 miles in the space of two hours and a half." Damage incurred in the flight was also reported with a tear visible in the one of the seams. Speculation at the time suggested that it was "burnt by the expansion of internal air, or otherwise it certainly would have gone a much greater distance".

A few days later the balloon was retrieved in Wrotham, Kent.

The scale of Sadler's 1784 creation and ambition was eventually revealed in the form of a monster 170-foot diameter balloon with a capacity of 38,792 cubic feet. It is worth reiterating that an apparently little-educated pastry cook had designed and built this vast craft capable of remaining safely airborne, although credibility points are justly deducted for Sadler adding a set of oars to his balloon basket to enable him to row through the air and "increase the motion". This, however, was breakthrough science - the cutting edge of science could not have got any sharper in the 1780s. Some doubters warned that Sadler and his aeronautical contemporaries would anger God and forewarned them they risked flying too high and crashing into heaven.

25 FEBRUARY 1784: THE ANNOUNCEMENT

In the same month another unmanned balloon was released from Birmingham, eventually coming to ground at Cheadle in Staffordshire. The relatively short distance accomplished suggests it was probably not one of Sadler's creations, though definitive proof hovers teasingly just out of reach.

Two farmers retrieved the balloon "and then attempted to blow it up". Whilst intending to inflate it, they deployed a pair of bellows and surrounded the inflammable air with lit candles. A contemporary newspaper recounts: "One of them approaching too near with a candle, the remaining inflammable air took fire, tore off the waistcoat, broke all the furniture, drove out the casement to a considerable distance, but did no damage to the bystanders except for singeing their hair."

Felix Farley's Bristol Journal then broke what it considered to be an exclusive story: "Mr Sadler, we understand, is constructing a new balloon. It is filled with hot air extracted from burnt wood - a method which is entirely new and hitherto has not been attempted in the UK." Whatever the *Journal's* story source - good old-fashioned reporter on the ground or a journalist hacking into a mail stagecoach interception - it was essentially correct. This "hot air extracted from burnt wood" gas technique would almost certainly have been discovered by Sadler in the basement of what is now the rather clumsily named The Museum of the History of Science ("Science Museum" would be easier for the person who has to answer the phone) in Broad Street, Oxford. Formerly the basement was Oxford University's first purpose-built laboratory, and Sadler gained employment there as a laboratory assistant.

11 MAY 1784: UNMANNED ESSEX FLIGHT

Buoyed by the success of his first unmanned experiments, Sadler repeated the exercise on 11 May 1784. This time the balloon reached just north of Maldon in Essex. There was another defining difference too. Whereas the previous flight was unmanned, so was this one - but not un-dogged.

With an eye on planning a future manned ascent, Sadler had decided to test whether there was sufficient oxygen at altitude for a mammal to survive a balloon flight by propelling into the atmosphere a dog in the basket. Luckily for Sadler, the RSPCA was not founded until 1824.

Two and a half hours after the balloon had commenced its climb out of Oxford as St. Mary's Church struck noon, it was discovered between the Essex hamlets of Tollesbury and Tolleshunt D'Arcy approximately ten miles south of Colchester. Had the balloon floated much further on the prevailing westerly, it would have reached Clacton and open sea - the fate of the passenger not a positive one no matter how good he was at doing the doggy paddle. A label affixed to the basket supplied details of the dog within, but when a local surgeon, Mr. Arnold of Tolleshunt D'Arcy discovered the fallen balloon, the mut was nowhere to be seen.

Whatever the fate of the airborne canine, Sadler had succeeded in putting a dog into space fully 180 years before the Soviets.

After releasing a series of unmanned test balloons, Sadler decided his balloon was ready for an ascent carrying a rather precious cargo: himself. With dawn's first light revealing the Dreaming Spires of Oxford intact again for another day, he took off from the site believed to be Merton Fields - or possibly the area now occupied by St. Hilda's College - in early October 1784. He almost certainly planned not to be seen in case the experiment failed, but typically a journalist was present - presumably returning from the pub at 5am. The esteemed *Jackson's Oxford Journal* reported the flight in quite astounding detail.

4 OCTOBER 1784: FIRST MANNED FLIGHT

Even before 1784 ended some doubt had seeped into Sadler's claim that he had flown. But it seems unlikely, teetering on the edge of incredibility, that such a distinguished periodical as *Jackson's Oxford Journal* would risk jeopardising its stainless integrity by reporting this English first as an exclusive if it had not happened.

Scandal sheets and lewd gossip are not confined to modern times, but Jackson's account is considered reliable. It is perfectly possible that Sadler was not seen, because no one knew in advance he was going to launch - and it was 5.30am opposite Magdalen College. How likely is it that a student would have been up at that time of the morning to witness the flight?

Sadler's inaugural manned flight was reported as an experiment, thereby instantly distancing him from the showmanship of other pioneer aviators. Referring to a "Fire Balloon raised by means of rarefied air", contemporary descriptions described not a basket, but "a kind of gallery provided with a stove upended over it for containing the fire".

Aware of the necessity to heat air molecules for lift, rather than embrace the erroneous conclusion drawn by the French Montgolfier brothers that smoke provided the upwards momentum, Sadler designed his own stove. Calculating the correct amount of heat required allowed him to ensure that the stove was no heavier than it needed to be, which in turn reduced the size of the balloon envelope. As an inventor and engineer, Sadler would have probably worked this out exactly, presumably algebraically (though how he learned such methodologies is only guessable and forms an alluring element to the Sadler story). His stove invention was transformational, allowing heat to be topped up to maintain flight and altitude, as was his clever addition of a lid controlling air flow. Unlike the Montgolfiers he was evidently aware that the stove only needed to generate heat not smoke into the envelope - hence the stove could be covered. This also reduced the risk of escaping embers that often proved fatal to his contemporaries.

Sadler started to fill the balloon in the dark with his specially manufactured "rarefied air" at 3am until the balloon was fully inflated at 5.30am. One newspaper reported: "The enclosed air having undergone a sufficient degree of rarefication, the intrepid adventurer ascended into the atmosphere - the weather being calm and serene." Aeronauts appear to have discovered surprisingly late in ballooning history the essentiality of that latter detail. Good luck in attempting to spot a balloon drifting above like an oversize soap bubble outside the few hours near dawn and dusk - the bookends of each day when most balloons are launched. And try spotting one in wind or rain. You hopefully never will, because they should not be launched in such conditions.

Yet nearly all of the frontiersmen of flight relied upon ascending at a set time and date, often selected weeks or even months in advance. This pre-planned flight schedule was necessary for raising funds by subscription and selling tickets granting access to the launch site. Ballooning required a large capital outlay, and this accepted method of funding - and profit - by public subscription was consistent in flights undertaken in both France and Britain. On occasions when launches were delayed for just an hour, crowds were frequently reported as a growing restlessly threatening, and riots did occur. Obviously this presented an insurmountable problem for the trailblazer. A strong wind or storm could easily result in disaster, and balloons did catch fire, trailblazer taking on a sinister literal double meaning.

Indeed, a few minutes into Sadler's pioneering flight, a breeze picked up and blew the balloon horizontally at some velocity. It became clear to those on the ground that the balloon opened up the possibility of hitherto unimaginable speed to mankind. Ever the scientist, Sadler had brought several instruments into the basket. In spite of intense coldness at altitude, he realised his thermometer was unreliable given the distorting effect of the gallery's oven. Yet his barometer readings enabled him to calculate that the balloon reached a maximum altitude of 3,900 feet, and after a sharp breeze it had dropped to 2,550 feet. Correctly calculating that additional heat was required to gain altitude, Sadler commenced stoking the oven.

"In these circumstances and perceiving that he was approaching a wood, it was found absolutely necessary to make use of the oars." Hmm. Sadler subsequently swapped his oars for two flags on all future flights, possibly learning that sticking oars on a balloon basket are as ineffectual as placing them on top of a double-decker bus. He descended after about thirty minutes in a field between Islip and Woodeaton.

The St. James's Chronicle and British Evening Post furnished their readers with considerable detail of the flight: "Just after dawn on Monday 4th October 1784 Sadler started preparation which would result by early afternoon the same day, in the pioneering accomplishment of being the first Englishman to fly." Witnesses reported that Sadler accidently dropped his fire fork overboard, thus immediately hampering control of necessary heat generation. "The loss was irreparable," concluded the *London Chronicle*, "and forced him to abandon his globe."

There are scant confirmed details on where Sadler had managed to build and test his components. Some sources have categorically stated that he used the kitchens behind his café in the High Street - again this appears to be a conclusion drawn more on reason than evidence. Sadler, on the other hand, preferred to draw his conclusions from evidence - empirically proven scientific observation being rather essential if you are reliant on it levitating you over a mile up into the sky.

This is how *Jackson's Oxford Journal* reported its world exclusive in October 1784:

Early on Monday morning the 4th instant Mr. Sadler of this City tried the Experiment of his Fire Balloon, raised by means of rarefied air. The process of filling the Globe began at three o'clock, and about half past five as all was complete, and every part of the apparatus entirely adjusted, Mr Sadler, with Firmness and Intrepidity, ascended into the atmosphere, and the weather being calm and serene, he rose from the Earth in a vertical direction to a height of 3,600 Feet. In his elevated situation he perceived no inconvenience; and, being disengaged from all terrestrial things, he contemplated a most charming distant view. After floating for near half an hour, the machine descended, and at length came down upon a small eminence betwixt Islip and Wood Eaton, about six miles from this City.

Later one source was to discredit Sadler, claiming his flight was fabricated. The Italian-born physicist Tiberius Cavallo was unreceptive to Sadler's claims and said so in his 1785 book *The History of Aerostation*. If attempting to order this book from the library, be careful not to order *The History of Aerosmith* - I did, and realised my mistake as soon as I saw the librarian walk this way.

Cavallo set about sniffily disclaiming Sadler's historical ascent. However, as J.E. Hodgson notes in his accomplished 1924 work on pioneering aeronautics: "*The Oxford Journal* was, even by 1784, an old established newspaper and of a character not likely to countenance a bogus narrative." Also it is surely pertinent that the same *Jackson's Oxford Journal's* obituary of Sadler in 1828 also makes clear reference to the 4 October 1784 date. Further overwhelming evidence of Sadler's first Englishman flight status was provided by respected scientific writer George Urquart in his 1786 work *Institutes of Hydrostatics*.

Yet the strongest, potentially jury-swinging evidence for the prosecution case that 4 October 1784 is indeed an unreliable date, long since chiselled into the stonework of English aeronautical history, comes via Sadler's own son John. Balloon enthusiast, writer, professional flautist and composer of an ill-considered "opera for flute" (it's a 'no' from me too), Thomas Monck Mason took up the case after Sadler's death, aiming to establish the exact date of the first flight.

Mason was an aeronaut himself, and in this capacity started a correspondence with Sadler's son John seeking date clarification of the first ascent. John stated it was 12 October 1784, and confirmed it took place "from Oxford gardens". Since this is merely eight days later than the official date of his father's ascent, it renders the fine detail immaterial as this later date still comfortably provided Sadler with the coveted pioneer status. And it is worth mentioning that John Sadler was being asked to recollect several decades after the event. Nor could Monck, who wrote the bestselling account of a later record-breaking, albeit accidental, balloon flight from England to Germany, discover any evidence to dispute Sadler senior's 4 October 1784 claim. In fact, if anything his book stress-tests the 4 October date as genuine. A plaque now stands adjacent to the launch site as official endorsement of the 4 October date.

Mason then went on to publish two books, saddling both with titles so long that readers probably had to take a break and place a bookmark half-way through the title before returning to finish reading it later. *Aeronautica or Sketches*

17

Commemorative plaque in Dead Man's Walk, Oxford (Richard O. Smith)

Illustrative of the Theory and of the Practice of the Aerostation Comprising an Enlarged Account of the Late Aerial Expedition to Germany. That's just one of the titles. The uneagerly awaited follow-up, equally efficiently titled, was *The Work and the Word or The Dealings and the Doctrines of God in the Relation to the State and Salvation of Man Summarily Reviewed and Reconciled and also Recommended in Accordance with the Dictates of Human Reasoning.*

However, Mason makes a singular yet astounding claim about Sadler, stating that he flew before October 1784. *Aeronautica*, published in 1838, contains the following passage: "Mr Sadler appeared a candidate for aeronautical honours having on the 12th September 1784 made an ineffectual attempt to ascend in a Montgolfier from a retired spot in the neighbourhood of Shotover Hill near Oxford, which was frustrated by the accidental combustion of the balloon almost immediately after it had quitted the earth and before it had attained an elevation of twenty yards. Had it not been for this untoward accident, a foreigner would not have had to boast the honour of having accomplished the first aerial voyage ever executed in England."

With the lack of any other supporting sources, this remains an isolated, and probably fanciful, claim. Oxford historian Mark Davies confirms that this is the sole reference to a September flight, though he concedes it was "logical enough to want to test things away from prying eyes".

Sadler's first manned flight, date aside, would unquestionably have been longer, though not as long as one of Mason's book titles, were it not for him dropping the toasting fork used for stoking the fire overboard. He immediately dispensed with cumbersome heavy stoves, and after only one flight in a hot air balloon, switched to hydrogen ballooning. This was the method he deployed for most of his flying life, although, with his son Windham, he later flew using innovative coal gas - a cheaper though less buoyant gas that behaved less temperamentally in changing temperature conditions.

Sadler is very much claimed by the Town, not the Gown, of Oxford. After all, Sadler was a pastry cook, like his father James Sadler senior before him, and gained additional employment in the town as a lab assistant. Lacking formal education, it is this dichotomy which is so inherent to Sadler's story: how did a man once described as barely able to use sufficient grammar to string a sentence together become such a successful self-taught pilot, scientist, engineer, designer, chemist, inventor and aviation pioneer?

12 NOVEMBER 1784: SECOND MANNED FLIGHT

Sadler's second manned flight took off in insanely dangerous conditions that nearly killed him. Still, a huge crowd jostling for vantage-points had swelled around the Physic Garden (later Botanic Garden) at the end of Oxford's High

Street. Flight preparations began "in the presence of a surprising concourse of people of all ranks. The Roads, streets, fields, trees, buildings and towers of the parts adjacent being crowded beyond description," reported a newspaper correspondent.

Centre stage in the Botanic Garden was Sadler's balloon. Surrounding it lay the apparatus necessary for pumping the envelope full of hydrogen, described by press reports at the time as "materials for exciting the inflammable gas which was conducted to the machine by several large tin tubes".

Commencing the hydrogen inflation at 11am, two hours later Sadler was ready for his second air voyage. He was backed by a mighty roar from the assembled throngs of Town and Gown - Sadler had chosen a University term time for his assent, so undergraduates would have been present (although his take-off time of 1pm might have been impractically early for most students).

Disappointingly for the crowd, though, he was enveloped by low cloud after only three minutes, but did fleetingly re-appear on four or five occasions through hazy cloud breaks. Journalists noted that "he moved with great rapidity", and we know why from another observed detail in contemporary reports: "before the wind which blew pretty fresh from the south west". It then started to rain, and Sadler later recalled that his balloon boat became flooded during the flight. These, then, were anything but safe conditions for flying a balloon. But since only three people had flown a balloon in England by this stage, these were lessons that evidently had to be learnt the hard way.

This horrid reality must have dawned upon Sadler during the flight, as he attempted to change altitude frequently in order to find less prevailing currents. Soon he was over the empty expanse of Otmoor, then heading towards Thame. In a desperate attempt to control altitude he started to jettison objects indiscriminately out of his boat. "He was not more than 17 minutes in his passage but found it necessary to divest himself of his whole apparatus and therefore had thrown out his ballast, provisions and instruments of every kind," observed one witness. His "provisions" included a bottle of decent brandy, Sadler's preferred method of staving off the cold, and a regular on his future trips. But it was looking likely that there would not necessarily be any future trips, as he struggled to contain the balloon while desperately attempting a safe reunion with terra firma.

Approaching Thame he crashed violently into a tree "and rebounded to a considerable distance". Spotting a hedge below, Sadler threw out his grappling hook. This partially anchored the balloon, but the wind's velocity dragged him along the ground, and shook him from the wooden boat. He was thrown to the ground but survived. His first hydrogen balloon did not survive and was "ribboned" - destroyed - in the landing.

Picked up from the grounds of an estate belonging to William Lee, twelve miles east of Oxford, Sadler was fit enough to be taken into Thame. After taking celebratory refreshments he returned to Oxford by post-chaise that evening. When he reached the outskirts of the city at 7pm, a waiting crowd unpinned the horses from his carriage, and then paraded him through the city. They "dragged the carriage through several of the principal streets of the city and were not content until they had compelled the inhabitants to illuminate their houses."

Newspapers of the age rushed to praise Sadler's achievements. But behind the gushing descriptions, they had a fundamental point to make: "Our English adventurer is the first person who has been his own architect, chemist, engineer and projector; that he exhibited a wonderful share of genius, intrepidity and cool resolution." Furthermore, he had accomplished the feat twice, with two different models of balloon and, crucially, fuel: his "rarefied air" (hot air) and now his "inflammable air" (hydrogen).

Particularly significant was the inflation time taken to ensure the balloon was filled with hydrogen. Listed in accounts of the time as being only two hours, this supports a contemporary source claiming that Sadler the engineer was the first to design and involve a cistern, rather than wooden casks, in the gas making apparatus.

The most remarkable aspect of Sadler's first hydrogen flight adventure, however, was that he merely shook off this near-death trauma and planned another flight almost straight away.

13 NOVEMBER 1784: POEM ON SECOND MANNED FLIGHT

We've all done it. Usually starting when we begin adolescence, perhaps upon entering the emotional turbulence of those early teenage years. We emit a scary strangeness to our parents, as we struggle to shed the skin of our childhood selves; our physical and emotional beings unrecognisable from our pasts as we emerge from the chrysalis of childhood into our teenage personae.

Usually we do it under the bedclothes, always in lonely isolation, shameful of discovery. Boys nearly always indulge in the activity whist thinking intently about girls. Likewise girls frequently harbour a deep longing for boys when they do it. We all do it, but no one would ever admit to it in public. It's what the lonely do. And even sometimes the not so lonely too.

That's right. We have all, at some time, done it. Yes, let's say it out loud. Let's embrace a new honesty, a *glasnost* of collective admission. Let's all admit to such a common, and defining teenage activity. My name is… And I once wrote poetry. (Sorry, did you say "poetry"? Sounded a bit different? Oh, you did say "poetry". You're sure about that? OK, just checking.)

Despite the fear of terrible reprisals if the activity was ever discovered, we have been moved to compose stanzas and misuse iambic pentameter reflecting on why nice boys/girls don't like us. Or to compare the girl who works at the garage forecourt shop to a summer's day, usually by perennially rhyming "blue", "true" and "you". Even in the fully exposed knowledge that should these poems ever be discovered in a drawer and circulated at school then you would have to lie about your age and fill in an on-line application form to join the French Foreign Legion. Illustrating this very point, the poet Alan Seeger - uncle of musician Pete Seeger and author of JFK's favourite poem "I Have A Rendezvous With Death" (you know... "I have a rendezvous with God, at some disputed barricade"... OK, perhaps not then) - ran off to join the Foreign Legion, presumably when it was discovered he wrote poetry. And he was actually quite good.

Henry James Pye wrote poetry. He was quite successful at it, so much so that he was honoured with the Poet Laureateship from 1790 until his death in 1813 - or so you would have reasonably concluded on that evidence alone. Until you actually read any of Pye's efforts.

Pye was almost certainly rewarded with the Poet Laureate tag for his obsequious support given to the Prime Minister of the day, William Pitt the Younger. Even that excellent public servant Wikipedia, although usually bland and neutral in prose style, permits itself a pop at Pye: "Although he had no command of language and was destitute of poetic feeling, his ambition was to obtain recognition as a poet, and he published many volumes of verse."

But the appointment was looked on as ridiculous, and his birthday odes were a continual source of contempt. Critical knives were further sharpened for Pye's back when Lord Blake declared: "Pye is undoubtedly the worst Poet Laureate in the English history." The Lakeland poet and nitrous oxide tripping bad boy Robert Southey quipped in 1814: "I have been rhyming as doggedly and dully as if my name had been Henry James Pye."

Today's Poet Laureates still receive the same salary: a barrel of sherry. Pye received this too, although he negotiated an actual monetary income to accompany it, securing the heady sum of £27 a year - which, based on my experience of poets, he probably spent buying more sherry. Poets tend to like a drink or five, though anyone reading Pye's poetry would be properly advised to consume a barrel of sherry first.

According to appreciators of Douglas Adams' *The Hitchhiker's Guide to the Galaxy*, inhabitants of the planet Vogon are often named as the worst poets in the known universes. They're not. In fact, Adams merely awarded them runner-up status as the second worst poets in the universes, after unwisely listing a real person and real poet, a former school friend and Cambridge University contemporary from Redbridge, Essex - complete with his full name and address - as the very worst poet in all the known (and probably unknown) universes.

Allegedly. This was supposedly not laughed-off as a joke and subsequent reprints after Pan's first edition in 1979 ensured the name was modified and became the fictionalised Paula Nancy Millstone Jennings of Greenbridge, Essex.

Herewith expressing a personal view, I would now like to propose that the status of the Vogons is bumped down a further place to only third worse. In my, admittedly inexpert, opinion, I classify Henry James Pye as the worst poet in the known - and probably unknown - universes.

Pye reoccurs (like the 4 in his namesake 3.14 - come on, arithmetic joke!) in late eighteenth-century Oxford history, and was a regular visitor to his old college Magdalen, ideally situated just across the road from the Physic Garden where Sadler undertook his first flight. Magdalen Tower, in an Oxford of fewer buildings than today, would have provided splendid views of the landmark ascent. Pye's epic poem about the ascent was published in the unimaginatively titled collection *Poems on Various Subjects* which stretches to two volumes produced in 1787. He prefixes *Aerophorion: A Poem* with the confirmation: "This poem was written on seeing the first English aeronaut James Sadler ascend in his balloon from the Physic Garden, Oxford in November 1784." Hence it was almost certainly composed upon witnessing Sadler's second, not first, ascent.

Aerophorion: A Poem displays an instant lack of confidence in his abilities relayed via his choice of title i.e. he felt compelled to clarify to the reader that it was a poem. Tunesmiths don't tend to title their songs "Strawberry Fields Forever: A Song" thus enabling confused listeners to remark "oh, that's what it is - it's supposed to be a song."

To be fair to Pye, it starts well with an excellent opening couplet that does justice to Sadler's ferocious ambitions. Then the poet's meaning quickly disappears like Sadler into the clouds, and remains obscured from view for several long lines, before re-emerging back into the bright sunlight with a couple of lines towards the end of a long and arduous flight of fancy. Then it disappears forever - before inevitably crashing badly.

Anyway... time for some poetry. (Don't feel bad if you start to skip the poem after a while - it doesn't make you a bad person. Or someone without taste.)

When bold Ambition tempts the ingenuous mind
To leave the beaten paths of life behind,
Sublime on Glory's pinions to arise,
Urged by the love of manly enterprise;
Swol'n Indolence and Fear, with envious view
The radiant track incessant will pursue,
The sneer of Malice to the crowd will teach,

And mock those labours they despair to reach.

Nor does the bold Adventurer dread alone
The poisoned shafts by scowling Envy thrown;
For decked in Wisdom's garb pedantic Pride,
And pompous Dulness constant to her side,
Shall try with looks profound each new design
By the strict rules of Compass and of Line,
And damn the Scheme, whose Author can't produce
The exact returns of profit and of use.

That's quite enough of that. I'll spare you further pages of dreadful stanzas and confused meanings. It reads like one man's war on talent.

On one poetry-hosting website, readers' comments are invited underneath. One "reader" has taken advantage of this, and simply critiqued the poem by adding the lone comment beneath this Georgian masterpiece: "This sucks - Dave from Swindon." Dave from Swindon should edit the *Times Literary Supplement*.

The Cambridge History of English and American Literature, published in 1921 in eighteen sturdy volumes, relishes in taking a big critical stick to the belittled bard Pye and bashes him repeatedly, and deservedly, with it: "Pye, though a convenient butt for the usual anti-laureate jokes, was in fact not so much a bad poet as no poet at all." Ouch.

Pye was saddled with enormous debt by his father's premature death. Soon afterwards the family home was burnt down in mysterious circumstances. It is unclear whether this was an attempt to destroy his poems. Or whether it was the worst insurance fraud ever: "Oh, we were supposed to insure the property first, then burn it down - not the other way around?"

Since no date exists for the authorship of his poem about Sadler - it was published in 1787 - it must have been finished within an hour or so of seeing Sadler fly. It really can't have taken longer.

2 INVERTING VERTIGO: MY FEAR OF HEIGHTS

Let's start with a question. Go on, it'll be fun. Ready? What do you call the condition experienced by sufferers who don't like heights, triggered by altitude exposure and often resulting in dizziness? "Oh," you're probably thinking, "I know the answer to this one."

To my knowledge, *QI* has yet to include this question. But I can imagine the scenario if they did, "So…anyone?" begins Stephen Fry, attempting to lure a professional panellist into a disguised trap so badly camouflaged you expect approach signs declaring "Trap Ahead" and "Last Service Station Before Trap". "I definitely know this one," thinks whatever established comedian has failed to learn from watching the programme's premise before. You don't get to be a professional comedian without an abnormally large showing-off gene, so the urge to press and gain a point for "Vertigo" is too much. "Vertigo," says an established comedian. Told you they'd do that.

"Oh dearie me no… no, no, no. So wrong it's the county town of Wrongshire, capital of Wrongland" Fry might exclaim (well he would if I was scripting the show), demonstrating his uncanny ability to be a reconstituted and unreformed luvvie and yet irresistibly endearing at the same time. Flashing lights and a klaxon exclaim that general ignorance has been exposed.

Because no matter how many people incorrectly purport it to be the case, the condition of height anxiety either inducing or triggering dizziness is not vertigo. Vertigo is a separate medical condition completely unrelated to heights. Really. This is not a medical fact I got off some bloke at a bus stop - nor did I research it solely on Wikipedia. Such is the misnomer's level of ubiquity it is fairly described as approaching totality. Yeah, it was news to me for decades too. Vertigo is a symptom rather than a condition.

True vertigo sufferers experience a spinning sensation, but it is triggered by an imbalance often caused by the ears or a particular series of head movements. One cause of vertigo is the rare disorder Ménière's Disease, where pressure on the inner ear results in a sense of disorientated dizziness amongst some patients. There are more causes of vertigo, but height exposure is not one of them. I, and what most of my fellow misinformed others, actually suffer from is a condition called acrophobia.

Although if you admit to "acrophobia", people might invariably reply, "I can sympathise - I don't like spiders either." Others will confess that they don't like open spaces, to which I softly point out their mistake. Agoraphobia

25

in the original Greek literally means "fear of the market place", as opposed to equinagrophobia, which is fear of being in a market and encountering an unexpected item in the packing area (usually - if you buy ready meals - a horse). There is also the fact that I might have made one of those phobias up - I think you can guess which one.

Yet "I suffer from acrophobia" sounds somehow cooler, a more sophisticated ailment, plus you gain additional respect once an ailment is given its clinical title. Oh come on, people often gain a sense of importance and defining identity from ailments (see men).

Fear of heights is sometimes diagnosed as a fear of falling. Sufferers know this, but often pretend not to; we prefer a deeper psychological evaluation, i.e. it's symptomatic of high IQ and empathy. That would be a nicer explanation, but profoundly untrue. The condition manifests itself by displaying a noticeable tendency to avoid high places, edges and approaching drops. I'm so terrified of drops I'm not even keen on drop scones.

Acrophobia stems from our primitive ancestral selves. My mammalian brain hates dangers, but likes food and girls. That's about it. Oh, and the novels of Elizabeth Gaskell. OK, not the last bit - but apparently that last detail endorses the possibility that there's still some hope left in me for girls. Unfortunately my sophisticated, urbane, Radio 4-liking brain is a bit of a wimp and allows the primitive brain to push him around and do what it says. He's the bully in the limbic system.

For those of us whose happiness is restrained by ancient anxieties no longer relevant to a modern world, such illogical phobias and default antithetical thinking can rather suck all the flavour out of life. And we do not appreciate others being comfortable with heights.

The person who devised the transparent glass floor is our Lord Voldemort. When we acrophobes rule the world, he will be brought to justice, albeit on the ground floor somewhere. People who design glass-walled lifts, we will come for you too (though only when the lift is on the ground floor, obviously). The person who installed that transparent glass floor on top of the Spinnaker Tower in Portsmouth, you are the Dark One who moves amongst us. We will come for you in the night (if you live in a bungalow).

We are secretly very ashamed and rarely reveal our condition. Being afraid of heights does, you may notice, immediately rule us out from all categories of superhero. "Hey, Superman, can you save this distressed damsel from the bridge?" "Er... I would if there was an enclosed lift, but that one's glass panelled and I don't really do stairs. Besides, there are loads more other damsels out there anyway."

In truth, the condition can be restrictive. Acute muscle tensing does occur.

Concentration and breathing, usually performed with blasé indifference, suddenly become unfamiliarly difficult. You require instructions to breath. Over-breathing triggers dizziness. A growing unbalance vibrates through your spine like an approaching tube train. Fear pounces from nowhere out of the darkened shadows of your subconscious mind and stages a coup d'état on the functioning conscious brain. Dizziness can quickly consume a victim. Heart rate soars upwards. Anxiety dials lurch to the far right. Needles flicker into red zones registering alarm. Internal klaxons sound. This combination is ubiquitously and incorrectly known as vertigo. If there's one place where you don't want to experience these symptoms then it's surely at a great height.

Hence the condition tends to manifest itself in an acute avoidance of heights. This is surprisingly problematic. I would prefer to be an avoider of snakes, and this isn't particularly restrictive within an increasingly urbanised lifestyle. But heights are my particular greatest fear, which would give the sadists of Room 101 a problem as the room number indicates that the locale of the ultimate Orwellian fear is only on the first floor.

Suffering from acute acrophobia does inevitably incur a block on entering certain professions. Any lingering dreams of becoming a steeplejack by the time you reach thirty are destined to remain unfulfilled through the passing decades, though even non-acrophobes tend to secretly agree that being a steeplejack is INSANE!

And beware, people who currently consider themselves comfortable with heights - or who are, as I prefer to express it, arrogant at altitude. Novelist Kim Curran, author of successful books *Shift* and *Control* (I assume her next novels will be titled *Alt* and *Delete?*), confided in me: "I thought I was fine with heights until I went up a crumbling ziggurat in Mexico called Ek' Balam. It's over a hundred feet high, no ropes to steady yourself and the steepest incline I've ever known. I made the mistake of looking down and... well, I had to descend on my backside, with my eyes closed. Hardly Lara Croft."

So there lies an unpalatable truth: even the safest cyclist with a high visibility bib, helmet and reflector can encounter the juggernaut of acrophobia unexpectedly swerving into the cycle lane.

Poet Sophie Clarke, winner of the Miracle Poetry Competition in 2013 with a poem inspired by her height anxiety, recognises my relationship with heights. "I can't stand anywhere near the edge of anything at a height, whether it be a cliff face or even a balcony with railings. Even if it's logically impossible, I'll feel like I'm going to fall through the barriers, or be swept off by the wind, or that I can't quite trust myself not to jump," she tells me. "I remember on school trips not wanting to climb to the top of buildings, like cathedrals or towers, and having to wait at the bottom with a disgruntled teacher. I'm not sure my classmates quite understood, and I certainly didn't want to draw attention to something I couldn't really articulate," she explains, citing a situation intensely recognisable to me, so reminiscent of my own experiences. "The anxiety manifests too in a terrible phobia of lifts, which makes a lot of things difficult - transporting luggage in hotels, getting to job interviews on the highest floors of tall inner-city buildings."

"That kind of thing can be quite debilitating, not to mention embarrassing. I've had my fair share of funny looks… 'Height' itself is something of an obsessional subject I am compulsively drawn back to. I've never actively sought outside help, but perhaps writing is a kind of necessary purgatory and/or therapy of its own," she informs me. "A lot of my poetry is about my experiences of climbing and mountaineering - my father has always been a keen hill-walker, so ever since childhood I have had this simultaneous fear and fascination of high places. Without wanting to sound too pretentious, it's a large part of my internal and external landscape."

All of these competing issues and concerns are spun together brilliantly with a poet's observational skills in the opening lines of her prize-winning work *I Too Have Dreamt of High Places*. "My parents taught me how to climb, up the north face of our three-storey house/They pulled the harness straps tight/In case you fall/I envied the lampposts their height/The window ledge shaling away in my hands/I couldn't go up and I couldn't go down."

But before the unsympathetic reject our psychological condition of acrophobia as unserious, remember that the fear is real and present even if the danger is not. Herein lies a consistency with most anxieties. Sufferers are aware of the "cognitive dissonance". We can even compute it in rational conversations. Fear is dangerous to us. Yet only heights offer a very literal danger, even though they are unlikely to kill us, simply because we are fearful of them. So the fear keeps us safe, but at a restrictive cost. And yet it is the fear itself that causes our lives to be uncomfortable, as it is extremely unlikely we will ever fall off one of those feared unpleasant heights. We can compute all this, and hold diametrically opposing views simultaneously. It's what us acrophobes do. That's me putting the "tit" in antithetical.

Author Denis Cronin in his 1980 book *Anxiety, Depression and Phobias and How to Cope With Them* acknowledges that: "Fear of heights is extremely common. The majority of people do not go to their doctor for treatment for such matters, but simply avoid those occasions which would tend to evoke the fear - like going up ladders, climbing mountains or visiting monuments." So far, so reasonable. Then he lurches off Reasonable Road, and takes a sharp turn into Vindictive Avenue, proposing: "Psychoanalytic theory suggests that fear of heights may mask a fear of undertaking responsibility, that such people are unadventurous, timid, with a tendency to avoid taking decisions." So far, so unreasonable. He then goes completely off road, departing any smooth surface of common sense, and judders over the rocky ground of prejudices masquerading as scientific facts.

If standing on the parapet of a tall building, the anxious person becomes worried in case he or she loses control and falls over. The physical fear, therefore, of being dashed to the ground from a building or into the sea from a cliff top, represents a deeper psychological fear of not being in control of one's own feelings, emotions and actions.

Oh, yeah? Well, if I was standing on the parapet of a tall building with the author of that vindictive diatribe, I'd be thinking of ways to distract the only witnesses.

This is a corrosively reductive theory that repackages the reasonable evolutionary caution of avoiding high drops as a severe personality disorder.

"The situation is thus seen as a threat," he concludes. Possibly. Or possibly not, as evolution would surely reward those who are able to scale height with their full physical and mental abilities unaffected. They are the ones more likely to survive and thus procreate their gene distributions. After all, the meerkats who used to post a look-out sentry elevated higher than their colleagues (or until their successful TV advertising careers cancelled the need to forage for food) suggest that a group stands a better chance of survival if its surroundings can be surveyed for danger from an elevated vantage-point. Ground dwellers like me, unless we can persuade our surprise lion attacker to consider going vegetarian very quickly by taking a "meat is murder" leaflet when picketing the watering hole, are in serious risk of gene extinction from our preferred height avoidance proclivities.

Yet anyone devoid of a fear of heights would be equally likely to remove themselves from the gene pool pretty early on - in a very messy way.

And as for that author's accusation of timidity. Frankly, how dare he accuse me of... oh, OK, it's no problem. He's probably right. Sorry to have troubled you...

Harbouring a strong fear of heights is incredibly common. Researching this book I interviewed many people who admitted to height phobias, and everyone - a 100% trial result - both (a) had never sought any treatment, and (b) were under the misapprehension that they suffered from vertigo and that altitude would trigger an automatic attack of dizziness. The fear of becoming dizzy at a dangerous altitude in turn accentuates the fear, turning the anxiety dial even further to the right.

I find the books about vertigo located on the library's top shelf. A mini-ladder is required to select them. Say what you want about librarians' famed timidity, but callousness in humour and a heightened (pun definitely intended) sense of irony is clearly within their remit. It's almost like they're screaming (silently and mutely, obviously): "We don't just go 'shush', point to a 'Silence' sign and operate a date stamp, you know." Apparently you can study a popular undergraduate degree in librarianship - how can it take three years to learn how to operate a date stamp? OK, it's jokes like that which make them keep the height anxiety self-help books on the top shelf to punish people like me.

Elsewhere in the psychology section I see a spine proclaiming a book's title as *Understanding Woman's Mood Swings*; maybe that gets filed on a different shelf every day, for no apparent reason, but they won't tell you where it is because you should know already where it is, because that would involve taking an interest, and it's your fault anyway for not knowing because you never listen and if you had listened then you might have heard where it was going to be filed today... (I think you get where I'm going with this routine: singledom.)

Eventually I source, then cross-reference, an overbearing weight of peer-reviewed evidence that disproves a common misconception. Vertigo is entirely separate from height anxiety. This means someone with a phobia of heights will not automatically trigger an attack of vertigo when ascending to a lofty position - with the ensuing symptoms of feeling dizzy and fainting. Yes, I am aware that becoming dizzy and fainting is not convenient at the best of times, but a particular definition of an inconvenient place to become dizzy and risk losing consciousness would be on top of something really, really high. So I am not going to get vertigo when I am high-up - on stairs, in a hot air balloon or on a ledge. This is a massive comfort.

Then Dr. Hannah Stratford, a phobia expert at Oxford University, tells me something that aids me enormously, proving that just a couple of short sentences can instigate a lifelong improvement when addressing my encountered difficulties with stairs and heights. She tells me that an irrational fear triggered by a phobia will definitely not cause me to pass out. Quite the opposite, as my brain is likely to manufacture a massive blood rush and provide a fight- or -flight-aiding adrenaline shot - my bodily equivalent of sinking a triple espresso with nine sugars.

There is one fascinating exception to the you-won't-faint-with-a-phobia rule, which shows how unknowingly clever our human bodies really are. She reveals this amazing fact to me later when agreeing to be interviewed for this book.

Holidays are a vulnerable time for us acrophobes. Escaping the dreamless drudgery of the workplace for a mere few short days each year, holidays invariably include activities misguidingly described as entertainment or fun that involve climbing high things. Even cultural breaks inevitably include mandatory climbs - church towers, view points, lookout stations, Ferris wheels or other selected implements from a torture box for the height phobic.

Activity holidays expect people to voluntarily separate themselves from their money for the privilege of parachuting, paragliding, abseiling and other horrors. One fellow holidaymaker asked if I wanted to go hang-gliding with him. I think I would have preferred to undergo an actual hanging - at least the ensuing death would be quicker. Whereas while negotiating the stresses and strains, balancing the conflicting hopes and disappointments of life for fifty weeks of the year back home it is relatively easy to side-step going up high things (as long as you allow time to avoid lifts and climb stairs very slowly). On holiday it becomes rudely unavoidable. "But," your travelling companions will say, "you can't go to Paris without going up the Eiffel Tower"; although that doesn't turn out to be technically true, unless the Eurostar now terminates half-way up it... (But this may soon be the case, as train stations now contain so many shops it is only a matter of time before they move the space-greedy trains and platforms out and convert them into more retail capacity.)

The first psychologist I see to research height anxiety, and to address my affliction ahead of taking a balloon flight, commences the session by being openly doubtful, bordering upon cynical, about my condition. Then he soon upgrades cynical to nasty. This is hardly the person-centred, people-focused Rogerian counselling I was expecting. In fact, he is transmitting a strong signal through non-verbal communication that my ailment is unworthy of psychological exploration.

The psychologist cites scientific research papers that conclude empirically that my symptoms may be manifestly linked to possible multiple personality disorders. Thanks. "But only mild ones," he seeks to reassure me later.

At the end of each dispensed scientific conclusion he quotes a research paper, always twin-authored. He sends me these later, decorating his dual-authored statement sources with parentheses and the published date i.e. (Swann & Gosbert, 1997). He states concerns about the legitimacy of some sufferers claiming a bona fide psychological condition (Mycliffe & Brown, 2001). He then opines that sufferers like me are often deluded, and have strong emotional problems (Harsh & Insensitive, 2013). I respond by imagining whacking him in the face with a frying pan (Tom & Jerry, 1966) or dropping an anvil on him (Itchy & Scratchy, 2014).

This does help provide me with some insight and determination - a determination to find another psychologist.

3 FRENCH FLIES: CROSS-CHANNEL PIONEERS

Ah, Paris. The city - or rather *la cité - d'amour. Je t'aime, Paris.* A sentence which, by the standards of my fellow Englishmen, qualifies me as bilingual. No Parisian ever contemplates leaving home without trousers, door key and an unnecessarily long, pointy baguette. But please, France, stop nicking our words and claiming them as your own: examples of English language word-rustling include *le weekend, le pub, le parking*; we wouldn't do that, it's just so passé, louche and laissez-faire.

Le Terror came to Paris in 1784. And again in 1994, when I attempted to go up the Arc de Triomphe. For me this was not a triumph. In fact Napoleon got a better result at Waterloo. Here's why.

Actually getting to the Arc de Triomphe alive is almost impossible due to French traffic. In order to drive a French car, you need to be (a) a holder of a valid licence, and (b) an untreatable psychopath. Then dispense with your rear and side mirrors, and your brake. Never give way, never stop, never care about remaining alive.

Reaching the island where the Arc de Triomphe stands hubristically with typical French arrogance amidst a dodecagonal layout involves negotiating eight lanes of traffic, fed by no fewer than twelve separate roads all converging into the roundabout with the monument in the middle. Presumably because of this there is a grave dedicated to the unknown pedestrian... I mean... soldier.

This dash is similar to, and shares an equivalent survival rate with, hatching turtles scrambling across a beach in a usually doomed attempt to return to sea. Fortunately, nowadays there are two underpasses and a Metro station.

Scaling all 164 feet of stone enabled me to stand atop a ginormous slab originally ordered by Napoleon to honour those returning from victorious campaigns by "a homecoming through arches of triumph". Rather than remembering those who died in the Napoleonic Wars, it prompted most onlookers to speculate that someone who built that ostentatious slab of self-praise for their military general must have a right Napoleon complex. Oh, I see.

Although ordered by the distinctly non-diminutive general (contrary to popular myth, Napoleon was of normal height for the era) in 1806, the project was severely delayed until 1836; typical builders: always late - they probably couldn't source a skip until then.

I recall somehow reaching the top, fortified by wine that had ironically been fortified itself according to the label, and then getting as near to the edge as

I dare - which involved actually working out the exact geometric point that kept me furthest away at all times from any of the building's rectangular edges. Terrifyingly, the perimeter wall was only around two feet high. I think that's worth typing again: the perimeter fence was two feet high. That was all the guarding required for this immensely high structure. That has quite an impact on me, almost as much of the 186 feet drop that I was currently fixating on. This was Health & Safety from 1836.

Returning to Paris more recently, and with utterly no intention whatsoever of returning back to the top of the Arc and reliving the ultimate acrophobic's nightmare, binoculars enabled me to confirm that far higher additional fencing has now been sensibly added.

The very first balloon flight took place near Paris. It was also dangerous, reckless and demonstrated craziness bordering upon the sectionable. It relied upon basic scientific ignorance, and yet it was revered as an incredible success - both a giant leap and a giant first step for mankind.

Jacques-Étienne Montgolfier (6 January 1745-2 August 1799) and Joseph-Michel Montgolfier (26 August 1740-26 June 1810) were brothers from Annonay near Lyon who ran a paper company. They had already encountered the newly discovered fashionable gas of the age, hydrogen, and knew it could be used to inflate miniature paper balls and send them floating through the air - based upon, it later transpired, hydrogen being fourteen times lighter than air.

But the properties of regular air could be altered dramatically by the introduction of heat. This had been observed at their paper works, where smoke could propel paper into the air through the chimney. Heating air arouses the individual molecules, and causes them to shift their behavioural patterns. One change was noticed by Joseph-Michel Montgolfier who reportedly informed a correspondent: "I observed the principles of hot air at work inflating an old wind bag, by observing my wife." His true vocation was not as a pioneer of flight, but as Les Dawson's opening act.

He had instantly discovered the properties of hot air, realising that it took on different properties to cold air, and could perhaps be harnessed to produce levitation in paper or fabric. He later confirmed this find by observing his wife's drying blouse becoming inflated above the fire-place. Writing to his brother Jacques he poured out the excitement of his discovery: "Bring me some taffeta cloth and cordage, *tout de suite*, and you will see one of the most incredible sights in the world!" Jacques-Étienne's response to dashing back to the small French town to witness a bit of cloth floating up a chimney is not recorded. But it would still require a robust leap of both imagination and materials science if they were going to adopt this discovery into fulfilling human flight.

Initially they designed small paper balloons, and used smoke generated from burnt wool, straw and hay, incorrectly surmising that the smoke provided the balloon's airborne lift. Although it clearly did not, as Sadler knew well, it did nevertheless serve to provide a sealing agent to their otherwise porous balloon made of thin paper.

Prior to the first launch containing human cargo, the Montgolfiers designed a giant 108-foot-wide balloon and placed it above a straw furnace in the town square at Annonay. As its name implies, Annonay was an anonymous parochial town to be chosen for such a world changing event. But it was the Montgolfiers' hometown, and the venue for this landmark first flight is annually celebrated today on the Place des Cordeliers where an obelisk stands marking the event. To this day, the Montgolfiers are still commemorated in the French word for a hot air balloon: *une montgolfière*.

On 4 June 1783 in what were perfect weather conditions for a hot air balloon launch, preparations began for an unmanned ascent. The scale was certainly ambitious, the sphere measuring 110 feet in diameter and weighing almost a quarter of a ton. The French astronomer Nicolas Camille recorded the event (but ten years afterwards), noting "it appeared only a covering of cloth, lined inside with paper - a kind of 35-foot high sack." As the hot air flowed into the sack, the shape it formed began to please Camille as "it grew ever larger in front of the eyes of the spectators and took a beautiful form, stretching inside on all sides and struggled to escape." The balloon is generally considered to have reached a height of around two thousand metres. What is undisputed is that it was the first public hot air balloon flight - though the absence of passengers or cargo ensured ascent was much easier than with a manned flight.

With an empty basket, the launch occurred quickly when eight rope-holding Frenchmen struggling to restrain the balloon from lifting off were given a signal to release their grip; being Frenchmen they were probably just distracted by a prostitute walking past. (In an increasing politically correct world, thank goodness we'll always have our wonderful neighbours the French as a legitimate comedy target.)

It landed just over an hour later, but the short distance travelled of just two kilometres is testimony to the almost non-existent breeze that day. Even so, the winds of scientific debate were blowing a gale, since many traditional scientists refused to believe this was possible within the rational laws of explained science. In order to fly, they argued, a balloon must have sufficient lighter-than-air gas such as recently discovered hydrogen. The balloon may have only flown two kilometres in an hour, but news was still travelling even slower; news of the achievement reaching Paris the next day.

On 19 September 1783 a paper balloon took-off in Versailles carrying three passengers. A sheep, a duck and a rooster all flew in the presence of King Louis XVI, Marie Antoinette and the entire French court. The balloon was suitably christened *Le Réveillon* after Jean-Baptiste Réveillon, the owner of a wallpaper business that enjoyed royal patronage and which provided the material for the construction of the balloon's entire envelope. Damaged by a rip in the wallpaper, and with its basket broken after colliding with treetops, the balloon gently floated to earth barely ten minutes after take-off, landing in the suburb of Vaucresson with its animal cargo physically intact.

It was thought that if a small mammal such as a sheep could breathe sufficient oxygen to survive at such altitudes, then so surely could much bigger mammals, including human beings. The balloon basket, however, would certainly need some serious cleaning before a member of the French aristocracy stepped into it as it had been used to fly very terrified livestock.

And so, in the presence of Louis XVI the first attempt was made to put a human into the air on 21 November 1783. Initially the French king decreed that two condemned prisoners should be trialled as the first people to fly. Although the prisoners were informed they would be given a royal pardon if (salient detail coming up) "IF they survived", they did not fly. Instead 26-year-old physics teacher and balloon-experimenter Jean-François Pilâtre de Rozier petitioned the monarch into allowing suitable volunteers from the scientific community to lead the way. Relieved that they had been spared the unknown and potentially deadly outcome of the balloon flight, the condemned prisoners were then swiftly despatched to the gallows - a fairly short-lived relief, then.

The involvement of Rozier's scientific mind was crucial, as he concluded, perhaps somewhat illogically to an outsider, that in order to raise more weight off the ground, the balloon would have to carry more weight. Hence he added an iron fire basket inside the balloon. This additional weight, alongside the necessary fuel, would indeed appear illogical - not to mention the increased danger of an open furnace in a balloon manufactured from paper. But the increased air temperature provided greater lifting propulsion, and also some slight control in the balloon's flight path: i.e. lob more straw on the fire to go higher and maintain a flight path. Rozier undertook several short test flights, during which he trialled various fuels for the fire, eventually concluding that cloth soaked in alcohol was the best performer.

That day a huge seventy-foot circumference inflated "gas ball" was lifted by a cumbersome straw-burning stove off the manicured lawns of the Château de la Muette, a few miles west of the French capital. The brightly coloured orb was

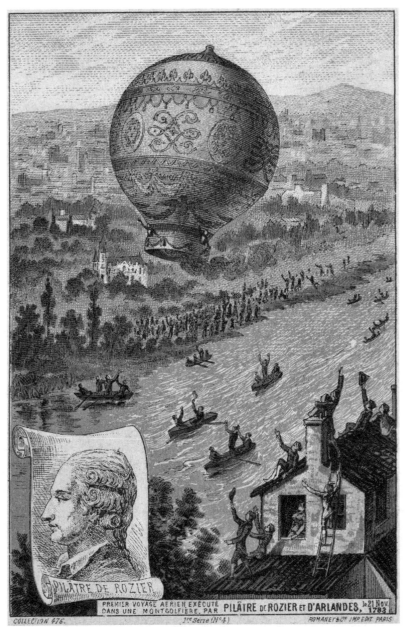

The first French manned flight (Library of Congress, Washington DC)

piloted by the Marquis d'Arlandes and Pilâtre de Rozier. Fortunately the weather was calm and conditions serene. Or they were when the flight eventually took off, Rozier having the foresight to cancel an early flight due to adverse weather conditions. After ascending to an altitude estimated at around 900 metres, the balloon landed without incident at the Butte-aux-Cailles nearly nine kilometres away after half an hour in the air.

Rozier's *bonne chance* did eventually run out, as it did for most of the original aeronauts with the notable exception of Sadler, when on 15 June 1785 his balloon suddenly lost gas and altitude, and crashed to the ground near Boulogne on the northern French coast. Alongside him was Pierre Romain who also perished in the crash, rendering these the very first aviation deaths.

It is worth recalling that the balloon, powering into the hitherto unknown skies where monsters could roam and oxygen not exist, was manufactured out of paper, hovering a few feet above the stove. After all, that was the Montgolfiers' business - they manufactured paper - and hence it was likely a publicity stunt for their company, in much the same way that it is possible to spot a balloon in today's dawn or dusk skyline emblazoned with the word Virgin.

Although the Montgolfier brothers are forever destined to enjoy pioneering status, and their own Trivial Pursuit answer, only one of them ever ascended in a balloon - and he only did that once.

According to the stereotype, Frenchmen are over-amorous and obsessed with *cherchez la femme*. This is an obsession somewhat paradoxically compromised by their disinclination towards using mouthwash.

This cartoon image of a typical Frenchman is fanned by Pepé Le Pew, the damagingly amorous fictional French skunk, constantly causing a stink with the beautiful ladies. Non-fictional Frenchmen do have a proclivity for liking the ladies too, of course, and that includes fighting for their attentions above the Paris skyline.

Real life Frenchmen Messieurs de Grandpré and Le Pique fought for the hand of Mademoiselle Tirevit in the skies above Paris on 3 May 1808, by conducting a duel in a hydrogen balloon.

The contemporary press described Mademoiselle Tirevit as "a celebrated opera dancer" who "was kept by Monsieur Grandpré but had been discovered in an intrigue with Monsieur Le Pique". Nice euphemism 'intrigue'. Presumably prompting a fit of pique - Le Pique having a fit.

Pistols were to be drawn at dawn, once they had gone through the rigmarole of launching twin hydrogen balloons above Paris one morning. Accompanied by their seconds, the aeronautical duellers rendezvoused in a field on the Parisian outskirts "to quarrel over Mademoiselle Tirevit".

Stymied by the practical difficulties of obtaining two balloons for a duel, the pair allowed a brief flowering of common sense in the otherwise arid desert of sense, and put back the duel for a month in order for the balloons to be sourced. They were both described as "elevated minds", but surely only in a literal sense.

A small Parisian crowd gathered on the duel day in a field adjoining the Tuilleries, reportedly expecting the novelty of a balloon race - not a deadly death match. Blunderbusses rather than pistols were selected for the unique duelling conditions, pistols decreed to be ineffectual at such range. Then at 9am both balloons were launched when the duelling duo's seconds cut the tethering ropes simultaneously. The globes drifted no more than eighty metres apart from each other. Once they had climbed to an altitude of 900 metres, Monsieur Le Pique "fired his piece ineffectively" - as Mademoiselle Tirevit could no doubt regularly testify.

Having spent his one shot, Le Pique could now only await his fate as a huge floating target. But his adversary did not leave him waiting for long, returning fire almost instantly and bursting his balloon. Consequently Monsieur Le Pique and his unfortunate second descended rather too swiftly and were both described as "dashed to pieces" on a house roof below. The victorious Monsieur Grandpré and his second then made a gentler and safe descent back to earth.

It was almost certainly the very first aerial duel, followed a few seconds later by the first aerial murder. It was one of several number ones for French aeronautics, since the French were also the first to harness the balloon for effective military use.

The Arc de Triomphe was, of course, built to celebrate achievements in France's somewhat bellicose history. By the approaching autumn of 1870 France was fighting a rearguard action in its war with Prussia, and Paris was ominously encircled by Prussian troops. A Parisian aeronaut ascended out of the city, immediately picking up a strong air current which flew him over Prussian camps where he dropped French propaganda leaflets.

On subsequent trips, Monsieur Jules Duruof carried a basket of homing pigeons. Scribbled notes listing the position of the Prussian lines, and estimates of their man and fire power were then despatched via the carrier pigeons' legs back to the French HQ. Within days of this reconnaissance accomplishment two of the city's principal train stations, the Gare d'Orléans and the present-day Eurostar terminal Gare du Nord, were put to work as improvised balloon factories - their high-domed roofs proving ideal for the large spaces required by hot air balloon production. And since the Prussians had excelled at sabotage, there were no trains left to disrupt. Which was fortunate, as even First Great Western have yet to use that old chestnut excuse: "We regret the cancellation of the 7.43 to Didcot Parkway - this has been caused by unscheduled hot air balloon manufacture to spy on troop positions in the Franco-Prussian War." It's only a matter of time though - you see. Using cheap cotton cloth, not the most impermeable of fabrics for containing hot air, over fifty balloons were soon ready for despatch over the Prussian lines in vital reconnaissance missions. Not all were successful, and one manned balloon accomplished the alarming feat of flying fully 2,000 miles until it landed in decidedly colder Norway.

Not all of the balloons managed to contain sufficient hot air to reach a safe altitude, and enemy riflemen picked off some of them, most notably shooting the eminent French politician Léon Gambetta through the hand while he hurriedly hurled ballast over the side of his balloon's basket, before he gained sufficient height momentum to escape and land safely back in Paris. As for Duruof, he survived until 1899, despite crashing - with his wife - in September 1874 into

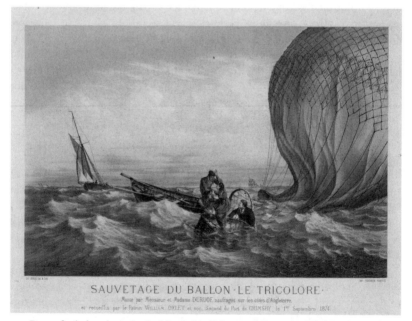

SAUVETAGE DU BALLON·LE TRICOLORE·

Duruof splashes down in the North Sea (Library of Congress, Washington DC)

the North Sea near Grimsby, where he was fortuitously rescued.

So important was the French aerial assault that the world's first anti-aircraft guns were created by the Prussians - crude improvisations that fired, with moderate success, at the large floating targets. Over two million letters were estimated to have left Paris breaching the siege, and providing vital communication to the outside world and other divisions of the French Army. Around 500 carrier pigeons successfully returned to base after being released from the balloons high above the Prussian lines.

Sadler is unlikely to have had access to any of the pioneering work being done in France in 1773-74, and it is remarkable that he was working on two entirely different balloon mechanisms simultaneously - akin to the Wright Brothers inventing an aeroplane and a helicopter in the same year. (Though, to be painfully fair, the French invented both a few months before Sadler.) Sadler was experimenting and producing coal gas, creating hydrogen, while simultaneously inventing his own highly efficient hot air balloon with a stove mechanism pivotal to controlling the balloon's propulsion. He was also adding crucial vents and values to the balloon, enabling the beast to be controlled rather than blindly rolling the dice of fate when it came to landings, which Montgolfier and others certainly did.

7 JANUARY 1785: FRENCH FARCE - THE RACE TO CROSS THE CHANNEL

Disappointment and setbacks were many in the pioneering days of aerostation, but if a man's character is judged on his reaction to adversity, then Sadler's personality test would score highly in this category. Having invested £500 of eighteenth-century money on building and equipping a balloon for this specific purpose, he was reported "having worked day and night" on the project of being the first to fly across the English Channel.

However not even Sadler could not beat the English winter weather. Setting off for Dover at Christmas 1784, Sadler found that his barge was literally frozen en route from Oxford to London in a prolonged cold spell. By the time a sufficient thaw had occurred to let him reach the capital, Sadler discovered the varnish on the silk balloon envelope had reacted with the ice and formed a substance akin to glue, rendering the expensive globe practically useless. Even the greatest men in history cannot overcome the British weather.

Upon leaving London for Dover the next day, news reached him that the Frenchman Jean-Pierre Blanchard had already crossed the finishing line and claimed victory for France on 7 January 1785. As if an illustration was needed to underscore how dangerous pioneering ballooning could be, Blanchard, as well as several other runners and riders in the race to be the first to fly the Channel, were all subsequently killed in later ballooning accidents.

Blanchard's route to the title was predictably unstraightforward. He also displayed a characteristic unwillingness to share the credit with his co-pilot.

Establishing base camp in Dover Castle in early January 1785, Blanchard and his flying partner, benefactor and sponsor Dr. John Jefferies, set about planning their attempt at flying across the Channel. Jefferies, an American medical doctor based in Britain, maintained a strong interest in meteorology and planned to take measuring instruments on the flight. But Blanchard was against such an imposition. And Blanchard had form in this area, once having thrown overboard the scientific instruments of his previous co-pilot, Dr. John Sheldon.

Paying for the flight also proved to be no guarantee of a seat for Jefferies. Blanchard locked himself in the castle and intended to launch himself solo over the Channel the next day. A legitimately outraged Jefferies was having none of this Gallic petulance, and he arrived at the castle in uncompromising mood and with a private gang of mercenaries. Dangling a purse bulging with cash helped persuade the castle governor to see Jefferies' side of the dispute - and Blanchard was restrained from his credit-stealing solo endeavour.

The next morning the two mutually suspicious aviators climbed into the balloon cart. Blanchard concluded that the balloon was too heavy for a launch and asked Jefferies to step out. Jefferies was right to harbour suspicions, and inspected Blanchard's jacket. Sure enough, a preliminary frisk revealed that he was wearing a specially adapted waistcoat filled with lead weights. Behaving more like a Scooby-Doo villain than a pioneering aeronaut, Blanchard had mendaciously attempted to make sure the balloon was overweight for take-off, his plan being to force Jefferies to vacate the basket. Once the ruse was exposed, Jefferies demanded that the leaden waistcoat be jettisoned before take-off. The pair then took off, exploiting favourable weather and an obliging wind direction.

Skimming the sea, the Frenchman and American soon started to lose altitude. They had clearly put more effort into fighting each other than making sure that their balloon was adequately inflated. Even after they had jettisoned all their onboard ballast early in the flight (except for three ten-pound sacks of sand) a note-taking Jefferies observed: "The barometer immediately sank from 29.7 to 27.3."

Throwing out ballast, Blanchard delighted in tossing Jefferies' expensive scientific instruments overboard. But although the balloon initially rose, it soon sank again, hovering menacingly close to the white waves below. Panicking, they detached the basket ornaments, followed by their coats and hurled them over the side. Even this resulted in insufficient levitation. Finally

Blanchard jettisoned his shoes, belt bucket and then, no doubt being French, his beret, onions, baguette and finally his trousers. "We were obliged," Dr. Jeffries recounted in a subsequent letter to the President of the Royal Society, "to throw out the only bottle we had, which fell on the water with a loud sound, and sent up spray like smoke."

How temptingly close the argumentative duo came to jettisoning each other mid-Channel is regrettably unrecorded by Jefferies.

Matching the trajectory of a Dambuster bouncing bomb for most of their Channel crossing, it looked likely that the attempt would end wetly. Jefferies later described planning to jump into the sea, resigned to a watery fate. Then, four miles from the coast, the pair suddenly soared upwards, regaining height when they encountered a different air temperature. At exactly 3pm they crossed the French shoreline equidistant between Calais and Cap Blanc Nez. Jefferies noted: "The balloon rose rapidly in a great arc." Encountering an intensifying wind, the balloon then ironically gained height and speed at the very time they needed to land.

They soon found themselves at a greater elevation than at any part of their course.

Once unsafely over land, they tangled with a high tree twelve miles from the coast. Their cart became embedded in a branch, making an impromptu tree house from which the bruised, scratched and intrepid aeronauts emerged to French acclaim (the locals were, of course, anxious to downplay Jefferies' part, given the fact he was an English-dwelling American). Pursuing horsemen had followed the balloon once it crossed into French airspace, and were quickly at the crash site. A day after the historic flight, the two aeronauts were rushed by the same horsemen back to Calais to attend a fete in their honour, where Blanchard was presented with the freedom of the town in a gold box. Jefferies received nothing. The town's municipal body purchased Blanchard's balloon and put it on display.

Yet Blanchard was only the winner by default. For a long time it looked likely that he would only claim the bronze medal in the cross-Channel race.

The most likely claimant to the title, even ahead of Sadler whose purpose-built balloon had been scuppered by the harsh winter, had been another French aeronaut: none other than our old friend Jean-François Pilâtre de Rozier, the very first human ever to fly.

Rozier should have been a shoe-in for the title, a favourite hotter than a stolen hot cake. In receipt of 40,000 crowns from the King of France and his backers the Académie des Sciences, Rozier had ample funding for the job. A special hangar was erected in Boulogne in November 1784 to house the monster globe. With a launch site already selected it looked like all other bets were off. But the hare became distracted, allowing the two tortoises Sadler and Blanchard to catch up then overtake Rozier in the race.

In Boulogne Rozier had met an English former convent girl, Susan Dyer, described as "the prettiest of English roses", and spent the next few months shacked up with her, repeatedly plucking his English rose. The couple quickly became engaged. His balloon neglected, it started to be eaten by rats. His funds were also being eaten away, and his Parisian backers were becoming increasingly impatient at the lack of news. This meant that Rozier willingly surrendered pole position and his place in history to Blanchard and Sadler, preferring the distractions of a three-month love-in with a pretty girl - which is satisfyingly national-stereotype-bullseye French.

With Sadler's attempt falling at the last hurdle, it was left to Blanchard to canter home alone towards to the winning post unchallenged.

Author Fulgence Marion's 1870 book *Wonderful Balloon Ascents or the Conquest of the Skies* has an interesting anecdote about Blanchard being rewarded by the Queen of France for being the first to cross the Channel: "Some days afterwards Blanchard was summoned before the king, who conferred upon him an annual pension of 1200 *livres*. The queen, who was at play at the gambling table, placed a sum for him upon a card, and presented him with the purse which she won."

Media reaction to the Channel crossing cannot accurately be described as undersold: "Enthusiasm about aerial voyages is now at its climax; the most wonderful deeds were spoken of as commonplace, and the word 'impossible' was erased from the language."

The petulant pair had succeeded in becoming the first to traverse the Channel by flight. And it was left to Dr. Jeffries to extract the scientific accomplishments from the historic ascent, when he later addressed the Royal Society - part of his strategy to counteract Blanchard's crude attempts to monopolise the credit.

Jean-Pierre Blanchard may have beaten Sadler across the Channel, but he also beat Sadler to the grave by several decades, falling from his balloon basket above The Hague in an unwise ascent during poor weather in Holland. Remarkably his widow Sophie Blanchard took up her deceased husband's profession, and became the first professional female balloonist. She was decorated by both sides in the French Revolution, firstly appointed "Official Aeronaut of the Festivals" by Napoleon. With the later restoration of the monarchy came her next official appointment in 1814, when she was granted the title "Official Aeronaut of the Restoration" by King Louis XVIII.

Unfortunately, she also became the first female casualty of aviation. Above Tivoli Gardens in Paris in 1819 she unwisely conducted a fireworks display directly underneath her hydrogen balloon. Regrettably, you can probably guess how that party ended - with a bang.

4 CASTLE COWARD: CHILDHOOD TRAUMAS

My very first meaningful counselling session is with a lady called Kate. She doesn't feel that I am a client who fits her model of counselling, so we do not continue with my treatment after a preliminary session. Which is odd, as I didn't know it was possible to get dumped by your counsellor, particularly if, like me, you are displaying clear self-esteem issues. Nevertheless, the very first advice I receive from my counsellor when I announce that I intend to take a balloon flight with chronic acrophobia is: "You just need a will to do it." Following her advice to the letter, I start positively by making a will.

Consistent with all the pioneering aeronauts, Sadler was used to his passengers making wills before going on a flight - a practice continued today for Ryanair flights. (Note to Ryanair's litigious supporters: that was a joke.) Well, at least balloon flight purveyors don't say: "And will you be requiring a basket with your balloon flight, Sir? You will? That'll be an expensive surcharge."

If I am going to face the biggest challenge of my life, then I need to plan. Therefore I take a bus into town to make a will. This turns out to include a sales pitch from a financial services expert, who at one stage genuinely utters the line, "because here at Bastard Bank we like to think that our customers' deaths are important to us." I really should have taped that. How typical that the financial services industry, not content with screwing us throughout our mortal lifetime, has now moved into securing the afterlife market too. Much pontificating then occurs on how my death can benefit people who are left behind when I'm gone - though mainly, I observe, shareholders of Bastard Bank.

So I make a will, guided through the process by a professional. Unsurprisingly this process does not fill me with confidence for my approaching balloon flight, but I have at least acted on my counsellor's advice - albeit with a stubborn literalness.

It is also worth observing that "counsellor" is not a protected job title in law. Although it is illegal to call oneself an architect or actuary without appropriate qualifications, bizarrely this is not the case for a counsellor, who, seemingly unregulated, can inflict damage on vulnerable people. All an architect can do, on the other hand, is design an ugly building somewhere (thank goodness there aren't any of those anywhere), and an actuary can devise some mis-sold insurance policy or modelling projections that end up ruining the economy and closing libraries to bail out bankers (likewise, thank goodness the current law protects us from that ever happening).

Kate wanted to steer me along the psychoanalytical route. Psychological archaeology was causing me some discomfort. All those deep digging excavations into my past and consciousness risked bursting a water pipe, and I genuinely felt hot tears flowing down my cheeks. Are women biologically more predisposed to crying, or is it just a cultural behaviour thing? Ask a woman and she'll inform you that it's because men give them more to cry about then they give men. In reality, males cry just as much as females throughout childhood right up until puberty. So The Cure were wrong about that too: Boys Do Cry. Only after puberty, women are biologically more predisposed to tears due to the twin reasons of having considerably larger tear ducts than men, and also possessing over 50% more prolactin - the hormone prevalent in teardrops - than men. Oh, and also because all men are arseholes. My wife has just reminded me.

So I decide to find another counsellor, and act on recommendations to test Cognitive Behaviour Therapy. Kate doesn't think I should be booking a balloon flight if I am this terrified of heights, a view fortified by my admissions of surging neurosis, and reinforced by my friends.

Yet I am galvanised into doing it, motivated by my desire to tell people about James Sadler. I want to restore his status as a household name.

I am eight years old and love castles. Two of the greatest things when you are eight come in castle format: sand castles and proper battle castles. So it is off-the-scale excitement today as we are going on a primary school trip to Tattershall Castle in Lincolnshire.

I can verify the exact date of my affection for castles, since I still have my school notebook: "I like castles. I love castles. Castles are nice. The End." Looking back it must have been obvious to all the teachers even then that I was destined to become a professional writer.

Everyone arrives, packed lunches predictably eaten by 9.30am en route, and we are paired into twos for the crocodile formation by a stressed teacher who, although I was understandably unaware at the time, was clearly going through relationship issues in public. Oh I can see that now. "If the girls could ensure they hold hands with a boy," hollered Miss Harrison before lowering her voice to near inaudibility, "you might as well enjoy their company before the crushing realisation of untrustworthiness inherent in their soulless beings emerges". That and her black panda eyes from running mascara, and the other teachers constantly comforting her with, "I know, they're all scumbags, he's just not worth it, you're better off without him".

I am paired with Caroline Hayes. This was not good. Another teacher continues to console Miss Harrison with, "they're all sexist pigs, dear." "We're not sexist or chauvinistic at all," I thought, somewhat precociously for an eight-year-old, and besides that's a remark typical of a sissy girl.

Caroline was a sissy girl, obviously. She also emitted the recalcitrant air of effortless superiority, being abnormally clever. She would probably have preferred to be reading poetry or Chekhov in Russian while the rest of us ran around then swung in tyres like primates. I sometimes wonder what became of Caroline. I'm sure she married beneath herself, as everyone seemed to occupy that position in her self-perception even back then - and often with some justification.

Paired off, and chattering at an even higher decibel level than Miss Harrison's sobbing, we move like a Chinese human dragon towards the castle. Hopefully they will be serving lunch soon, as we've already eaten ours.

Whereas the castle has seen off many marauding armies and foreign invaders, it is vulnerable to attack by noise and crisp crumbs from primary school kids. Whatever medieval armies or Civil War conscripts it repelled in history, a bunch of loud primary school kids are not going to be held back, even if they attempt to raise the drawbridge.

"Welcome to Tattershall Castle," announces the guide, realising that this audience are prepared to give him their attention for five seconds - eight seconds tops. So he moves quickly to the gory stuff. "This was a dungeon where lots of men had horrible things done to them." "Good," confirms Miss Harrison, "I hope they all died in agony," she concludes. Another teacher places a sympathetic arm around her.

"The castle was built by Cromwell in the fifteenth century," the guide continues, ignoring Miss Harrison's public breakdown.

"Surely," interrupts Caroline, "Cromwell was around in the mid-seventeenth century, not the fifteenth." Told you she was clever. "Very good," says the tour guide in a timbre that translates the uttered words into their actual meaning: "There's always some bloody precious precocious know-it-all brat determined to expose the fact I only got the guiding notes last night, and there was too much to read let alone learn what with the bloody cat being sick everywhere again."

Later it transpired the castle was indeed built by Cromwell, albeit Ralph Cromwell. Ralph, not Oliver, was a Privy Councillor, then Treasurer of England between 1433 and 1443, serving under Henry VI where he held the title of Chamberlain of the Royal Household. Earlier he had accompanied the king's predecessor Henry V at his victorious battle at Agincourt in 1415. This is generally a good thing to remember as it annoys the French.

Not content with designing the castle and its battlements, Cromwell also landscaped the grounds, planned the moat and built the nearby church - leaving me with the impression that Cromwell was evidently a bit of a control freak.

47

Tattershall Castle boasts both an inner and outer moat, but this fortification still ignores a common oversight in castle defences: the weakest point of any castle, where it is least defended and thus most vulnerable to attack, is always the gift shop. Although, admittedly, I am not a military historian.

"Any questions?" asks the guide. "No," he answers patiently, "there were no landing docks designed for rocket ships." Then Caroline asks a question: "Why are the inscriptions in pseudo-medieval French misspelt?" "Um... so, where would you all put landing docks for rocket ships, eh children?" the guide responds. Caroline sighs the sigh of those destined to be permanently disappointed by the level of idiocy surrounding them, and totters off to the gift shop in presumable hope of sourcing a decent Medieval French Dictionary.

Ralph Oliver died shortly after the castle was finished. Soon afterwards government autocrats arrived to inform his grieving widow Lady Joan that the castle would now be confiscated, women having no property ownership rights in law back then. It's quite difficult to comprehend such insensitivity.

The Great Tower of Tattershall Castle, with its illustrious red bricks - a rare and expensive material for castle construction in the era - stands an impressive 130 feet tall. Therein lies a major problem for me. Reaching the promised panoramic vista on top necessitates negotiating exactly 150 steps on a dark, twisting and seemingly continuous spiral staircase, corkscrewing its way to the flattish roof behind the battlements.

Others kids are running up the stairs. A teacher calls out, "stop running on the castle stairs!" Great, that's yet another place we can't run - along with corridors. Miss Harrison doesn't care if we run or not; instead she optimistically asks the guide: "Don't suppose you have an alcohol licence for the tea rooms?"

I am not running. Instead I am actually pleased the teacher has decreed there is to be no running on the stairs. I clutch the handrail. And then I stop. My feet are locked. My tongue is frozen. I am unable to move or communicate. Both reactions are shockingly involuntarily. Even at eight years old, I know this is something I should definitely be worrying about. I feel sick. There is a real risk of vomiting. The teacher at the rear asks me why I have stopped. I cannot tell her or, it appears, speak at all. Craftily, the teacher tells me she can hear the sound of the children on the roof already, encouraging me to conform to peer pressure and follow the other kids.

When I do not move, she asks me again why I have stopped. Then she asks me if I am scared of heights. "I don't know," I manage to answer truthfully. "I think you may be," she counsels. I nod, shameful and truthful tears cascading done my cheeks. The tears flood out, though still not approaching the level of Miss Harrison's, who belatedly realises she should probably hold it together as an adult role model when in charge of impressionable young children. She holds my hand and leads me carefully back down the stairs. "Come on," she says, "we'll get a milkshake from the café," before adding, "it's not just the moats in this place that are dry."

What I really don't like about myself is that I was angry with Miss Harrison, because my anger displacement transferred onto her because I was unable to reach the top of the castle - a rare chance to say "I'm the King of the Castle" in situ. It was not her fault. She was the one being kind to me.

As promised, she sympathetically gets me a drink - not a milkshake but a foamy, frothy Cresta (there was an advertising jingle in the 1970s, "It's frothy, man"). I pour the suspiciously bright fuchsia liquid into a glass. Miss Harrison orders herself a substandard 1970s coffee. This was the pre-cappuccino age when coffee only came in a jar and shared the colour, properties and taste of river silt. I surmised the reason it was called "ground coffee" back then was because it tasted like it was made from the actual ground - an insipid frothy mud.

Then a castle estate worker enters the café. A ludicrously handsome man just exiting his twenties, his natural rugged outdoor good looks garnished with a tan and muscles. He stares at Miss Harrison like a man who has just noticed the sky for the first time - and Miss Harrison must have appeared as a glorious sky, worthy of J.M.W. Turner reaching for his easel. She appears equally transfixed, suddenly unable to hear the question I am asking her.

Miss Harrison quickly positions, primes, loads and fires her big guns - not the cannons on the castle battlements, but her more destructive big guns. She treats him to the full flirtatious hair flick and that pretend I'm-adjusting-my-hair-in-an-imaginary-mirror thing followed by an unnecessary reapplying of a scrunchie that women sometimes manipulatively do because they know it makes them look good. With all that hair tossing, body shimmer, raking fingers through her silky mane the handyman views her like a salivating lion watching a gazelle supping demurely at the watering hole while winking at him.

With our evolutionary smugness, we've got home espresso machines now instead of Mellow Birds instant coffee granules (nowadays you only offer someone an instant coffee if you want to insult them). Yet for all the veneer of superiority humans like to bring to their evolutionary progress, our mating rituals transplant us right back to the monkeys. It could have been a scene from the Serengeti half a million years ago. As, equally, could have been the responsive behaviour of her potential mate. Miss Harrison was arching her back and thrusting up an ample display of décolletage.

The guy responds with a darting snake tongue and cartoon eyes-on-stalks. Fortunately for an already over-populated world, just at the crucial moment when this mating ritual is reaching its conclusion, marked by the handyman scraping his right hoof across the Tea Room parquet floor and charging towards his quarry, the other teacher reappears in the café. Immediately, and speechless, she literally drags Miss Harrison off, leading her away like a dog who has just been discovered attempting to get through a hole in the fence to liaise with next door's bitch.

Once out of the room she starts to speak, pointing out at some volume to Miss Harrison, that (a) more than one teacher should be supervising a class of very young children on a 130-foot high roof (told you it was dangerous) and (b) how could she possibly be thinking about men and dating again "after what she's just been through" what with her pledges and vows of sending SAEs to nunneries only a few moments earlier? "And why aren't you wearing your glasses?" she enquires. Miss Harrison is more busted than I was that time I was milk monitor and gave my friends double rations. That plan would have worked if there had been some milk left once half the class had been served. For quite a while after that fateful day, I was widely tipped for a career in politics. An embarrassed and busted Miss Harrison puts her glasses back on and is pulled up the stairs by the other teacher.

I am left along with a disappointing can of Cresta and an even more disappointed handy man. "That went well," I feel like saying to him, "not your lucky day is it. Plus you get to spend the best years of your adulthood in the 1970s which, as a decade, definitely sucks."

But I liked Miss Harrison - she was kind to me. Then I realise why she was reluctant to go upstairs too and out onto the roof. In retrospect I can recognise a fellow acute acrophobe when I hold their sweating, shivering hand on a stairwell.

I often wonder what happened to Miss Harrison. I heard she moved to the Falklands one week before the Argentine invasion. Perhaps she had gone there to escape a guy and believed it would just be her and the penguins. Afterwards I was told she moved to Holland and got married to a local man. Typical of an acute acrophobia sufferer to want to live in a country mainly below sea level. She married a Dutchmen, the Dutch being, according to UN statistics, the tallest nation on earth. Why? There's nothing there that they need to see over!

Back on the bus, the kids talk about the views. "So, what have we learnt today?" asks a teacher. Other than that it's definitely worth Miss Harrison paying the extra and investing in water-proof mascara? Well, I've categorically learnt that I suffer from acrophobia. And bathmophobia. Big words for a small person.

Whenever I go past that castle today, decades later, I still feel a shivering sense of shame and regret. After - or if - I do my balloon trip in honour of Sadler, I will return and conquer those stairs too. And finally get to see the view I missed out on all those decades earlier. And discover if it's possible forty years later to get a decent cup of coffee in their tea room.

I am fifteen, desperate for sixteen. Greedy for life experience, yet restrained from most potential teenage experiences due to a combination of anxieties: the usual teenage cocktail of angst and insecurities mixed with a peculiarly unique fear of stairs. It never dawned upon me to discuss it, i.e. admit it to anyone, either the helpful and resourceful (health care professionals) or sneering piss takers (my peers). Placating my nagging mind's insistence on performing Obsessive Compulsive Disorder completion rituals clearly did not help me fulfil my teenage potential either.

Travelling home on the school bus I am wondering, not for the first time, if it is normal to consider my peer group desperately immature. Sometimes during these journeys I peer out from behind my teenage eyes and dirty bus window to survey the immaturity surrounding me, wondering if I am the only one with a gift of seeing how jejeune everyone is. No, I don't want to hide someone's bag, throw some unfortunate's possessions out of a window or make stupid noises. I just don't. Right now, I'd rather be in my forties. I've seen how people in their forties behave and it's considerably better than this. They read, have meaningful conversations, listen to Radio 4 and tell people about it afterwards without getting beaten up. Plus they get to eat things like rye bread and olives. And sip wine appreciatively with meals.

Predictably, this attitude guarantees that I have few friends among my peer group. And since education in my home town enforces a strict apartheid gender policy, I know scarcely any girls. The few times I have stolen access to girls in this forbidding town, I have discovered they are more empathetic than boys, and on average noticeably less immature as a species. Hence I prefer their company.

There are four principal secondary schools in my hometown and all operate along stern single sex divisions, which hardly prepares anyone in their formative years for dealing with the world at large. I can't help noticing subsequently, perhaps more than I'd admit to my wife, that there appear to be several women in the world. No one made any provision for that eventuality during my entire secondary school education.

However, even in my early teenage years I am capable of recognising a girl - I saw a picture of one once. This sounds obvious, but not in the pre-Internet age it wasn't. You know how today people leave copies of *Metro* on Tube trains (presumably in Paris people leave copies of *Tube* on the Metro)? In our day it was hedges and porn magazines. By rights, today's teenagers should have to access a laptop hidden in a hedge. Top shelf magazines were how we discovered female anatomy. Most boys of my generation were in their early twenties until they realised that naked women did not come as standard with two staples in their midriff. Though, ironically, there is now a fashion among women to have belly button piercings - girls voluntarily putting the staples back.

Already in my early years I had learnt one thing. There is nothing in nature as beautiful as a woman. Sunsets, mountain ranges, rainbows, giraffes - all fine efforts, God, but nowhere near as beautiful as a female human called Charlotte Jones. Charlotte has dolphin-blue eyes, and I discover myself harbouring incommensurable affection for her. Charlotte is more attractive than any human surely ever needs to be.

Her name chimes with my favourite song at the time: Charlotte Sometimes by The Cure. The Cure were my top band, fronted by Robert "Mad Bob" Smith, a man, like Albert Einstein, who showed what it is possible to achieve in life if you don't waste time brushing your hair. Robert Smith also wore bright red pouting lipstick, badly applied, which always gave him the appearance of someone who had put on lippy in the back of a car while going over speed bumps.

Charlotte was the genuine girl next door type, mainly because she was the girl who lived next door - and my own age. Although in our rural isolation next door constituted an eight-minute walk, as we lived in a remote part of Lincolnshire's empty flatlands miles from the town where we attended separate schools. Furthermore, the boys' and girls' schools were on extreme polar-opposite sides of my hometown, to discourage even the most accidental of fraternisation between the genders.

Twenty houses and an inn constituted the hamlet where I grew up and Charlotte had suffered the cultural shockwave of moving here from London. Only once did it make the news. When Jeffrey Archer was an inmate at an open prison in the locality, he allegedly treated two of his prison warders to a pub lunch in our hamlet. This caused much outcry in the press, but surely it wasn't the first time that Archer had paid for a screw. (My marks out of ten for that joke: /10.)

Maybe Charlotte was not a classic beauty, the type that a careers adviser would tell: "You should be an artist's muse - the hours are good". But I thought Charlotte was stunningly beautiful, and crucially female. Looking back, my earlier pre-Charlotte infatuations were not well chosen. There was Sandra who may not have been the most refined of sophisticates, blowing her bubble gum into a balloon equivalent to Sadler's circumference, and laughing crudely at her friends even cruder jokes. Yet I felt Cupid pulling back his bow string and aiming at me. This was probably because she had one major attribute going for her: she was female. And I had virtually no access to females in my emotionally isolated teenage life. Refined, urbane culturists like Charlotte Jones were as exotic as unicorns. Though my friend pointed out that Sandra was definitely up for a snog. Unfortunately, this involved climbing up a water tower one afternoon. So that didn't happen.

Boarding the school bus one afternoon I spot Charlotte, flicking her long chestnut mane over her shoulders and carrying a book of Rimbaud's poetry. In French. Wow, she is so cool, sophisticated and debonair. And she wears perfume too - what an all-round class act. Charlotte and I allow a feral pack of schoolboys to ram their way onto the bus before boarding ourselves. The problem with today's bus journey is now there are no more seats on the ground floor. "Plenty of seats upstairs!" trills the driver, in a pitch similar to the bell. I pretend, unconvincingly, not to have heard him and stand up. This is infinitely preferable to saying out loud, in front of numerous bullies and morons devoid of any developed sensitivity: "I won't go upstairs because I am really scared of stairs and heights. If you'd please only hit me one at a time, bullies. Thank you."

A week earlier I saw Charlotte's long legs striding past KFC where she threw me a pitying glance as my friends and I classily ate out of a bucket while sitting on the pavement, grease stains dribbling down our white school shirts. She was so much more sophisticated than us. Had a Kentucky Fried Grouse opened, maybe she would then have frequented it - but not KFC.

Not only did she own a Miles Davis LP that I once saw her carrying under her refined arm as she alighted at my bus stop one evening - still reeling from her move to these isolated, unedifying wastelands from worldly London a few weeks earlier - but I also saw her talking to another girl about French cinema. My peers all listened to Status Quo; cultivated Charlotte represented a challenge to that status quo orthodoxy. This is why I like girls - because they talk about French cinema and don't like Status Quo.

The next night Charlotte boards the bus, but goes upstairs. So I won't be eavesdropping on her conversation tonight. Nor the next night when she also rushes up to the top deck. Eventually one evening I find her downstairs. She has progressed to Italian cinema and mentions The Bicycle Thief to another girl. I eagerly rent it for the weekend, and make notes, write observations, learn pre-prepared soundbites. I am ready for Operation Impress Charlotte. She watches Vittorio De Sica's 1948 black and white masterpiece in an era when my contemporaries were almost exclusively watching Porky's I, Porky's II and, with the predictability of leaves falling in autumn, Porky's III. My heart actually made a noise it pined for Charlotte so much.

On Monday she boards the bus, but goes upstairs. Tuesday, she quickly scurries up the staircase like a hamster darting up a tunnel eager to escape a pursuing snake. She repeats this behaviour, scampering upstairs on both Wednesday and Thursday. On Friday she starts to scuttle up the bus stairs again. Moments later her lovely light-brown knees, still tanned from an obvious middle-class family excursion to somewhere warm, descend the steps, and I see her dark green school skirt surprisingly reappearing into view. Presumably there was no room on the top deck; it was fully colonised by rabid, acne-ridden school kids. So she sits on her own in front of me downstairs.

Friday I'm In Love. Another Cure song plays in my head competing for air time with Charlotte Sometimes in my internal jukebox. This is my chance to talk to her. She pulls her long free-flowing hair upwards and applies a hairgrip. Behind her I am sitting in a bus seat conquered by her enticing beauty, admiring the back of her gorgeous neck, contemplating how Charlotte misses out on this view: the back of her own beautiful neck. I rehearse opening lines internally. My heartbeat doesn't appear to be helping, suddenly racing at 200 loud pounds per minute, booming like a bass drum incessantly struck to a fast dance beat. It is so noticeably loud that it will surely drown out any words I attempt to orate.

Then, in a voice I hardly recognise as my own, I open with "Hello". "Hello" is my grand, rehearsed, practised to the point of obsession in front of the mirror for weeks, line. My big opening. As opening chat-up lines go, it's a standard. Not a classic, but a standard nevertheless. I decide to build on my one-word opening, and succeed in adding one further comprehensible word to make: "Hello Charlotte." Unfortunately she appears to expect me to add to my initiatory two words. This is where preparation is the key. There is also traceable alarm in her expression, her look audibly wondering: "How do you know my name, weirdo?" I know her name purely because I overheard her friends call her that. I prefer "observant" to "eavesdropping", "taking an interest" to "stalker".

But she ignores my disconcerting use of her name, allowing me to go straight to my prepared line which has finally come back to me, after the abject panic triggered by the unfamiliarity encountered in speaking with an actual human female of my own age: "I heard you were really saying something... I mean talking Italian." This is supposed to be a key speech in my teenage years and I'm involuntarily reciting Bananarama lyrics. Go away Bananarama, you're not helping.

I try again: "I heard you saying something really interesting about Italian cinema and *The Bicycle Thief*." She eyes me like an unordered side dish placed before her in a restaurant. I continue and make one of my prepared spontaneous observations about Italian cinema, enabling me to reach the final of the Britain's Most Pretentious Man Contest. Then I fall silent.

After a full quarter mile, she says something: "Shy Boy". Clever. You see, she had responded to my Bananarama Tourettes by saying the title of that band's then current Top 5 single. This, alas, was completely over my head. It was decades later - on the cusp of 2014 to be exact - before I worked out the smart significance of her response. She really was decades ahead of me. Sighing pitifully when I fail to understand the concept of her witticism, she arrows me a look which suggests her intellect shines with the intensity of a thousand suns compared to mine: a lone speck of dust. Oh well. I conclude she's intellectually superior, a tad snooty, out of my league, perhaps mildly obnoxious and vastly more attractive and popular than me. So why do I suffer the huge inconvenience of liking her so much? At least she didn't freak out completely when I called her by her name. I seem to have got away with that one. We get off the bus together at our abandoned rural outpost and spin in different directions - me to the right and her to the left.

Monday and Tuesday of the next week she goes upstairs. On Wednesday she sits downstairs, but as soon as I sit on the only vacant seat next to her, she immediately puts on her new Sony Walkman and music leaks out of her headphones. I had never seen a personal stereo device before, and Charlotte could not only have been Lincolnshire's earliest adopter, but likely the very first person in the UK to annoy every other bus passenger with an inconsiderate inability to keep their personal stereo device personal.

She's listening to The Cure! Wow. At least we have something in common. I decide I must tell her this - only of course she cannot hear me. Plus the song title *Boys Don't Cry* doesn't turn out to be true - it transpires Charlotte has made it her teenage specialism to disprove the premise of that title. Indeed, she probably kept a skip underneath her bedroom window into which to toss boys' broken hearts.

Most would see the instant application of headphones as a snub - and they would be right. But I deploy a positive re-frame technique instead. After all, this allows more preparation time for me to struggle with a timeless dilemma. Yes, human beings can use radiometric dating to discover the earth's exact formation date, colonise space, cross continents in hours, map the genome. Yet I'll only be really impressed when scientists finally figure out an answer to the most timeless yet basic human question: how do you tell a girl or boy that you like them? (Then they can move on next to making broccoli taste like chocolate.)

The next night she travels on the top deck. As usual we both get off the bus in our backwater, the only two people to end their journey in this landscape so isolated and deserted it resembles one of the photos sent back by a Mars probe. From the unfashionable, less desirable part of Mars. North, south, east and west, nothing but flat fields of crops, a featureless undefined landscape without buildings or culture. Charlotte and I are surrounded by this arable desert, an unbroken breeze constantly blowing low across the fields. Everything here is destined to be played out beneath a huge, melancholy-inducing sky squatting above us. There is nothing hidden in this landscape; no hills, no obscuring trees - consequently everything is constantly in a state of existing revelation. No surprises hidden or wrapped, no mystique preserved. Though this area is so uncompromisingly flat that the local authority is officially named "Holland", it is an ideal dwelling choice for height anxiety-ridden acrophobes like me.

Surely Charlotte will see fate has given us something in common: this culturally estranged nowhere, this no man's land between two forgotten borders. We are connected by it; the only two people in the world to share this remote school bus stop.

It turns out this doesn't impress her. We go in separate directions again, only tonight I call her name. She stops, and slowly swivels to face me, but doesn't speak. I guess that's because it is down to me to initiate the next line, since I called out her name. "Charlotte," I repeat, "er… I… um… ahem… I… er…"

All I have accomplished is to check that her name works. I say "Charlotte" aloud in order to receive brief attention from someone called Charlotte. Yeah, her name seems to be working properly. But she's already starting to swivel back around. She's making a twenty-degree angle turning away from me. I flounder: "I was… er…" Thirty degrees, "like um wondering… er… if…" Forty degrees. "Er…" Fifty degrees. I had genuinely rehearsed my lines too. Really, I had. Sixty degrees. You don't leave this to chance, you have to have a line prepared. Seventy degrees. Not a good time for an actor to dry. Eighty degrees. Or a lonely teenage boy at an even lonelier bus stop either. Ninety degrees. She's disappearing from view.

In the end they say that life comes down to a small collection of vital moments, with only a few random pressured seconds allocated to each. The moment you applied for that job, made that proposal, accepted that offer, took that trip, didn't see that cyclist, and asked that girl out.

When they arrive you have to be standing in the right spot at the far post when the ball of opportunity comes to you, and despatch it past the goalkeeper of bad luck into the goal of fate. And then not be flagged offside for nicking someone else's chat-up lines.

I only have a few seconds left for a potential Big Life Moment. Her back is now half-turned. Then the words come to me in a flow: "They are showing a Fellini film at Blackfriars in town this weekend and I wondered if you'd like to go?" There, I had asked a girl out. "With me," I clarify; hopefully unnecessarily, but in case she doesn't realise I am proffering a date rather than a local "What's On" service.

Why is there nothing harder, or more painful or difficult, than the ageless dilemma of how do you tell a girl that you like her? You risk scorn, rejection, humiliation and heart-stopping agony - and future awkward bus journeys - if she doesn't like you back. From now on receiving painful treatment at the dentist, climbing an industrial chimney, ascending in a hot air balloon - or even going upstairs to the top deck of a bus - ought to be a comparative doddle. Maybe Sadler only did what he accomplished to impress a girl called Charlotte.

Charlotte surveys me. She looks up and down at my scuffed and unpolished shoes, then back up to my face where she maintains her scrutiny for a lengthy three or four seconds. Staring in silent, undisguised contempt, she holds her gaze with an expression that someone would reserve for viewing a fresh dog turd on their expensive, newly laid carpet. Slowly she turns around, gradually reaching the full 180 degrees until her back is facing me, and casually walks away, not even legitimising my painful heartfelt request with any answer.

That contemptuous silence resonates so potently I can hear it today, blowing across those open, flat fields like a breeze strong enough to knock me off my feet. The moment is still loaded with a hurtful capacity sufficient to bring a good mood instantly toppling down, capsizing the happiest of thoughts. Its flinching acidity is undiluted by the passing decades. Great: first your voice breaks, quickly followed by your heart.

On Thursday I board the bus. Charlotte gets on with two friends. Before systematically scurrying upstairs, she points at me, which results in her two friends collapsing into laughter. I don't like girls any more. They're much nastier than I expected. I may send for a "How to Become Gay" leaflet. I'll buy a Soft Cell album.

Instead I returned to my obstreperous male peer group. Desperate to fit in, I bought a Status Quo LP. It was rubbish.

Looking back, on second thoughts I can't be certain I hadn't asked her if she wanted to see a Fellaini rather than Fellini film - the former being a crazy-haired Manchester United and Belgium midfielder. On third thoughts, I may have asked her if she wanted to see a fellatio film.

Soon afterwards Charlotte's house displayed a "For Sale" sign, and within a mere month she had moved from Lincolnshire. I never expected to see her again.

Years later, I did.

When living a dreary existence in a small-town Bedfordshire house with an aggressively hostile, steep, open-spiral staircase - the worst possible dwelling choice for an acrophobic bathmophobe like me. Plus the walls were so thin, the builders had presumably just overcome the failed delivery of wall partitioning one day by gluing back to back wallpaper to divide a house into two semis, thereby saving on the budget by not supplying a wall.

It was a Friday night and I was watching *Blankety Blank* on BBC1. I recall exactly why I was watching *Blankety Blank* on my own on a Friday night - it was because my life officially sucked. The quiz show's format was dependent on the perennial British obsession with mild innuendo. A suggestively rude caption being completed by a contestant whose suggested - and suggestive - answer scored a point for each of the six celebrity panellists' answers it matched. Although the word "celebrity" was often deployed in its most elasticated form.

Contestants were required to write down a single word that they thought the assembled celebrities were most likely to have selected as a response to complete the earlier statement. Something like: "The naked au pair discovered my husband had a massive…" And the answer would be "heart attack". OK, perhaps not as extreme as that example, but you know where I'm coming from if you ever saw the show. And chances are that you did. Pivoting on a contestant's ability to match the word choice of a celebrity panellist, the show ran for 23 years from 1979 to 2002

Next door's television sound would leak invasively into our lounge through the porous walls. Alison next door would ritually have distinctly audible sex on a Sunday morning, and very occasionally midweek (if, I assume, her partner Robin's birthday fell outside a weekend). Then Alison and Robin divorced; and she kept the house. Ironically, the sex sounds increased dramatically after that.

Imposing television noise bled through our permeable walls to such an extent that viewing any programme would depend on our neighbour's decision to watch the same channel: otherwise it was like listening to conflicting separate stereo feeds. Some nights I would answer questions on the quiz show our neighbours were watching. Talking to my flatmate I would intermittently break away from our conversation to answer *University Challenge* questions from next door with "Cardiff City in 1927", "Rhodesia" and "they're all slang terms for Jeremy Paxman".

Alison soon settled on a new boyfriend, and after the carnal noises had peaked in the first few weeks of their budding relationship, a romantic autumnal chill evidently set in and sex reverted back to a strictly Sunday morning activity she performed along with the rest of the weekend chores. Weeks later there was a rare noise signifying midweek sex, like spotting a flower blooming at the wrong time of year, or an exotic bird in the wrong continent. I think I got our new neighbour a birthday card that lunchtime.

One night I am having dinner - a microwavable meal for one either from a supermarket's Lonely Gits meal-for-one selection or Oh Poor You economy range, while occasionally answering questions out loud: "the Treaty of Versailles", "Gary Lineker", "darkest Peru". Then I attempt to read a newspaper silently, saying out loud between each paragraph "Siege of Stalingrad", "A Midsummer Night's Dream", "Danger Mouse and Penfold".

Then the neighbours switch channels from the quiz and put on *Blankety Blank*. Giving up, I put it on too - might as well have pictures rather than just an audio feed. Stunned, I instantly recognise one of the two introduced contestants, giving viewers an over animated wave and toothy game show smile. It's Charlotte Jones.

Unmistakably her, before they confirm her name - that same aloofness that she cannot convincingly step out of for the TV cameras, her natural good looks relatively undiminished by the passing years. Les Dawson then introduces her by name. Host Les then reads out a short phrase, confirming the show is spiked with mild innuendo: "A blind man was so excited to hear he was in a nudist colony that he fell over and bent his... blank." Stick is clearly the answer. All the celebs write "stick" apart from Lorraine Chase who can't spell - or write - so she draws a picture of one. Charlotte doesn't say stick, she says something abstract like "hovercraft". A nation collectively gasps "what an idiot". Charlotte has scored nil out of six and immediate elimination.

Les Dawson used his tenure as host to pleasingly undermine the show with comments like "I bet, love, you wish you'd stayed home and watched *Crossroads* instead." Charlotte certainly wished she had stayed at home and watched a Fellini film because she had just suffered a horrid humiliation, played out on TV to a squirming nation. Charlotte's ignominy was deliciously drawn out, elongated as six raspberry bleeps accumulated to display her 0/6 score. Her game show facial expression was punctured by a leaking smile and hissing resentment, with every revealed answer mismatch.

As she was the losing contestant, her fate was for her part of the set to swing around while she disappeared out of view, her torment incongruously accompanied by inappropriately upbeat jangly music. Yes, fittingly she did the 180 degree disappearing-from-view silent swivel - this time for the entire Friday night peak time BBC1 national audience to witness, not just me at an abandoned bus stop in rural Lincolnshire all those years earlier. Yes, she continued with that courageous wave to camera, prompted by the floor manager, but she was incapable of hiding the stinging pain of disappointment in her eyes.

The hurtful humiliation. The burning rejection. Oh, I could see the hurt. Did it make you cry, Charlotte? Did you cry for fully three hours afterwards and refuse to leave your room to have your tea? Did you Charlotte? Because if you did, it's called karma, Charlotte. Karma.

I'd still go out with her if she asked, though. Obviously.

5 BALLOONOMANIA: THE ORIGINAL MAD HATTERS

2 MAY 1784: FRENCH BALLOONING BACKLASH

Although balloons were still fashionably new and exciting to most, a backlash was already brewing. The French, never a nation to avoid an opportunity to become surly, rallied, perhaps over-exaggeratedly, against balloon traffic gridlock.

This quickly built momentum, with stories blaming hot air balloons for causing wild fires that spread like, um, wild fire. Eventually the king became involved and threw his crown into the ring. King Louis XVI issued a royal proclamation in Paris on 2 May 1784. A subsequent official announcement appeared pinned to posts, and duplicated in most French newspapers the next day:

> Notice is given that His Majesty forbids the fabrication, or the sending up of any aeronautic machine under the pain of imprisonment. His Majesty strictly enjoining such persons as desirous of making any experiment of that nature, to apply him for permission. As he thinks proper. A decree of police, dated the 23rd April 1784 and published yesterday prohibits the conducting or raising of any balloon to which are hung lamps or spirits of wine, or any other combustible matter. The above ordinance also forbids the raising of any other balloon, without previous permission. The reasons for these prohibitions, are the dangers which are likely to follow from the falling of these machines upon thatched houses, haystacks or other inflammable materials. These precautions are not intended, however, to let this sublime discovery fall into neglect, but only that the experiments should be confined to the direction of intelligent persons.

30 AUGUST 1784: BALLOONS AS PUBLIC TRANSPORTATION

The presses were hot with Sadler's achievements by the summer of 1784. A nation was quickly becoming obsessed with ballooning, and adopted Sadler as its British hero. And remember, this is an age devoid of celebrities; people were inevitably happier then - there was no Piers Morgan. And yet the newspaper letters pages were just as full of axe-grinding, moaning NIMBYS as they are today.

A correspondent took the trouble of dipping into his ink well on 30 August 1784 to fulminate: "It is said the proprietors of large coaches are preparing a petition to prevent the use of Air Balloons as common vehicles of conveyance, and that the commissioners of turnpikes in general will join in the petition, praying that Balloon owners may be restricted from taking passengers, except to the Moon."

Like the later railways posing a threat to the canal system, feared as possible providers of agitation (the Duke of Wellington warned that railways would "cause the lower orders to move around" with the implication they would stoke revolution), balloons were seen by many as a potential revolutionary threat to traditional transport industries of coaching and shipping.

15 SEPTEMBER 1784: SADLER'S RIVAL LUNARDI

Balloonomania erupted in the UK after the flamboyant Italian Vincenzo (or Vincent) Lunardi moved to London to work for the Neapolitan Ambassador. Although Sadler was the first Englishman to fly - and was a genuine scientific engineer unlike the reckless, amateurish Italian showman - Lunardi can rightfully claim to be the first to ascend in Britain. He achieved this title at Moorfields, London, on 15 September 1784, a mere three weeks before Sadler. Nevertheless, Lunardi possessed a demonstratively showbusiness ethos compared to Sadler's Renaissance Man image. There is a marker stone still standing at Standon Green End to commemorate Lunardi's first landing near Ware, in Hertfordshire. (And don't say "Ware?", because that joke only works orally, not in print.) Lunardi had practically landed on the exact site of today's South Mimms services - handy if he wanted to pay £9.80 for a post-flight tuna baguette.

The press enjoyed portraying Sadler and Lunardi as pitted rivals; the following poem from a 1785 newspaper typifies such delineation:

Behold a windy competition,
Two puff makers in opposition,
The whole must end in vapour,
By various means their puffs they utter,
This uses water, flour and butter,
And that pens, ink and paper.

Notice how Sadler is reductively depicted as a pastry cook, whereas Lunardi is exposed as the manipulative penman. Lunardi's alleged self-written account of his flight was dismissed by numerous sources, one batting away any attempts at the author's legitimacy by remarking "anyone who has spoken to him for only a minute knows it cannot be his work."

Lunardi is considered to have made thirteen ascents, though it all went predictably wrong in 1786. Some say he was fortunate not to encounter disaster

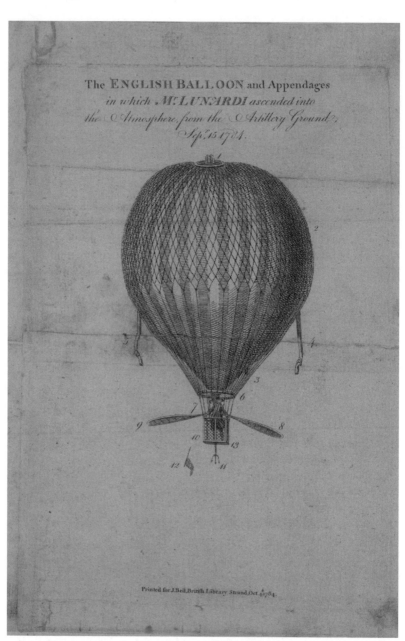

The ENGLISH BALLOON and Appendages
in which Mr. LUNARDI ascended into
the Atmosphere, from the Artillery Ground,
Sep. 15 1784.

Printed for J.Bell, British Library Strand, Oct 4 1784.

Lunardi's prototype, complete with his oars (Library of Congress, Washington DC)

earlier. Taking off, Lunardi accidentally trapped a spectator in a guide rope. The unfortunate involuntary stowaway then plummeted to a messy death from an altitude of three hundred feet. The unlucky man was named as Ralph Heron, who inadvertently became the UK's first aerial death.

The Italian was sufficiently aware of the vast dangers he had been beckoning towards him (solo flights in a primitive valveless balloon) to record a last will and testament on the eve of each flight. Revealing that he was also the hedonistic showman, he decided key weight could be added to the balloon basket by including bottles of wine and brandy in order to toast his successful climb to the heavens - though he forgot to pack one equally crucial item: a corkscrew. Never one to give danger the respect it deserved, the reckless Lunardi merely snapped the neck of the glass bottle and glugged down its contents - and thus became the very first in a long tradition of pilots discovered to be drunk.

Devoid of an accurate altimeter, reasonably on account of the fact one had not yet been invented, his mood settled on a seemingly ingenious way of charting his exact height. Clicking his stopwatch into action, he tossed the empty bottle over the edge. Calculating that it took four minutes to shatter on the earth, he surmised this meant he was at an altitude of four miles. No, I don't know why either.

What really cost him his reputation in the UK was the unexplained disappearance of a cat. No matter what you achieve in the UK, forget how highly the British value their pets at your peril. Lunardi took a cat up with him during his ascent, and returned to the rocky ground of earth with quite a media bump - because there was no cat in his basket. Pressed to explain the balloon's lack of feline content, he span a transparent and infelicitous mistruth about his decision to land the balloon to drop off the cat and then re-launch. As his primitive balloon possessed no valve to deflate the air pressure, this would have been almost impossible. Basically, Lunardi was vilified, his aeronautical achievements lining up in distinct second-place to moggy murder. Somewhat unfairly treated, Lunardi pressed ahead with future pet-free flights. This was akin to Neil Armstrong being the first man to walk on the moon, but only being remembered for once accidently stepping on a hamster.

Aiding British ridicule was the undeniable fact that Lunardi was an egotistical womaniser, once declaring "I am Lunardi - who the women all love." He was young, handsome and not only relished his own hype, but simultaneously both manufactured and believed it too. Brooches flipped open to reveal his portrait - always worn with several shirt buttons undone to expose his chest, very much of the puffed-up variety, and satisfyingly exposed for his swooning female adorers. These brooches had chart-topping sales figures during balloonomania. A garter belt, emblazoned with his portrait, also became a bestselling lingerie item. He caused women to fan themselves into knee-twisting faints, often hitting the floor hard in his presence, and when they raised a seemingly hapless arm for the Italian to pull them upwards they would often yank him forward where their open arms and heaving bosoms awaited the softest of landings. Lunardi wrote: "Women of this country are more difficult to resist with their coquetry, than Italian women. Many of them wish to accompany me."

In popularising ballooning among the masses, Lunardi undoubtedly contributed to its anti-intellectual status, as did the various occurrences of mass riots reported with relish by the press. Focus was being lost from ballooning as the product of enquiring scientific minds. Sadler can be credited for reclaiming aeronautics from showbiz to scientific enquiry.

Although he remained an unreconstructed Latino dandy perfectly fitting the eighteenth-century image of playboy aristocracy, Lunardi demonstrated a modern PR consultant's acumen. Prior to his landmark - or rather skymark - ascent he exhibited his balloon at a theatre in the Strand, charging a hefty one guinea admission fee which also included a seat at the take-off. Post-flight, the balloon was again exhibited with a public pay-to-view, this time in the Pantheon in Oxford Street.

Nearly 200,000 people were claimed to have viewed his take-off, though the claim was significantly made by the self-mythologising Lunardi himself. There is little doubt, though, that the public imagination was very much of the captured variety. The Prince of Wales attended the launch, the Prime Minister was rumoured to have rescheduled a Cabinet meeting to view the balloon soaring above London and Dr. Johnson's sagely dispensed advice, to save a guinea and see the balloon for free, was thoroughly endorsed.

After over two hours of flight at the mercy of the currents - though Lunardi remained adamant he could row through the air even though he could probably hear the sniggers of Dr. Johnson and Boswell from 1,000 feet below - he somehow managed to land in Ware.

Never one to miss cashing in on a marketing opportunity, Lunardi granted interviews to anyone who would provide a willing ear and produced his own lengthy, yet undisputedly ghost-written, account of the flight *My First Aerial Voyage in London 1784*, complete with characteristic proclamations of self-importance, but also sartorial grandiloquence. J.E. Hodgson observed in 1924: "Lunardi's effusive literary efforts were the subject of some not wholly deserved ridicule. Sadler, on the contrary, seldom uses his pen."

No matter how reckless Lunardi was prepared to be in an attempt to pump hot air into his balloon at an equivalent rate to inflating his ego, the death of a cat and a ground worker finished his career. Like Blanchard who had also planned to capitalise on the mid-1780s British appetite for balloons by briefly

John Francis Rigaud's portrait of Lunardi, a male assistant and a lady friend (Yale Center for British Art/ Paul Mellon Collection)

moving to the UK, Lunardi quickly fled England too. Neither ever returned. This left British ballooning in the more scientifically capable hands of Sadler.

29 SEPTEMBER 1784: SHELDONIAN THEATRE

Perhaps the most astonishing detail about mankind's quest to reach for the skies is the speed of progress once initial flight had been accomplished. After hundreds of thousands of years enviously watching birds gallivanting around the sky, the Montgolfier brothers had ascended in a hot air balloon (although if you'd asked them at the time, they would have described it as a smoke balloon) for the first time in public on 21 November 1783. Amazingly, within twelve days a manned hydrogen balloon ascent had also been successfully pioneered.

It is unlikely that Sadler consciously planned to be the UK's first balloonist - his enquiring scientific mind was more interested in obtaining the correct instruments to accompany his ascent than in winning the race to be the first Englishman in the skies. Even so, aware of the publicity this brought him, he was certainly complicit in later attempting to win the race to cross the Channel and, afterwards, the Irish Sea. His probable indifference towards being the first English ascendant can be guessed at by the fact that Sadler planned his first manned voyage on a date after a scheduled attempt by a fellow countryman.

Dr. John Sheldon was a fittingly eccentric English gentleman to be attracted to the dangerous new sport of ballooning. Quite how eccentric can be determined by one detail: he kept his late wife's embalmed body in his London house, and would wheel her into the room to put astonished dinner party guests off their starters.

To Sheldon ballooning was a new sport, not a new science. The doctor commissioned an umbrella maker to manufacturer a balloon, based upon the Montgolfier template. The result was an 85 foot high by 80 foot diameter monster orb. Two attempts at launching were made, and if either had been successful, Sadler would have lost his tag line "the first Englishman to fly".

The first intended ascent occurred on 16 August 1784 in the garden of Lord Foley's residence in Portland Place, London. As the gathering crowd's impatience grew, Sheldon's attempt to raise the balloon on a very hot day in the middle of a heatwave helped ensure the orb remained stubbornly flaccid and impotent. This was a success compared to the full 18-certificate horror show that happened with the next attempt six weeks later on 29 September 1784.

After several hours and with dusk encroaching, the flight was announced as cancelled when insufficient "lifting gas" had been pumped into the obviously porous balloon envelope. A bad tempered crowd dispersed noisily. Only then did Sheldon and his accomplice Keegan suddenly overcome the inflation problems, and the guide rope holders collectively announced there was sufficient propulsion to engage a lift-off.

At this point, disaster struck. Fragments of incandescent straw escaped from the huge seven-foot burner, designed on a scale deemed necessary to provide sufficient propulsion to pull such a cumbersome monster from terra firma. Like the Montgolfiers, who deliberately chose straw and sheep's wool for smoke-emitting properties when burnt, Sheldon mistakenly believed smoke, not hot air molecules, provided the balloon's ascension.

In front of a huge crowd, the balloon did go up... in flames. The illustrator Paul Sandby callously satirised Sheldon, depicting him with a giant balloon bottom - his charred backside going up in flames in an illustration titled "The English Balloon".

Sheldon was by no means the only failure. Several Frenchmen, determined to enjoy their self-considered superiority obtained from being the first nation to reach the skies, decided to show the English how it could be done on their own soil. One such Gaelic visitor, the Chevalier de Moret announced an ascent from Five Fields Row in Chelsea. After numerous delays, rumoured purely to provide more publicity and ticket sales opportunities, the balloon itself proved incapable of inflation. In truth, it displayed no attributes of being airworthy. The paying and baying crowd concluded quickly, and justifiably, that they were in the presence of a charlatan. Riots occurred, and the Frenchman was pursued back over the Channel.

All this accumulated ostentatious failure ensured a quickly polarised press. "Everyone should laugh this new folly of ballooning out of practice as soon as possible!" thundered the *Morning Herald*, whereas the *Chronicle* applauded ballooning as "the furthest humans have thus far succeeded - we are indeed fortunate to live through these times". Meanwhile, the *Daily Mail* probably ran with "Does ballooning give you cancer?"

1 NOVEMBER 1784: BALLOON HATS SOAR IN POPULARITY

Before Beatlemania there was balloonomania. Britain and France collectively went proper-balloon-mental in 1784 and throughout most of the following year. Whenever a trend sweeps a nation, three things inevitably follow in its slipstream: hysteria, exploitative memorabilia sales and people eagerly prepared to satirise it. All three were present in an article that appeared in the *Daily Chronicle* that year, which reported women wearing miniature inflated balloons levitating above their hats. One newspaper advert in 1784 proclaimed: "AIR BALLOON HATS, either trimmed or plain, or the wires to make them, may be had, in the greatest variety of colours, at Hartshorn and Dyde's, Wigmore Street, and in the Circus, Bath; where likewise may be seen a large quantity of particularly fine Goat's-beard Muffs, from two to three guineas."

Meanwhile a brisk trade was reported in balloon-related paraphernalia:

hats, cups, brooches, sketches, snuffboxes, ceramics, medals, cigarette cases, fans, tobacco pipes, garter belts and even bidets all came with a balloon motif. Basically if you wanted to make something sell in the mid-1780s, paint a balloon on it.

Reports had reached Britain of French ladies wearing balloon-shaped bonnets to commemorate inaugural flights, and several British aristocrats were incomprehensibly keen to be seen supporting the trend - with their heads if not their minds. Because to wear a balloon hat certainly constituted a blind leap into trusting fashion.

The *Morning Herald* in March 1784 found the target irresistible, fulminating against the fickleness of fashion: "Balloon Hats now adorn the heads of much of the parading impures as can afford them; whilst the more inferior tribe have invented a hat which is, not improperly, called 'the bastard balloon'! Being a humble imitation of the green-balloon fashions are about their zenith and must soon burst and be forgotten!"

Numerous creative varieties followed. Sadler would certainly have been aware of the fashion, and no doubt accepted it as further endorsement of balloonomania defining his age. In an era desperate for heroes, yet with a paucity of celebrities, it is worth reflecting that Sadler would have been as big in late eighteenth-century Britain as the Beatles ever managed to be two hundred years later. Sadler's appeal was utterly ubiquitous. A surge in patriotism greeted his achievements, not unlike a flag-draped nation during a successful English team at a football tournament. Union jacks fluttered around anywhere Sadler had consented to ascend.

The balloon hat was also known as the "Lunardi Hat". Manufactured from a straw base representing the balloon basket (straw being Lunardi's fuel of choice), draped fabric representing clouds would trail from the side of the hat, cascading down from an elongated brim irregularly topped with added esoteric decoration, often a small spherical balloon. The hat's popularity soon extended to British shores from France, hence the common presence of the 'parading impures' that so riled the *Morning Herald*'s fashion correspondent.

During the Regency period ladies' balloon hats were predominantly constructed from silk, felt, ribbon, linen, straw and bad taste. Decorated according to the wearer's fancy (with lace, feathers, fruit, flowers, foliage, etc.) they were inappropriate for any occasion, as common styles were crowned with a miniature inflated balloon floating above the hat. Oversized berets (tams) were also popular. These could be made of velvet or some other heavy fabric, and trimmed with feathers or jewels. Adding some sort of balloon emblem was considered *de rigueur*.

Deterred by Lunardi's flamboyantly showbusiness approach, the scientific community did not all rush to embrace balloonomania with the enthusiasm shown by the rest of a nation collectively gripped by all things balloon-related in the last quarter of the century.

There were other dissenters. One notably grumpy refuter of such hype was Prime Minister Horace Walpole. He famously caught sight of a balloon and pronounced it "certainly no bigger than my snuff box" - a remark which questions Walpole's relationship with perspective: "If stuff is near, it looks bigger - no, Strawberry Hill has not suddenly got smaller whilst you walked further away from it." Walpole was renowned for being dismissive of aeronauts, branding them "a mere job for getting money from gaping fools". Upon learning that Lunardi had actively endangered a cat's wellbeing during his ascent, Walpole menacingly concluded: "Lunardi... has every right to venture his own neck" but, by implication, not that of his feline accomplice.

Whereas many foresaw a more exciting future due to man's eventual conquering of flight, Walpole was mainly concerned that the first people to put the new technology to use would be smugglers. Walpole speculated in a letter to a friend in December 1784: "This enormous London, that must have some occupation, is most innocently amused with those philosophic playthings, air-balloons. But, as half of a million people that impassion themselves for any object are always more childish than children, the good souls of London are much fonder of the aeronauts than of the toys themselves. Lunardi, the Neapolitan secretary, is said to have bought three or four thousand pounds in the stocks, by exhibiting his person, his balloon, and his dog and cat, at the Pantheon, for a shilling each visitor. Jean-Pierre Blanchard, a Frenchman, is his rival, and I expect that they will soon have an air-fight in the clouds, like a stork and a kite."

Blanchard was equally detrimental to ballooning's early image. He claimed in a later London flight to have accomplished his pre-flight boast of landing on the same spot as his launch-site - thus demonstrating hitherto unseen piloting skills. In reality, he had hired two horsemen to tow his balloon back to the starting point from a landing achieved several miles away. Subsequently an unimpressed mob destroyed his newly opened "London School of Ballooning" and he hopped back across the Channel, where the King of France had equipped him with a life-long pension.

Writing to a friend, Walpole is distracted by seeing another balloon over London from his Strawberry Hill mansion, and concludes:

I saw the balloon from the common field before the window of my round tower. It appeared about a third of the size of the moon, or less, when setting, something above the tops of the trees on the level horizon. It was then descending; and after rising and declining a little, it sunk slowly behind the trees. But I chiefly amused myself with ideas of the change that would be made in the world by the substitution of balloons for ships. I supposed our seaports to become deserted villages; and Salisbury Plain, Newmarket Heath and The Downs, arising into dockyards for aerial vessels. In these days Old Sarum will again be a town, and have houses in it. There will be fights in the air with wind-guns, and bows and arrows; and there will be prodigious increase of land for tillage, especially in France, by breaking up all public roads as useless.

Sadler achieved some semblance of balance, like a pendulum swinging from extreme to extreme, between daredevil recklessness and scientific innovation. His proclivity for advertising dates well in advance of his ascensions meant he was utterly exposed to the vagaries of the weather. Taking off in a gale renders a safe landing unlikely. Yet he was a highly skilled pilot. This ability saved not only his own life, but those of his travelling companions. On one occasion, his cargo was MP for Norwich and Secretary for War in Prime Minister Pitt's cabinet, William Windham (1750-1810), a self-confessed balloon fanatic. Windham later recounted: "From the moment of hearing about balloons I felt in common with anyone of even the smallest imagination the wish of adventuring in one." Sadler had the expertise, Windham had the money.

5 MAY 1785: MOULSEY HURST

Showing that Sadler's social status had risen with comparable speed to his balloons, he was now hanging around with new best friend William Windham, prominent Whig and even more prominent wig-wearer. The two planned an ascent together, selecting Surrey as a launch site.

Windham was so convinced of the peril he was about to place himself in when stepping into a balloon gondola that he busied himself on the eve of the flight by making a will and composed a letter, "only to be delivered upon my death", to Lord George James Cholmondeley. It contained instructions "to leave my suits to my brother Peregrine, my guns to my Uncle Grenville, and the rest of my estate to my mother to dispose of as she sees fit after my death." The letter was eventually delivered, 25 years later rather than the next day, in 1810 after Windham had died. His in-the-event-of-my-demise correspondence proclaimed his faith as a committed Christian. In fact, Sadler was the one taking more of a risk, placing himself in unnecessary additional danger by ascending with an inexperienced flyer. It did not end at all well.

The pair ascended before a huge throng of spectators from the grounds of Mr. Dodswell's gardens in Surrey between Sunbury-on-Thames and Kingston at Moulsey Hurst, a location already established as a site for cricket, prize fighting and other mass entertainments for a holidaying or weekending public.

After spending two and half hours filling his balloon with hydrogen, by 9am Sadler was prepared for the launch. Oddly, Windham does not appear to have been identified by the newspapers at the time, nearly all subsequent reports referring to "Sadler and a gentleman". Only some days after the flight was Windham identified, when a correspondent from Oxford wrote to the *Whitehall Evening Post* and identified him as "Honourable Mr Windham, formerly of this University". Windham had attended University College in the High Street, located only a few doors from Sadler's café in the same street, so may have encountered him as a young man in Oxford - although social lubricant ensuring frictionless movement between Town and Gown would have been extremely rare then. (It's still quite rare today.)

The Oxford correspondent confirms that the balloon was large enough to have carried four passengers. Teasingly, however, he doesn't go on to state categorically that the pair's intention was to cross the North Sea. The report rather confirms their route over London and Westminster towards Kent - later verified by witnesses - and states that the pair had taken "mathematical instruments" on their voyage. It concludes: "on the utmost danger of being carried into the North Sea the balloon happily met another breeze that landed our adventurers near the North Sea after having travelled nearly 200 miles from whence they took postchaise and returned to town that evening."

The Times was keen to point out that "Mr Sadler and the gentleman were provided with proper instruments for philosophical experiments." At that time the word "philosophical" possessed a sufficiently wide definition to cover the area we would today describe as science - rather than implying that Sadler might have become philosophical and remarked to Windham: "If your lack of skills as a aeronaut ensure we fall into the North Sea and there's no one around to witness it, would you still emit a sound when I punch you?"

A correspondent reporting for a different newspaper observed that:

Mr Sadler and his companion came down in a field near Rochester where a labouring man was at work. Who was very much alarmed at the balloon. And it was with great difficulty that they could prevail him to lay hold of a rope which they threw him for the purpose of assisting them in their descent which he at last consented to do and held until they alighted but before they could procure a ballast for the balloon pulling rather strong and the man having no great relish for his employment let go his hold when it ascended with great rapidity leaving the aerial travellers behind taking the direct course over the German Ocean.

(The German Ocean was a former name for the North Sea until Germany's persistent military misdemeanours - the nation spending the first half of the 20th Century on Europe's naughty step - lost the country its eponymous ocean when it was renamed the North Sea.)

Startled agricultural labourers suspicious that Sadler's balloon was an unfriendly alien appear as a leitmotiv during his landing episodes. Presumably such lone labourers were the equivalent of those Texan rednecks proclaiming their conviction to cheap documentary filmmakers that they were abducted and probed by visiting aliens. Sadler, like earthbound aliens, appears to have regularly picked upon a lone village idiot, thus guaranteeing that the idiot's story, free of confirming witnesses, would not be believed when later recounted in the village pub.

A few days later, more of the story emerged, and it was apparent that Sadler and his companion had been the architects of their own misfortune. The *Whitehall Evening Post* of 10 May 1785 states: "in addition to our previous report of Mr Sadler, we are assured as to the authenticity of this account". The landing may have been sudden because the two intrepid aeronauts were "intimidated at the sight of the seas". The looming vast greyness of the North Sea appears to have panicked William Windham - not the first time an MP has experienced a panic and instigated a U-turn over the prospect of continental Europe.

Spying the North Sea coastline ahead, Windham started to randomly throw items overboard in the mistaken belief this would help facilitate an impending landing. And there was a lot of ballast to throw overboard. Sadler had packed the balloon with over 300lbs, which led the newspaper to conclude they were "planning a longer excursion than any of his predecessors". Rumour had it that the pair had intended to reach the continent - a pioneering accomplishment if it had succeeded. *The Times* was adamant in its speculation that this was the intention: "By the course they went it was expected that they would reach the continent the next day, and if the wind continued as it then was, they will descend in Flanders," it announced, before concluding with outrageous hubris, "unless they should be inclined to go further."

The reporter claimed to have observed evidence: "Mr Sadler and co. took out provisions for a two day voyage." *The General Evening Post* asserted that "it was the intention of Mr Sadler to remain in the atmosphere longer than anyone has yet done", citing again the huge onboard ballast as evidence for this supposition. Certainly the ballast, the early morning take-off (Sadler typically preferred early afternoon ascents) to maximise daylight and the extra provisions are circumstantial evidence to support this theory, though it remains speculation. Such an attempt would offset any lingering disappointment over Sadler becoming a non-runner in the cross Channel race a few months earlier. It may seem odd that in selecting a co-pilot for such a lengthy journey he didn't pick someone with more ballooning experience - but Windham would have been likely to provide the crucial funds.

Yet, with considerable ballast aboard, the pair pressed on with their sudden decision to land, and not risk crossing the German Ocean. Another reason for Sadler suddenly attempting to crash land could well have been a driving wind, thus forcing an inflight reappraisal of the risks provided by the North Sea. Once over open sea, landing would almost certainly have proved deadly.

But the *Whitehall Evening Post* also reported that Sadler discovered his valve was malfunctioning "with the pipe not discharging the gas fast enough". Sadler forced as much air as he could out of the envelope, while probably bellowing at Windham to stop jettisoning any more sandbags. Hitting the ground at a much faster descent speed than Sadler knew was safe, they bounced into the air again as the wind sent their envelope back skywards. This same procedure occurred several times, before Sadler shouted to Windham to jump clear of the basket the next time there were close enough to earth.

This they both accomplished, fortuitously sustaining only superficial injuries, escaping from the basket. The balloon immediately surged upwards and rapidly departed out to sea.

The pair eventually found themselves on terra firma only a few miles short of the coastline. With a broken valve, depreciating provisions, driving wind and panicked misunderstanding of how ballast worked, Windham's earlier decision to write a will had, at one point, looked like a remarkably expedient one.

A few days later the balloon was seen again, bobbing on the surface of the North Sea where it was rescued by a passing schooner. Under the minimalist headline "BALLOON", the owner of the ship bound for Sunderland announced its discovery (and profitable cargo) by placing the following advertisement in several newspapers: "Mr Sadler's balloon taken up in the sea. The owner, by applying to John Blunt, Cross Lane, St Mary at Hill, Thames Street, may have information thereof." Never has an omitted word been so heavily implied: "Reward".

Despite the accident, such was the closeness of the relationship between Sadler and Windham that Sadler's son was christened Windham after the politician, who in turn was appointed as godfather. Windham, an Old Etonian and a disturbingly unreformed supporter of bull baiting, did not perish in his balloon flights with Sadler, but instead had an honourable death in 1810 - dying of injuries sustained in rescuing books from a library fire.

But if Sadler had made a powerful ally in the MP, he succeeded in making equally powerful enemies: Oxford University among them. Windham later wrote: "I hope for the advantage of Sadler who I really consider as a prodigy. And who is oppressed to the disgrace of the University, I believe from pique and jealousy of his superior science." As we shall see, other potent enemies were to follow; the Royal Navy literally threw him out of Portsmouth, even though he had provided them with vastly more efficient re-engineered firepower. Lord Nelson had earlier gone public in supporting Sadler, his cannon and rifle designs thought to be instrumental in enabling the British to defeat Napoleon. If it wasn't for Sadler, we could now all be eating croissants and *pains au chocolat* for breakfast. Oh. We do anyway.

But for now Sadler was a household name. Everyone, regardless of status, would have known about James Sadler in late eighteenth- and early nineteenth-century Britain. And therein lies his uniquely classless appeal. He was an egalitarian fascination: democratic in an undemocratic age. As a Lincolnshire newspaper eloquently described his popularity across the spectrum of class in 1811: "Spectators flock from the titled Peer to the humble cabbage seller to see Sadler".

Another observer, possibly perched on one of the many trees used by onlookers to gain a vantage-point at his second manned flight in 1784, wrote that Sadler was "watched by a surprising concourse of people of all ranks; the roads, streets, fields, trees, buildings, and towers of the parts adjacent being crowded beyond description." Sadler was not only always a hot ticket in whatever town he visited, but also a unique ticket - one that had equal appeal among all classes, genders, ages and intellects.

A sign of Sadler's celebrity, and confirmation of the public's affection for him, occurred moments after he had survived yet another dangerous flight. Obviously suffering too many bruises and suspected fractures, and realising that the description of his antics as "death-defying" would eventually lose its second word, he was to give up flying a few months later. A crash landing in Heckington, Lincolnshire, in 1811 happened with such an impact that Sadler was bundled out of the balloon seconds before it rose upwards again with his stranded co-pilot still aboard. Losing a shoe in the crash, Sadler approached the local miller and "begged if he could borrow a shoe". "No," came the unambiguous response. The mean miller would not sell him a shoe, even if he was the intrepid celebrated aeronaut. Sadler offered him a generous shilling, which the miller refused. According to the local Lincolnshire paper of October 1811: "The inhuman boor refused seven shillings for a shoe, taking more, though it was not worth two pence." The profiteering perpetrator was, however, "recognised amongst the crowd and forced to refund amidst the execrations of all present." Hence the money-grubbing miller was fingered by Sadler, and the mob forced him to pay back his exploitative gains. A vignette which portrays the level of affection the public held for Sadler, even if there were individuals like a Lincolnshire miller immune to the aeronaut's celebrity appeal.

In a pre-photographic age, Sadler would have been recognised due to his portrait being sold as a mass-produced sheet of paper. Although formal portraits can be idealised images, they do at least give us a glimpse of him - captured at different ages in his career. Sadler flew well into his fifties, which for the early nineteenth century would be quite an age to perform daredevil stunts with almost guaranteed violent crash landings. As, indeed, it would today - at any age.

Portraits serve to embalm time, and they at least allow us to glimpse the man's physical characteristics. He always looks kindly - proud without bordering upon arrogance or hubris. Maybe that's how the portrait was supposed to portray him. But it's an image that my research has not contravened. Maybe when Sadler was rejected by such powerful enemies as the Royal Navy and Oxford University it was because he was an uneducated pastry cook, a man devoid of breeding or education. Maybe he represents the pivotal point in history where this changed, ushering in if not an egalitarian, then at least a meritocratic approach alongside all the usual passes to success: status, opportunity issued by breeding, nobility and education. The eighteenth-century public and today's certainly shared the same affection and taste for a risk taker.

Although an American might once have observed that dinner parties are what the British do instead of having friends (it's OK, since he was an American, there's a high statistical likelihood he's been shot by now), Sadler certainly would have appeared on the dinner party A-List of his period. He was written about and praised by John Constable and Lord Nelson; he was revered by his self-confessed fan Percy Shelley; and he so impressed Dr, Samuel Johnson that the Good Doctor practically rose from his death bed to meet him and present him with a vital artefact.

The poet Samuel Westley wrote to the composer Vincent Novello in 1812 informing him, "he has puffed my deserter's meditations to the size of

_James Sadler, Esq.
First English Aeronaut.
Drawn & Engraved by B. Taylor._

Published by the Act May 1 1812 by B. Taylor Nº 7 Drury Lane...

Mass-produced print of Sadler, 1812 (Library of Congress, Washington DC)

Mr Sadler's balloon" – showing, even incomprehensibly, that Sadler was in the public's consciousness as a household reference. His contacts book must have been the envy of royalty.

Indeed, Sadler was even granted an audience with the queen. On 2 August 1814 he was invited to meet Queen Charlotte, the wife of "mad" King George III, and her princesses. After dining in the grand Mayfair house of Princess Sophia of Gloucester, "they returned to the queen's palace where Mr Sadler was introduced to them and gave a full account of his aerial voyage sixteen miles beyond Gravesend to Her Highness." Sadler had also brought along his balloon basket to show to the Queen, and demonstrated his pilot tasks. "Sadler explained to Her Majesty how he travelled and his operations within the balloon," revealed *The Morning Post*.

In the latter half of the eighteenth century, the biggest celebrity in town, the one everyone aspired to pleasing most and whose acerbic tongue and pen was most feared - was the Good Doctor. Dr. Samuel Johnson spelt the word "balloon" incorrectly, with only one "o". He should have used the dictionary - if he had one about. He genuinely refused to incorporate any French words into his landmark two-volume 1755 dictionary; such was the extent of the famed lexicographer's dislike of the French. The words "champagne" and "bourgeois" were deemed unworthy of entry, omitted as a *fait accompli* by the *enfant terrible* of words. Johnson, we have seen, was previously a balloon sceptic, branding aeronauts as showmen and charlatans intent on fleecing a susceptible public vicariously aroused by blanket media coverage. Balloons were portrayed as relentlessly modern, representative of mankind's ability to go onwards and upwards, in both a literal and figurative sense. But these accomplishments were often merely filled with hot air (yes, also in a figurative and literal sense). And Johnson aimed his verbal vitriol onto them at an early stage. The Prime Minister of the day may have taken time out to see a balloonist sail over his Downing Street garden in the 1780s, but Johnson pointed out that anyone prepared to be distracted by such side shows in the sky was a "lackbrain clotpoll". It is not necessary to consult the dictionary - his or anyone else's - to decipher those two words.

And although becoming increasing curmudgeonly as he aged was a vital part of the Johnson brand (his hometown of Lichfield in Staffordshire is bizarrely included in Johnson's dictionary and defined as "city of the dead"), it doesn't deflect from the fact he had a point. He also defined oats as being food for horses in England, but the staple diet of the people in Scotland. And when a benefactor of his precious dictionary refused to provide him with promised funding, Johnson merely exacted his revenge via the lexicographical route and defined the word patron as "commonly a wretch". The word dull is simply explained as "to make dictionaries".

Johnson had been initially intrigued by balloons, even enthralled by them, declaring that they had the potential "to bring down the state of regions yet unexplored". He imagined "the earth a mile below me, without a stronger impression on my brain than I should like to feel." But he quickly became agnostic to the widespread belief that balloons were the force for the future, before offering open hostility to aeronautics, even thundering in a 1783 letter: "I know not that they can be of any particular use." Sadler was to singlehandedly rotate Johnson's view.

Later, only a few weeks from his deathbed, the Good Doctor donated a scientific instrument to Sadler for aeronautic usage: an expensive barometer. When losing altitude at an alarming rate over a stormy Bristol Channel with darkness approaching, Sadler was forced to hurl Dr. Johnson's precious gift overboard as a life-saving attempt to jettison ballast and regain height. Sadler later lamented that this act had caused one of the greatest heartaches of his life. One newspaper, *The Caledonian Mercury*, reported that Sadler had earlier refused an offer of 200 guineas for Johnson's gift.

Other celebrities of the age scrambled to embrace fashionable flight. The Lakeland poets, who dressed and acted like a Camden-based indie rock band strutting around the Lake District, admitted inspiration from aeronautical pioneers, often adopting the balloon-as-metaphor approach in their work. Samuel Taylor Coleridge declared balloons "uplifting and terrifying", which is an accurate description (although he may have been at the laughing gas again, as was his proclivity). Indeed, it is debatable whether Sadler ever got higher than the Lakeland poets with their nitrous oxide habit.

Lake poet William Wordsworth begins his 1817 poem *Peter Bell* with the image of a balloon boat (wooden boats being the forerunners to later, crucially lighter, wicker baskets).

> There's something in a flying horse,
> There's something in a huge balloon;
> But through the clouds I'll never float
> Until I have a little Boat,
> Shaped like the crescent-moon.
>
> And now I 'have' a little Boat
> In shape a very crescent-moon

Fast through the clouds my boat can sail;
But if perchance your faith should fail,
Look up - and you shall see me soon!

His sister Dorothy was not exempt from catching the then commonly circulating balloonomania infection, and eagerly wrote about the subject in her capacity as a compulsive letter writer. Twice a day she would make the hilly eight-mile round trip on foot between Dove Cottage in Grasmere to the post office at Ambleside to check if she had received any correspondence - the equivalent of today's compulsive email checking. (Though imagine her reaction after enduring an eight-mile walk in characteristic Lake District rain, only to discover that the two items she collected were both junk mail letters offering cheap Viagra.)

In Hilary Term 1811, while reading chemistry at University College, Oxford and experimenting as a side-line in the then fledgling science of electricity, Percy Shelley witnessed Sadler fly. Inspired by what he had seen, Shelley enthused: "Why are we so ignorant of the interior of Africa? Why do we not despatch intrepid aeronauts to cross it in every direction to survey the whole peninsula in a few weeks? The shadow of the first balloon as it glided over that unhappy country would virtually emancipate every slave, and would annihilate slavery forever."

Later that same term Shelley was expelled from Oxford, sent down for distributing his pamphlet *The Necessity of Atheism*, and for conducting a prank in the High Street where he tiptoed towards townswomen whilst they were distracted in conversation with each other whereupon he swapped over new-born babies in their prams. Women, eh? You never know what's going to upset them.

Oddly, whereas the period from 1780 to 1820 is packed with balloon enthusing celebrities, famous people seem less prone to "come out" as balloon aficionados in modern times. With, that is, the notable exception of Richard Branson.

6 VIRGIN ON DISASTER: SEX AND PHOBIAS

I lost my virginity in a Lincolnshire farmer's field. This is not uncommon in Lincolnshire, although what was less typical for the county was that my experience involved a female human, not a farm animal.

No, it was not with Charlotte Jones, but it was within view of her house. It was also in a cornfield, so like most occurrences in my life the action took place on ground level. Amazingly a hot air balloon contributed to the experience.

People really do still make love among the cornfields, the wind sweeping patterns on the wheat, allowing the swaying corn stalks to resemble a tidal wash. Corn offers a good place to hide, devoid of patrolling parents standing on sentry duty outside bedroom doors, ready to barge in like a police drugs raid if they suspect any suspicious noises from inside may indicate illicit snogging activities within. In former times it was not uncommon during harvest season to see hastily re-dressed couples fleeing from the chasing blades of combine harvesters when their afternoon's wheat-hidden amour risked ending with a different sort of thrashing than that envisaged by angry parents.

A girl I knew in my hometown told me on the one daily bus that linked my parochial small town to London (and any semblance of cosmopolitan ambition) that her parents had once called her downstairs for a "meeting". She had only ever previously been summoned to "chats" so knew this must be important, particularly as there was also Battenberg cake - which passed for middle-class aspiration in a pre-Waitrose age. This was clearly meant to be a meeting where portentous life advice was about to be dispensed - and with it would almost certainly come awkwardness.

Sure enough, she was asked, aged sixteen, by her parents: "Are you still chaste?" Being unfamiliar with such an archaic expression, she genuinely thought they meant "chased" to which she replied, "don't you think I'm a bit too old for that?" Before adding, "in the past with my schoolmates, obviously, I did it all the time with every girl and boy there. But I've grown out of it years ago." Her parents nodded disapprovingly but agreed that "in the modern age" she probably was behaving consistently with their fears implanted by *Daily Mail* columnists. The best their generation could hope for was that there would be some downhill stretches as they resignedly lugged their handcarts towards hell. "But," they insisted, "we hope you gave the matter serious thought beforehand." Perplexed, she took some Battenberg back to her room.

Years later she realised what they must have actually said, but only after her parents had died - and left their house to her two brothers.

Frankly virginity, and subsequent loss thereof, is overrated. Here's a glove-slap-in-the-face challenge to that perceived status quo: the first time you do something is unimportant. That's because the initial time you do something is rarely the best, any more than the second or third. It takes time, practice and experience to become competent at something, and to extract meaning and purpose from that evolved competence.

Quite why people willingly believe they should save their virginity for a special occasion, ratcheting up the pressure higher than James Sadler ever literally reached, is illogical. The first time you cook an omelette, drive a car, draw a picture or ascend in an untethered balloon is unlikely to represent the pinnacle of achievement in that chosen discipline. The same is indisputably true of sex.

Understandably, for a sensitive individual, this experience in the cornfield meant a lot to me, though probably less to my "conquest" - a term laden with gender politics - and inaccuracy in this situation - as I am certain I was her conquest, probably to win a bet. Her whispered amorous sweet nothings drifting like scented blossom petals in a refreshing summer breeze: "Hurry up, I want to watch *Brookside*. Oh for God's sake, it unhooks here - bras aren't that difficult to remove, surely!" My eyes darted across her bare chest, flickering like lizards' tongues. When we had finished - the beginning and ending time could only be separated by an atomic clock - I received the traditional post-coital enquiry: "Is that it?" Then she realised this might be construed as an insensitive remark to a boy currently feeling vulnerable after failing in an activity in which culturally no boy or man is allowed to fail. "That was very... um... enthusiastic," she said, fumbling for a compliment.

My conquest was a few years older than me, and clearly doing this out of a not entirely misplaced sense of pity. Her mechanical actions displayed the emotional investment she would have spent in defleaing her dog. Rather than gushing affirmations of romance whispered like droplets of poetry into lovers' ears, she uttered that unintentionally discerning line that women often say during post-coital intimacy: "So, do you feel better now, sweetie?" - rather confirming the clinical, almost medical, procedure that has just been overseen. Before pausing to ask, "are you sure that's it? Shouldn't it take longer?" Luckily I have no feelings.

She was a nice girl who was basically being very kind to me, unaccustomed as she was to discovering unfamiliar hands inside her blouse. And I was relieved to have shaken off my virginity, ridden myself of that "loser" badge which the condition appears to pin to boys - although without goal-line technology in those days to prove otherwise, there's still a chance I hadn't done enough to lose my virginity.

And losing one's virginity can be difficult enough for socially awkward, shy boys, but it is particularly complex for those constrained by the inability to negotiate stairs, given that bedrooms rarely tend to be located on the ground floor. A few days earlier she had suggested we go up the tower of one of the highest spires in Lincolnshire - a formerly welcome landmark for sailors on the Wash built high enough to contain a lantern for shipping in ancient times. I actually made it up the first two flights of stairs such was my determination to hide my phobia from her. Then I hyperventilated, and had to descend the stairs literally sitting down. Maybe she just felt sorry for me, but she was sympathetic and understanding. Her kindness still impresses me, and resonates, today.

Post-coital under a pewter sky - one of those endless, melancholic skies of the featureless Lincolnshire flatlands. Then two strange things were suddenly noticeable on the horizon, both becoming larger in that sky as they came towards us. Someone had just set fire to the stubble of the neighbouring cornfield that had already been combine-harvested. Making love at the side of a burning cornfield ought to provide a rich palette of descriptive colours, tones, and imagery for a writer - but all I can recall is that smoke really does get in your eyes. That song was right.

They're not allowed to burn cornfields any more. And they seem to have passed a similar ban on woman having sex with me dating from roughly the same period. The old adage, adopted for the twenty-first century: "Red sky in the morning shepherd's warning, red sky at night shepherd fined for pumping cacogenic pollutants into the atmosphere with illegal stubble burning in contravention of EU legislation."

Fleeing from the field, she lost a shoe. Running over stubble is difficult, but it's more than just precarious if barefoot. Already trickling blood was visible below her ankle. I called out to her to stop running, and stay stationary against her instincts to avoid the approaching acrid smoke and her fear of discovery. Nobly, I went back like a soldier returning to a fallen colleague, and retrieved her shoe. Moments later we shared an affectionate Cinderella moment as I re-shoed her. Then, at a time when we really needed to start running again, before smoke and embarrassment consumed us, we stood looking upwards marvelling at the sky.

For there was the other strangely unaccountable object in the sky looming larger by the second as it soared towards us. A giant hot air balloon.

"Do you think they were spying on us?" asked my "conquest" picking straw out of her hair and tutting as she discovered more and more tell-tale ears of corn and husk on her angora sweater. "My dad will kill me if he finds out," she added - the implication being that he very much would find out from the accumulated crime-scene evidence in her clothing and hair. Or from the voyeuristic balloon informants. "Well, I'm sure that just because you're covered in corn is merely circumstantial evidence unlikely to lead to a sex conviction," I said, sagely. "He'll kill you too," she confirmed. "Oh, OK, I'll help brush down your clothes once we're out of this field." I allowed a respectful two seconds to pass before adding, "Do you think we could, er, try again? I think I might be better at it the second time." My implication being that although I'm unlikely to have evolved into an experienced provider of female gratification in the last five minutes, there is a small chance that at least the next time she will actually notice we've had sex.

"No!" was her, in my view, unnecessarily firm response. "Why not?" I whined. "Three reasons," she countered, eagerly listing them: "This field is literally on fire, there's a balloon full of voyeurs and *Brookie* is on soon."

Fortunately the balloon was red and white, but without any identifying marks. It would have been an unpalatable yet scrumptious irony if the balloon had taunted me with one giant word emblazoned across it: Virgin.

The (lost) cherry on top of this particular experience was that she did say she had enjoyed the afternoon and wanted to see me again. The problem was the next time I saw her she had got a new boyfriend, who was older, taller, richer, wittier and handsomer than me and had a car, job and house. I don't know what she saw in him that I didn't have.

I assume he also got asked if he "felt better now?" and his answer would be invariably much better than mine. Oh well. You lose some, and you lose some. Then you lose some more. Maybe it was understandable she didn't want to rendezvous in a cornfield for bad sex. Perhaps I had caused her to become wheat intolerant.

Much later, knowing what I do now about balloons, it was strange to the point of being inexplicable to see a hot air balloon in the location I did that day. Although the weather conditions (relatively windless) and time of day (dusk) were consistent with the optimum conditions for balloon flight, it should not have been there - perilously close to the sea. We were only a mile from the seafront marshes and next stop, The Hague. Fly over the North Sea with a prevailing, inescapable westerly, and you're in trouble of the potentially fatal variety. And boy, can that wind blow off the Wash into the Lincolnshire Fenlands. I distinctly recall one day when I was eight years old, that for the fist time ever the wind briefly stopped blowing, and everyone consequently fell over.

It was debatable whether I truly lost my virginity in that field, but undebatable that something else was lost in that field: the balloon crew. My kind de-cherrier was wrong about the balloonists being voyeurs (voyeurs who had certainly been prepared to go to a lot of expense and trouble). Instead, they had picked up a stronger wind than anticipated and been blown miles off course with the result that the coastline was approaching menacingly fast.

This was almost exactly the situation that Sadler experienced in this part of the world too. Akin to Sadler nearly two hundred years previously, they were aware that they had one choice of action to avoid an unsatisfactory plop into the Wash - get the balloon to earth as quickly as possible, even if that meant hitting the ground at shuddering velocity.

Balloons had been associated with carnal longings several centuries before my cornfield experience. Convenient for a press just as intent on salacious gossip 250 years ago as now, the first English female to fly was a glamorous actress, who reportedly shocked eighteenth-century ground viewers by becoming prostrate with her gentleman aeronaut before disappearing into the cloud line. Although a more innocent and entirely truthful explanation for her sudden horizontal position was produced upon landing - namely she fell over into the basket when attempting to swap places with her male co-pilot. You can guess which version the press preferred. Years later I spotted in the local paper that my "conquest" had married. It was in November 2003, the exact same month that the final episode of *Brookside* aired. Presumably she now had time for marriage.

Even today stairs retain the capacity to cause me potentially fatal levels of embarrassment.

Sitting in reception at a highly prestigious private school I am experiencing two primary concerns. Firstly, since I've been sitting here for fifteen minutes, do I risk aggravating the stern matriarchal receptionist again to check if I've been forgotten? The second is a pervading regret in this august academic establishment, that I resisted any attempts in my life towards receiving a formal education. The autodidactic route is okay, but the reunions are rubbish.

I am using my trip to Gloucestershire to go scouting for locations that Sadler would have seen - he once famously closed the entire town's schools, shops and factories when he brought his balloon near here.

Eventually, a flustered teacher greets me. Panting like an over-exercised dog, he is only capable of pronouncing words one at a time: "So… sorry… been… mad… here… today." I'm ushered through a door, and then descend shallow steps into a long corridor, natural light flooding in from the left to illuminate an immensely long, seemingly endless corridor. So, this is what arguably one of Britain's most famous private schools looks like. Unlike Eton, or rather my perception of Eton, everyone is dressed comparatively normally - the utilitarian green uniforms wouldn't look different on kids on any school bus around the country throwing peanuts at each other. Whatever they spend their near £30,000 per annum school fees on, it's not uniform designers.

"The girls are really looking forward to hearing you speak," he confirms. I suspect that's a lie, but I'm still immensely grateful for the remark. I am here to address some of the Sixth Form.

After we've walked for so long that I am ready to ask if we can stop for a sit down, I'm about to be led up another flight of stairs. Problem! I am being directed to the edge of the stairs, towards a low banister and, even worse, a high balcony that overlooks A Sheer Drop. A chain of book carrying pupils are busily descending on my right, like a group of leaf carrying worker ants. So switching staircase sides to ensure I'm safely away from the edge is impossible, as I cannot block their path. "If you'd like to follow me," he chides, perplexed as to why I am suddenly frozen and glancing at his watch in a more aggressive side of passive aggressive gesture.

Once again, I feel powerless to admit my predicament. Shame gushes over me, soon occupying my entire being. My emotions mottled with several shades of anxiety. What if I did say something? "I'm scared of being on this side of the staircase." He'd probably ask some of his pupils to help me. Requiring a schoolgirl to hold your hand to enable you to go upstairs is probably the ultimate life fail for a forty-something independent adult male. Cowardly, I pretend to adjust and re-tie my shoe lace, which noticeably involves untying it first, in order to pointlessly re-tie it. Which I think he may have spotted me doing. Until a train of pupils have descended and I can cross to the far side and ascend next to the wall, I remain frozen. Then I do the traditional phone check, which the modern age has given me as a face-saving justification for waiting for stairs to clear before I can grab a hand rail and go away from the edge. The teacher notes this eccentric behaviour and deducts me respect points - though I doubt if he's worked out why. My shame remains hidden.

I am ushered into a panelled room covered with prints. Recognising these from Christ Church, Oxford - the only place in the world where a college chapel doubles as a city's cathedral - they form the Edward Burne-Jones window depicting the story of St. Frideswide the patron saint of the city. Only they are not prints. This being a plummy public school, they're originals. They have about twenty Pre-Raphaelite originals, ignored on a classroom wall. All we had on the walls at our school was graffiti proclaiming: "Nobby is a bender."

The teacher introduces me by declaring, "Richard never went to university," ... thanks for that... "or did A-levels"...was it truly necessary to impart that?... "or passed any O levels or GCSEs at all." (Special thanks, cheers for that, mate.) The girls visibly wonder why they've booked a speaker whose non-qualifications are being paraded with such emphasis. Is it to show them that slavish dedication to study coupled with academic application is to be discouraged because you can be successful anyway? Maybe next week they will book a female speaker who can tell them: "You don't need to study, girls, or focus on going to university. Instead just take a two litre bottle of cider to the park and get fingered on the swings. Then become pregnant by some bloke who works at the fairground. Worked for me."

Or perhaps I am here as a warning: a visitation from the Ghost of non-study Past, showing how people inevitably end up when rejecting education i.e. pitiful, cheaply dressed struggling writers forgoing professional haircuts and intent on taking biscuits for later from school staff rooms. And unable to go upstairs.

"Richard is a successful author and scriptwriter," the teacher continues. "And he'll also tell us about the real Oxford, from the Town's perspective not the University's prospectus." I wrote that last line for my intro - flattered he used it.

Then it dawns upon me that I've never spoken to eighteen-year-old girls before. Depressingly, that was also pitifully true when I was eighteen myself. "Hello," I begin. No one says "hello" back. This reminds me that eighteen-year-old girls ignored me when I was eighteen, and they appear to be doing exactly the same now. They stare at me. I stare at the Pre-Raphaelites. This is awkward. I need to say something, but have no idea what. "So... er... who boards here?" Most hands shoot up. That's a lot. They seem to be keeping their hands up for a long time. Then it hits me: I'm supposed to ask one of them to speak. "Er, yes," I say pointing to a plump oriental girl at the front. The others put their hands down. One pupil exaggerates the strain, while a blonde rubs her arm muscles to show how uncomfortable it was having to unnecessary keep her hand raised for fully four seconds. I rightly predict she will be causing trouble later. "What's it like being a boarder?" I ask.

"It's alright, I suppose," the Asian girl replies. I ask another sixth former. "It's OK. Suppose it's alright," is her response. This is the upper sixth *crème de la crème* English set and so far their vocab extends to four words. Another Asian girl puts up her hand. "Yes?", "It's alright, I suppose."

I ask who's applying to Oxford. Half the hands go up. Cambridge? About the same number. A hand stays raised. "Yes?" "Why didn't you go to university?" Hmm... that's a nice scarf. "There will be an opportunity for questions afterwards," interjects the kindly teacher, like the bell signifying the end of a round in a boxing match just as an opponent has completed his backswing before landing a knock-out punch.

"Richard can begin his talk now," which clearly means "Get on with it. If you've got nothing prepared we're about to find out." "So, please welcome properly," pausing whilst he clearly looks down at his notes for my name, "... Richard O. Smith. He's an author and you may have heard some of his jokes on TV and radio. He'll talk to you about the Ottoman Empire and subsequent ramifications into post-Byzantine monarchical statehood." There's a few seconds of cold silence and then "Ha! Ha! Ha!" Everyone laughs. Clearly they've stung many visitors before with that one. It's their familiar comforting little joke. And it works better as an ice breaker than most commissioned ships in Greenland's navy.

I begin speaking and make the mistake of looking at the blonde girl, whose face has now moved from a frown to an active scowl. Later she upgrades her facial expression further, from scowl to venomous.

There is a part of my routine where I have to swear. Having encountered school kids regularly on the bus, I am fairly sure they are familiar with swear words. My joke relies on a taboo word, and unwisely I have already started the routine. It's too late to stop now, and I can't think under the glare of the public speaking spotlight of a possible detour. Committed, I deliver an "f" bomb to the room. The teacher sitting at the table on the stage with me shudders like he's just received an electric shock from his chair, forcing him to suddenly hinge upright. Some of the girls laugh, but I hear competing exhalations of breath. It is the only occasion when the blonde girl laughs. Mainly because she thinks I've got myself into trouble.

After that, I make a note not to swear anymore. Mentally censoring my act invokes a two-second delay from brain to mouth - like a radio phone-in programme. Inevitably this ensures my timing suffers, but the audience are wonderfully generous and polite. Apart from Blondie, obviously, who sits with arms crossed staring directly above at a turned-off light. One day she's going to make her future husband very unhappy.

Performing comedy to Radio 4-savvy middle-aged people in arts centres and village halls is, it turns out, different to gigging to a group of seventeen- and eighteen-year-olds. So I attempt to change direction slightly, and do a Lady Gaga joke I once wrote for *The Now Show* that got edited out of the broadcast. It kills (knew it shouldn't have been edited out!) and I feel a buoyancy returning to my confidence. Everyone laughs, apart from Blondie plus the teacher whose face expresses slight anxiety - and I realise for the first time that there is an obscure, unintentional double meaning to the punch line, which although undeliberate could be interpreted as a very rude joke about gay sex. But surely that reference is so opaque, so encoded and so unlikely to be detected, especially in such hallowed, refined surroundings as these, that it's not worth a second thought.

As soon as I finish my talk, the teacher leads the girls in a round of appreciative applause, and he then announces: "This is Clarissa. She'll look after you now." Clarissa is eighteen, but dresses, acts and speaks like she's fifty-eight. She uses sixth form uniform liberties to be creative with scarves. Lots of tiny little scarves. My wife would know the proper fashion name for them, but I have no idea what this clothing accessory is called. Clarissa's delegated job is to lead me back to reception. En route her phone rings. "Sooo sorry," she announces, "but I have to… Ya? Ya. Ya. Ya. Don't care, you tell him there are other vets in Gloucestershire! Ya. Ya. Tuscany is not a problem, but Perpignan could be. Ciao." She presses a digit on her phone then emits a theatrical sigh. "Sorry. Mummy's taking a bit too much on at the moment. There are problems with her polo ponies when we're supposed to be leaving for Tuscany, but she also wants to fit in a couple of days at daddy's bolt-hole in France beforehand. So, is there anything I can get you?" "Yes," I think, "access to your life."

Then even by the standards of a teenager, she manages to really shock me with what she says next: "Are you OK going down the stairs if you stay on the side away from the banister?" "Yes… hang on, how did you know?" "Oh, I have a big problem with heights too," she says in a reassuring it's-no-biggie tone. Clearly £30k a year school fees are worth it if it imparts this much deductive observational skill. No one has ever noticed I'm bathmophobic before. Or have they? Perhaps my self-deception was more extensive than even I realised, and everyone thought "oh here's that guy who is terrified of stairs but we mustn't let on we know in case it hurts his feelings, and so he can go on pretending that no one notices."

Clarissa leads me into the school's small single-room museum, where I have time for one question before she has to leave. Maybe she has to go and buy another tiny scarf. So I want to use my one question opportunity well and ask a good one: "What's it really like being a boarder? How much do you miss home?" Drawing breath to respond, she pauses - then freezes like a suddenly distracted squirrel. Hesitating to assemble the correct words, to express herself with the profound poignancy I'd expect of someone aspiring to read English at Oxford, after further deliberation still she finally replies: "It's alright, I suppose." Before eventually elaborating that she misses her friends during the holidays. Two of those aforementioned friends then join us, and she informs them, "You should have come. He was really funny." That's nice of her.

Mercifully there are no more vertiginous steps to negotiate - just a long corridor lit from the right-hand side by yellowy autumnal sunlight, and an easy shallow flight leading back up to reception. Immaculately mannered Clarissa says goodbye and thanks me for visiting the school. "That talk was really brilliant. Really funny," she confirms. "Thank you," I say with genuine gratitude. "Ya, all the girls agreed you were great. We especially liked your gay sex joke."

88

Although a reductively nutshell definition, counselling is predominately about helping a client manage their anxieties.

A famous nineteenth-century psychoanalyst born in Vienna of Jewish extraction took this view. This shrink also coined the phrase "paranoid schizoid position", which theorises that a baby is born with anxieties. Can you guest the therapist's name? That's right, it was Melanie Klein. (You said Sigmund Freud, didn't you? Don't pretend you didn't! I know I did.) We all have inherent anxieties from birth, yet some of us have our anxiety levels set too high. And turning down the thermostat on those anxieties is frustratingly difficult.

I am often staggered by the ability of my brain to coldly fib to the rest of my body, telling it to prepare for dangers that plainly do not exist.

Anxiety covers potential experiences with an impervious membrane of fear, suffocating ambition. In its extreme form it disqualifies meaningful engagement with the world, invalidates potential experiences by the mind rushing to signal imagined dangers. It sees imaginary pitfalls where none exist and recognises monsters where none roams.

Scenarios which the majority would consider either neutral or pleasurable - unthinking participation activities, driving a car, getting on a train to meet a friend - are hugely problematic activities, mined with dangers. For decades I could not go upstairs on a bus, yet sometimes anxiety meant it was hard enough for me to even contemplate boarding a bus at all. Other people go on holiday. This is normal. These are collectively sought-after activities, their normality endorsed by the majority.

But not by me. Anxiety has undermined my ability to have these experiences in my life. Yes, it does make me inexpressibly angry as a consequence. Society punishes people by taking away their passports or banning them from driving. I have broken no laws, but receive the same punishments, alongside a life sentence of extreme anxieties.

Unsticking myself from these fears requires immense effort. And acrophobia forms only part of this. Living with general anxiety is akin to encountering a permanently malfunctioning warning light, a distracting red flash constantly flickering when there is really nothing malfunctioning to be warned about, except the warning light itself. The fact that the alarm is always false somehow misses the point, or perhaps is itself the true point.

Should a malfunctioning burglar or car alarm regularly be activated, then announcing "it's OK everybody, it's only a false alarm so there's no genuine threat or danger," isn't really going to placate the neighbours. The damage has already been done by the invasive alarm constantly mis-triggered. The fear is real, even if the danger isn't. The alarm is horribly disruptive, irrespective of whether or not there are any actual burglars. At its worst, anxiety deflavours life, sucks all

89

the nice chocolate from it and just leaves the hard unrelished bits underneath. You get the stone but no cherry.

Anxiety disallows freedom. Sometimes it feels like living in a cage where the cage door has been flung open decades ago, and yet I remain dutifully sitting on the perch. It's the freedom that taunts you, the realisation that you cannot participate in the world, engage with it, go up to it and ask it to dance, and be capable of dealing with the consequences. The transition from child to adulthood unquestionably meant much less to me than others, because I was still trapped with character attributes (fear of dark, stairs, going out, heights, socialising). Hence few of the prizes normally obtained by reaching adulthood were available for me.

Do I sound bitter? I hope so, because I am. I would shiver uncontrollably. Painful psychosomatic headaches would flare up suddenly. My legs would flail like Bambi on a frozen lake. Just being in small room or at the theatre I would feel uncontrollable nausea, palpitations and a frightening sense of imminent vomiting, later diagnosed as emetophobia.

There are numerous occasions - several within the last few weeks - when I have gone to a pub to meet friends, seen them through the window, but have felt crippling anxiety that forbids me from entering the pub, even though I really, really want to see these people I know very, very much. Especially as an occupational hazard of writers is often enforced alienation in the day job.

I'm terrified to be standing in the street, or getting the bus home. But I have to get home as quickly as possible. Naturally, when I get home, and the anxiety starts to subside, it is immediately replaced with feelings of acute and reoccurring regret. Needless to say, this is not something I tend to share with people. So when I tell counsellors about it, then it shows a deserved confidence in them. But I have not previously admitted this to anyone, strangers, friends nor, more dishearteningly, mental health professionals. There are three prominent reasons for this: shame, embarrassment and the likelihood of not being believed.

Quite understandably, people cannot dissociate the ability to speak to a capacious room packed with paying people for an hour doing successful stand-up from an inability to go into a pub or board a bus. And most of the time I cannot comprehend it either.

Not forgetting the unacknowledged reality of visiting a GP with my anxieties: "I'm here because I can't go on holiday," while people are waiting outside to see the same doctor who might have cancer.

Occasionally it is possible to encounter people who gain importance and purpose from their phobias. I am sure they exist. But the overwhelming majority of people, particularly those with malfunctioning anxiety receptors, do not. I just want to be better. I want to start tasting the flavours life has to offer. Enjoy its colours. Meet life and go to the pub with it - not perennially hide from it most of the time.

Education, as well as counselling, are my twin weapons in the fight back against restrictive phobias. So, what is a phobia? How prevalent are they? And how can we control them rather than let them control us?

Living with a fear of heights appears to be one of the most commonly experienced anxieties in Britain. This conclusion was not initially drawn from empirical peer-reviewed scientific evidence, merely anecdotal conversations with friends, colleagues, contacts and the occasional friendly-looking stranger bothered on public transport after I had been drinking. However, after years passed without any noticeable decrease in my altitude anxiety, I started to adopt a more scientific interest in the subject. Consulting published research, it transpires that acrophobia is certainly up there among the nation's chief fears, but not the chart-topper. Not even close.

The most common fear in Britain, and there are numerous surveys and research polls to qualify this statement, is… (pause to build dramatic effect)…. (just a little bit longer)… glossophobia. Hmm. I sense you have a question. And are feeling a bit like those underwhelmed characters in *The Hitchhiker's Guide to the Galaxy* after waiting thousands of years to receive the answer "42".

Glossophobia is the technical name for… Well, see if you can guess which one it is from the Top 10 list below. And no, it's not the fear of being kept waiting for an answer.

A traditional Top 10 chart rundown of Britain's most common phobias includes an irrational fear of spiders, snakes, heights, open spaces, dentists, needles, death, germs, enclosed environments, flying and public speaking. Glossophobia is a clinician's name for the last category in that list.

Year after year in the UK, glossophobia claims the top spot as Britain's no. 1 phobia, repeatedly knocking "fear of death" down into second position. As has probably been observed before, this means that at a funeral the average Briton would rather be in the casket than deliver the eulogy.

Other phobias are considerably more off-piste, such as top materials scientist and all round good bloke Prof. Mark Miodownik whom I had the good fortune to work with when writing and recording the BBC2 series *Dara O'Briain's Science Club*. He has a fear of cheese. Dara callously demonstrated this off-camera for additional studio-audience laughs, watching Prof. Mark retreat in abject consternation from a haphazardly waved cheese square like a panicking man in a monster movie fleeing into the streets.

Not all fears are irrational. I have a terrifying fear of Piers Morgan - but that's both normal and rational. This does prompt us to question society's attitudes. Why is claustrophobia sympathetically tolerated, whilst other phobias are insensitively categorised as an indulgence and riper than a gorgonzola left out of the fridge for three weeks for comic humiliation?

These more obscure phobias don't allow sufferers to possess the sense of bonding inclusivity available to those phobics who suffer any in the legitimising Top 10. We're the popular phobics - the ones experiencing a condition legitimised by common participation. Yet whatever your phobia - snakes or a fear of playing snakes and ladders (although the latter would technically be ophidiophobia coupled with acrophobia) - the underlying and defining aspects remain the same. Starting with a realisation that the fear is most damaging in itself: i.e. it is the fear that we often fear the most with any phobia.

Phobias are psychological impediments. A phobia is an irrational, abnormal, excessive, persistent, unrelenting, unreasonable fear.

To demonstrate the extent of phobias, and just how far they can blight aspects of life, I turned to the *Oxford English Dictionary* and psychology textbooks which define myriad phobias affecting the daily functioning of numerous otherwise healthy adults. Humans have delivered aversions to many things, and continue to evolve to fit newly invented fears; a recent update of the OED includes words defining computer hardware aversion: terminology for terminal fear of terminals.

There are so many anxieties, each recognised by its own defining word in the OED, that it risks inducing gateophobia in most of us. Gateophobia, by the way, is the fear of insanity - not, as you would reasonably expect, gates. Although a man freaked out and demonstrating uncontrollable splenetic rage by gates would be fairly described as "insane" (or a former Tory party chief whip) - unless it was a responsive aversion to the "music" of Gareth Gates, which would be reassuringly normal, and a confirmer of functioning sanity.

For most phobias we can thank the Greeks for the words we use to describe them. Agyrophobia is an aversion to crossing the road, whilst alektorophobia is the fear of chickens. Therefore presumably agyroalektophobia is the fear of telling a "why did the chicken cross the road?" joke. Sadly it's not.

Aichmophobia is defined as an irrational fear of a pointed needle, although, personally, I'd be more fearful of a non-pointed needle. That would definitely hurt a lot more. Meanwhile, wiccaphobia is the fear of witchcraft, not the fear of dubious encyclopaedic facts. No, I didn't just get that wiccaphobia fact from a well-known on-line knowledge resource.

Spinophobia is an irrational fear of being without a backbone or becoming spineless. I'm a busy man, so please take a moment to add your own Nick Clegg joke here.

Coimetrophobia is a fear of cemeteries. Extreme sufferers wouldn't be seen dead in one. (See what I did there? Oh, please yourself.)

Alliumphobia is an abject fear of garlic, which is of course indistinguishable from the word francophobia meaning an uncontrollable terror of French people. Surprisingly, bathophobia is not another francophobic word describing French people i.e. it is not the defined condition of being fearful of baths. That is abluthophobia - and a relatively common condition among very young children and the 65 million who currently inhabit France, obviously. (You may have noticed how so much comedy - even billed satire - is extracted from mere reinforcement of stereotypes.)

In fact bathophobia is a fear of depths. My friend once bought a posh looking watch from a charity shop for only £4.95 and, gleaming with pride, showed me the uniquely designed and "surely worth a lot of money" watch. I pointed out that it looked uniquely designed because it was a diver's watch i.e. it told not the time, but the depth. Hence if someone asked him "what time is it?" he could reply, "I don't know, but we're both currently one metre above sea level if that helps."

Acronyms can be unfortunate. Ask the Cambridge University Netball Team. (I'll wait.) But their overuse constitutes a ubiquitous war on clarity. People genuinely dislike the over-reliance in communication on acronyms which risks creating a we-know/you-don't-know division. Surprisingly it is a phobia without a name, though campaigns have started to have the condition recognised with the word acronymophobia. This is far too literal - paradoxically, a suitable name for fear of acronyms should have that aforementioned we-know/you-don't-know club exclusivity to it.

Some have suggested acrophobia - they can't have that, as it already exists as my condition: the fear of heights. Perhaps a suitable name for the phobia of encountering acronyms ought to be pedantophobia, since many a pedant enjoys pointing out that it's not an acronym unless the collection of letters spells a pronounceable word. Totally What Annoys Them would therefore be a true acronym as you can pronounce the lettered abbreviation as a word to a pedant: TWAT.

Bathmophobia, as we have already learnt, is a legitimate fear of stairs, and climacophobia is the condition of being fearful of falling downstairs. And, um, I suffer from this, although not as acutely, or cutely, as I did when a young child. Being terrified of stairs is borderline socially acceptable for a three-year-old, but becomes increasingly difficult when you enter your forties. This is why I prefer not to tell anyone and suffer in silent humiliation - in common with other phobia suffers - I know, just when you weren't expecting a serious point to be made!

Hexakosioihexekontahexaphobia - and they surely could have accomplished the job with fewer letters (presumably the lexicographers were being paid by the hour rather than word when they forged that noun in the word factory) - defines the fear of the number 666, though it should also be the fear of spelling unnecessarily longwinded words or, should anyone attempt slipping this into general everyday conservation, fear of meeting Britain's most pretentious man. Though you wonder when anyone would ever select using the word ahead of merely saying "I'm phobic about the number 666" given that relatively short number of syllables would always be destined to win a pronunciation race ahead of "I've got hexakosio..." until concluding fully twelve seconds later in "... aphobia". This will lead to the inevitable requested follow-up explanation: "I'm phobic about the number 666" proceeded immediately by "why didn't you say that in the first place?" Nor is it a good one to use in classified adverts, telegrams (should you ever time travel) or in any other format where you are charged by the word. There is also a likely risk of inducing hellenologophobia (fear of scientific technical terminology). Oh, and also fear of Greek things like salty white cheese cubes, taramasalata, ouzo and EU bailouts.

Ergophobia is being fearful of work, which to a German is interchangeable with the aforementioned hellenologophobia. Germanphobia is a frustratingly rare, and yet welcomed, phobia - not in the sense of advocating racial discrimination against our European sausage-munching brethren, but because it is transparently named: Germanphobia is, refreshingly, exactly what you would expect. Although Germans may stereotype Britons as being ergophobic, which leads to potential Germanphobia.

Hypengyophobia is a fear of responsibility, unatoxophobia is the fear of tidiness, eosophobia is being fearful of daylight, while autoerotinteruptusphobia is the condition of being irrational fearful of discovered self-pleasuring. All four combined at once is also known as "being a teenager".

Suffering from a fear of trains and train travel experiences is known as sideromophobia - or being a First Great Western passenger (or, as they prefer to call you, customer). The fear of being called a customer rather than passenger is simply "being normal".)

Samhainophobia is not the rather specific and impolite fear of Sam Hain - a bloke of that name used to run a chip shop in a Bedfordshire town where I once lived. He seemed fairly easy going, so I'm surprised he has been rewarded by being singled out for individual scorn by the *Oxford English Dictionary* - their chief lexicographer must have had a seriously bad bag of chips there. Instead samhainophobia is the fear of Halloween. Paradoxically, being fearful of an event that exists to generate fear is already getting into the spirit of the event that sufferers are supposed to dislike. If you really wish to scare and terrify modern children senseless when they visit your door trick and treating, instead of giving them sweets, try offering them some pieces of actual fruit and veg. Ding, dong. Open door. Announce: "Healthy raw vegetable crudités, children?" "Arrrggghhhh!!!!!"

Lachanophobia is the persistent fear of vegetables. Rather than being trauma triggered by an unfortunate radish-based accident in earlier life, this condition is extremely prevalent among some groups of sufferers, where it is also known in technical clinician's language as either lachanophobia or "being Scottish".

Hippophobia is obviously a fear of a particular animal. That's right. A horse. Obviously. You knew that. What? Yes, a horse. There appears to be no word for fear of hippopotami. Which is odd, because they're bloody dangerous!

Rather callously in my opinion, psellismophobia is the technical name for expressing a fear of stuttering. It is also an impossible word to pronounce without inducing an involuntary stutter.

Proctophobia is the fear of bottoms, which cannot be a phobia that afflicts Kylie Minogue or top twerker Miley Cyrus, since that pair - or rather quadrant - of celebrity buttock owners have exposed theirs more often than a rebus monkey over the past decades. Fear of moons - the big white circular rock orbiting earth, rather than Kyle's or Miley's hot derriere, is selenophobia. This is a relatively rare condition, although it would have been unfortunate if any of the extensively trained twelve Apollo astronauts suddenly discovered upon lunar touchdown - especially original pre-Michael Jackson moonwalker Neil Armstrong - that they suffered from this unusual phobia. "Sorry guys, but I don't think I want to step on the moon after all, so if we could just go home instead. We haven't put much time or effort into this Apollo project, have we?"

Hylophobia is a fear of woods and forests, a condition presumably accentuated during childhood when all those stories take place in shadowy forests. Alternatively, isopterophobia is the specific fear of only wood-consuming insects. Sufferers would therefore be terrified of a woodworm, but register no fear when deciding to pick up a scorpion.

Malaxophobia is a fear of foreplay - a condition that I suspect afflicts exactly half the population. You know which half. I am surprised that Ann Summers don't market a Foreplay Timer for women to buy their menfolk ("twenty minutes of compulsory warming up exercises, or the only thing you're banging tonight is your own head in frustration.") Hmm… That's my *Dragons' Den* pitch sorted out.

Pentheraphobia is the fear of a mother-in-law, also known as Les Dawson's entire forty-year showbiz career.

Homophobia we recognise as a prejudicial fear against gay people.

Meanwhile hodophobia is the fear of road travel and hobophobia is, fittingly, the fear of beggars. Hence, feeling bigoted towards a driving gay tramp renders you hodo-homo-hobo-phobic, which is extravagantly bigoted, but also sounds rather mellifluous.

Disappointingly, hohohophobia is neither the fear of Santa Claus nor prostitutes. Indeed, suffering an abnormal fear of prostitutes is cypridophobia - the same word being indistinguishable from a fear of contacting venereal disease. Suffering acute cypridphobia must also cause awkwardness whenever a known sufferer starts developing allergic reactions to a lady in social situations, particularly when she's hosting a posh middle-class dinner party.

Meanwhile, hippopotomonstrosesquipedaliophobia is, disappointingly in my view, not the fear of hippos. In fact, the later word (I can't type it again without inducing RSI) is authentically the fear of long words. Irony overload. It is also a magnificent source of points in Scrabble, although your opponent may reasonably request an explanation for why you currently have 35 tiles in your rack.

The chronic fear of dancing is known as chorophobia, while the fear of *Strictly Come Dancing* is called "having good taste".

This might also induce sesquipedalophobia, which is a fear of deploying long words. Again, this is a particularly cruel clinical name for the condition, as sufferers attempting referral for treatment must constantly endure terror when informing administrators, counsellors, receptionists and doctors of their condition. Fear of users of long words is not, alas, pretentiouswankerphobia.

Mycophobia is a fear of mushrooms, rather than a fear of people called Mike. Orthophobia is the fear of property, yet no phobia has yet been coined to describe estate agents

Paraskavedckatriaphobia is the fear of Friday the 13th - the calendar date not the over exploited movie franchise series. Parthenophobia is the fear of meeting a virgin woman, which explains why so many afflicted sufferers prefer to move to Essex as a popular cure.

Elsewhere, tiny distinctions between the spellings of phobias can reveal crucial differences. For example, genophobia is the fear of sex, whilst geniophobia is a fear of chins. These are crucial distinctions, unless you are married to either Bruce Forsyth or Jimmy Hill, when they constitute pretty much the same thing.

Two other phobias share a close similarity in their description if not condition: Europhobes are well-known in the British press for being sceptical about Britain's membership of the European Union, though Europhobia should not be confused with Eurotophobia - the latter being a fear of a female's genitals. That is also known as NigelFaragephobia - er, to clarify: both the former and... oh yeah, why not... the latter phobias.

Medomalacuphobia is the fear of losing an erect penis, which must be the

96

panic invoked when realising, "now, it must be somewhere around here - I'll try thinking back to when I last saw it - oh yeah, before I got fat."

Official NHS health advice guidelines state that if an adult male is unable to see his own penis, then he is classified as morbidly obese and should address immediate weight loss. However, if like me you have an eighteen-inch penis, then this advice is flawed - as even though I may be clinically obese, I can still see it. OK, not really. Maybe it does help sufferers to think back to the last place where they definitely remember having it, although that will probably be on the Internet. Being frightened of losing an erection is different to megalophobia, defined as the condition where sufferers fear large or big things. No - before you say it - none of my girlfriends have encountered that phobia.

Glimpsing a man's penis may induce an attack of phallophobia in a woman (fear of seeing a penis), which is a preferable response to inducing an attack of microphobia, a fear of unusually tiny things.

Women explaining to the majority of men that their erection does not induce an attack of megalophobia - the aversion to large things - is known as... well, insensitivity, mainly. Complimenting a man on his size risks him being doxophobic: doxophobia is the condition of harbouring an irrational fear of praise.

Consecotaleophobia is the mortal fear of chopsticks - the eating implements not primitive piano playing. Katagelophobia sufferers deserve mocking because they suffer from a fear of ridicule. Meanwhile a limnophobic person hosts a specific fear of lakes; presumably they are fine with ponds, marinas, seas, rivers, tarns, canal basins, lidos, pools and puddles, but freak out at the suggestion of seeing a lake.

Anyone enduring mnemophobia would endure painful psychoanalysis treatment when asked to recall when they first experience mnemophobia and subsequent triggers for the condition - it is the fear of experiencing memories.

Zemmiphobia is an abject fear of the naked desert mole rat, and a hard one to elicit sympathy for - or indeed claim incapacity benefit for the infliction and time off work - given that the rodent is a resident of one extremely small deserted area of Eastern Africa.

Maybe that's enough technical phobias. If so, you could be suffering from verbophobia: a fear of words - and undoubtedly a lexicographer's sick note of choice.

With so many fears given official acknowledgment by the dictionary, you seriously wonder if a significant amount of the population are just afraid of their own shadow. Actually, that's included too: sciophobia is the fear of seeing shadows. Since pupaphobia is the fear of puppets, a sciophobic pupaphobe would not enjoy an evening of shadow puppetry. And if that's too many technical names for phobias, then you could be suffering from nomatophobia, a fear of names. And in case you're wondering, phobophobia is a fear of phobias.

Apologies for any of the highly opinionated remarks expressed above if you suffer from allodoxaphobia, the fear of opinions. There are too many aggressively held opinions masquerading as facts in the world, and I for one would like to promote more allodoxaphobia.

And it's probably time I unstuck myself from epistemophobia - that's an aversion to knowledge - and educated myself about phobias: their causes, definitions and treatments. I want to learn why phobias are so prevalent and what current advances in psychology have discovered. Find out the latest score in the Nature v. Nurture contest.

I need to do this if I have any real ambition of shedding my phobias so that I can ascend in a balloon to replicate James Sadler's achievement and look down on the same view that Sadler had of Oxford's skyline. Let's do this thing.

7 THE MISSING YEARS: SADLER'S CURIOUS CAREER

What impresses people is generational. When the first street lights appeared, thousands of people flocked to see them, then stood beneath them, looking up in silent wonder. Some had travelled huge distances to observe the street lighting. Now if you stood and stared at a street light, passers-by would probably call social services. But is the wonder any less now than then at this unnatural capacity to make the darkness vanish?

James Sadler was at the forefront of this modern wonder, pioneering research into burning coal gas as an illuminant. He worked on a process that became known as gasification, where subjecting coal to a process of chemical reactions would force out combustible gas. Coal gas became such an efficient and popular fuel for domestic use that it remained in regular use until the 1960s when the discovery of North Sea gas prompted household cookers and other gas appliances to be transferred to new models designed for burning natural gas.

He had garnered enormous success and fame (but probably not money as Sadler's motivation appeared more scientifically driven than commercial in his first years of aeronautics). For someone who invented so much that was put to practical use, he appears to have lived a frugal existence, utterly reliant upon his friends' generosity in later life in order to move back to Oxford. The number of flights he took between 1784 and 1785, and then from 1810 until his second aeronautical retirement, varies between accounts and newspapers. Totalling his balloon voyages is rendered impossible by the lack of distinction in the reports between Sadler senior and his sons. We are further confused by a third Mr. Sadler, his son John, who also occasionally flew the family balloon, adding a third flying Sadler to Windham and, of course, his dad. On at least one occasion, father and son swapped before take-off, resulting in contrasting reports that credited different aeronauts for the same voyage. Undisputed evidence as to why he suddenly curtailed ballooning remains simply unknown, abandoned to speculation.

Or did Mrs. Sadler simply put down her (probably clogged) foot and point out that he had a wife and family, which would be quite hard to support if he changed his status from "aeronaut and pastry cook" to "deceased"?

By the time he eventually returned to flying Sadler had not been in a balloon basket for a considerable time. Recommencing his aeronautical activities exactly one quarter of a century later, he was then at the advanced age of fifty-seven. The one activity that had made him a national celebrity and able to count MPs and

Cabinet Ministers as close friends was ballooning. So why did he abandon the activity for so long? Certainly one contributory reason was the abrupt ending of support from Oxford University.

Sadler had encountered a bumpy ride from the University. After he had initially gained its approval, there were plenty of witnesses prepared to testify that the University was jealous of Sadler's accomplishments and of headlines gained by a working-class Townsman. Sir John Coxe Hippisley observed: "Sadler has been harshly used… there is not a better chemist or mechanic." Others used the word "pique" to describe the University's attitude towards him. A letter sent to his friend and Cabinet Minister William Windham had shed light on this fallout with the University, alluding to "pique and jealousy of his superior science". The author of the letter was Colonel Richard Fitzpatrick, who had just found himself on an unexpected solo flight.

24 JUNE 1785: CORPUS CHRISTI COLLEGE, OXFORD

After the University initially championed Sadler's achievements in 1784, the relationship appears to have curdled. Was this due to an incident at Corpus Christi College on 24 June 1785? This was a day of undoubted importance in aeronautical history, as various University dignitaries including the Chancellor had been invited to attend alongside Fellows of the Royal Society - all in the presence of one Dr. Horsley. The refined were dressed in their finery, awaiting Sadler's planned ascent.

Regrettably, Sadler had either overestimated the balloon's capacity to carry four passengers or had been unable to refuse requests from such high-status members of the scientific community to be passengers. Lifting four adult dignitaries - none of them a stranger to the dessert trolley - was a tall order for Sadler. The results were predictably farcical.

From first light until Sadler signalled at 1.30pm that the balloon envelope was sufficiently inflated to attempt take-off, people and traffic "had been incessantly pouring into the city of Oxford". One newspaper observed: "The operation was greatly impeded by the pressure of the crowd." Even fencing off a large part of Corpus Christi had only temporarily kept the encroaching multitudes at bay, all desperate to glimpse Sadler.

By 2pm "everything having been adjusted, Colonel Richard Fitzpatrick and Sadler seated themselves in the car, only for the balloon to be found incapable of ascent." According to a contemporary press report, it appears no one was able to inform the Colonel that his large girth was rendering flight unlikely: "The Colonel being resolved not to quit his feat, a due proportion of ballast was added". Again they tried to launch from the college gardens, but the weight was still too much. What happened next appears strange bordering upon imprudent, even by Sadler's standards of demonstrative recklessness.

Already the balloon's inflation process had taken nearly two hours longer than expected, and still it stubbornly refused to leave the ground. One by one, Sadler had to persuade the promised passengers to step out of the basket, until only Colonel Fitzpatrick remained. Sadler had taken the surprising decision to vacate the basket himself and allow the Colonel to pilot the balloon with "an unpremeditated solo flight which was managed with admirable judgement, though with no more than a few brief verbal instructions given by Sadler".

Perhaps Sadler proposed to show that ballooning was for all men, not just an isolated few daredevil pilots. Maybe he became so annoyed with the Colonel that he was prepared to let him ascend solo to prove a point - the point that he was unlikely to return uninjured. Sadler merely handed Fitzpatrick "his flag" and stepped out of the balloon, leaving the intrepid Colonel to ascend on his own after a brief oral tutorial from England's foremost aerial voyager. *The Times* describes what happened next: "The colonel manifested a cool intrepidity both before and after the balloon had been launched and continued waving the flag as long as he could possibly retain sight of the spectators below. After 47 minutes he sank gently into the horizon," a detail that suggests both a lack of wind and Fitzpatrick's sudden aeronautical skills.

Three days later, Fitzpatrick wrote to Windham:

Grosvenor Place, London
June 27, 1785

I have gratified my curiosity in a flight from Oxford; where your protege Sadler (who, by the by, I consider as a Phenomenon) behaved very handsomely, and finding his process not answer his expectations and the balloon only capable of carrying up one person, very obligingly gave me up his place, and after receiving some hasty instructions, I ascended by myself, in view of all the University, as well I believe as of the whole county...

I had told Sadler that I would not take his balloon very far, and my intention was to have flown about two hours, but as I wished to ascend as high as possible without danger to the balloon; after having first try'd the valve to see if I was master of the use of it, I continued rising for three quarters of an hour, when I suddenly perceived from my flag, that I was descending. I discharged gradually five of my bags of ballast, throwing out papers between each, without finding that I appeared to diminish the velocity of my descent, till the 5th, when the paper I threw out floated instead of rising, to my great satisfaction, since I perceived something had happened of which I was ignorant. I then determined to reserve my two last bags till I was certain of being very near the earth, and fixed one of them to the anchor in order to drop it and break the fall of the machine. When I saw the shadow of the balloon increasing very fast, and could plainly distinguish objects, so small as horses in waggons and in the fields, I threw out my sixth bag, but unluckily when I was preparing the seventh upon the anchor, it slipp'd off, and fell without it. Within a very few seconds I came to the ground on the side of a steep hill, in a corn field. The shock was trifling, but the unevenness of the ground overset the Car, and rolled me gently out. Disentangling myself from the cords, I held fast the side of the car, and with some difficulty held the balloon till some country people came to my assistance. I then perceived a large rent in the lower part of it, which accounted for my descent, and which, I suppose, by a more judicious use of the valve I should have prevented. The curiosity and astonishment of the country who flocked in by shoals were prodigious. I got Sadler's balloon, however, safe in a stable, and waited at a little publick house two hours for his arrival.

Adieu, Dear Windham.

Sadler, who had given pursuit in a horse-drawn carriage from Oxford, quickly appeared at the pub and retrieved both balloon and unplanned pilot, and travelled back to Wantage in Oxfordshire. Relief, as well as the balloon, must have been in the air for a long time that day, as it was midnight before Sadler, realising it was too late to reach Oxford, opted to stay in Wantage for the night, missing the planned celebrations of the flight's success in Oxford.

Fitzpatrick's family were hardly danger-rejecting risk-assessment carry-outers. His brother John Fitzpatrick, the 2nd Earl of Upper Ossory, was an Irish peer. Elected as an MP for Bedfordshire for nearly thirty years, he also spent forty years as the appointed Lord Lieutenant serving the monarch in the county. He also spent an equal amount of years womanising, culminating in a high-profile affair with none other than the Prime Minister's wife Anne Fitzroy. This affair produced an illegitimate child, and the mother's eventual scandalous divorce. A special Act of Parliament was required for granting her the divorce in 1767 from Prime Minster Augustus Fitzroy. Not that the PM's bed sheets were whiter than white, as he reacted to the divorce by marrying within eight weeks his lover Elizabeth Wrottesley. A vicar's daughter, Elizabeth produced no fewer than nine surviving children. Hence Sadler probably knew that recklessness was in the Colonel's genes, before allowing him the unique distinction of going up in his balloon without knowing how to use either ballast or vent.

But however much of a bumpy ride he received figuratively from Oxford University, this was nothing compared to the literal bumpy ride Sadler encountered on his final flight prior to his self-called 25-year time-out from aeronautics. On 10 September 1785, after taking off from Worcester, he only just survived a terrifying ordeal.

25 AUGUST 1785: WORCESTER

Sadler was big in Worcester. Yet a Worcester flight caused Sadler such a jolting shock to his flying confidence that he curtailed all ballooning for over a quarter of a century. But that was still to come.

In August 1785 Sadler travelled to Worcester for his seventh manned flight. With the second Manchester flight nearly killing him, and the Corpus Christi flight not at all going to plan, coupled with news reaching the UK from France of the deaths of prominent fellow aeronauts, even a daredevil stuntman like Sadler must have been hosting some anxieties as to his choice of future career.

Taking off in the private grounds of a Worcester estate, "on Thursday afternoon about half after one, Mr Sadler ascended with his balloon amidst the acclamations of a large crowd." On a cloudy day, Sadler was reported as making little progress until he threw out three large bags of ballast, at which point he suddenly soared upwards. Ever the combined gentleman and crowd pleaser, he courteously saluted the crowd with his hat and disappeared into the grey cloud blanket. Unlike the Colonel, he knew what to do: vent the globe continuously to neutralise the hydrogen pull causing the alarmingly steep ascent.

However, 37 minutes into the flight, Sadler was low enough "to converse with field workers who told him that he was over Burford, near Tenbury, 21 miles from Worcester." After re-ascending by tipping overboard the last of his sandbags, a few miles later he drifted low over the estate of Gilbert Nicholetts known as The Broomtrees. Indeed, he was so low as to receive a shouted invitation to dinner. Sadler, careful to doff his hat, politely declined and continued for another three miles until he threw out his anchor over the village of Stretton Gransome. Unfortunately, the next part of the story does not reflect well on the agricultural workers of this Herefordshire hamlet.

Upon seeing the shadow of Sadler's balloon appearing on the field, "forty people were working at the harvest there but they fled with the upmost precipitation." Only an old lady remained, and Sadler persuaded her to grab hold of his mooring rope and help steady the balloon. Eventually, deciding the balloon was not a ferocious dragon despatched by the devil, the farm labourers gingerly returned and aided the old lady with docking the balloon. Wisely forsaking the superstitious dragon fearers as dining companions, Sadler walked the three miles back to The Bromtrees and dined with the Nicholetts. *The Times* reports that when Sadler arrived, the entire family were all "fitting". Hopefully, this is a simple case of the eighteenth-century letter "f" being interchangeable with the letter "s", rather than Sadler demonstrating an early attempt to invent strobe lighting.

The next day, Friday, both Sadler and balloon were returned to Worcester by the afternoon, launching some considerable weekend-greeting festivities. As he reached the outskirts "the populace took the horses from his carriage and drew him about the streets in triumph."

This sort of admiration must have been hard for Sadler to give up, but within a few weeks, he had done just that - for nearly 25 years. A correspondent writing to a newspaper gushes praise upon Sadler's exploits in Worcester, clearly star-struck by seeing his balloon. But the report ends with the descriptive detail: "Though the day was remarkably cloudy at his ascent, as soon as Mr Sadler got above the clouds the sun shone with great force." This description surely works, too, as a load-bearing metaphor for Sadler's career and life: escape from the greyness of his kitchen worker environment, soaring above the dreamless drudgery into the sunlight, basking in the warmth of the public's adulation.

10 SEPTEMBER 1785: WORCESTER

When Sadler took off "in his beautiful new balloon amidst the acclamations and applause of thousands of spectators" there was an early omen that this flight would prove troublesome. Back in Worcester, his ascent was immediately hindered by a pear tree, and it took several minutes to untangle the balloon from its branches. After that initial setback upon take-off, Sadler soon soared over a cooing crowd, his supporters turning out in incredible numbers again to witness first-hand an acknowledged hero of the age.

Then things started to go wrong, badly wrong. Firstly, he was forced to keep the value open throughout, and then "meeting with a very cold assemblage of vapours, hastened his descent much more quickly that he would have wished".

Nine miles from Lichfield in Staffordshire, Sadler realised he would have to land. But there was a problem. His entanglement with the pear tree had meant his grappling iron, a makeshift anchor he favoured as his primitive landing gear, had been damaged, and rendered ineffective after losing several prongs on the pear tree. Sadler "was dragged nearly five miles over a rough and extensive heath, and at length thrown out of his car. By this unfortunate accident his balloon escaped him." Moreover the balloon was never to be seen again, and the expense of manufacturing one balloon per journey was clearly impractical - something that was evidently dawning upon Sadler by this stage. This was another likely cause of his future sudden decision to prematurely curtail his aeronautical activities.

Lord Uxbridge, dwelling nearby, immediately despatched his carriage to the crash scene to rescue Sadler. Lord Uxbridge's son subsequently became famous at the Battle of Waterloo when a French cannon ball removed his leg in 1815, causing him to exclaim, "By God, Sir, I have lost my leg," to which the Duke of Wellington supposedly replied "By God, Sir, so you have." That exchange probably passed for psychotherapy in those days. Having suffered a 25% reduction in the limb department, the ever-stoical Lord only uttered one cry during the subsequent primitive surgical procedure, observing during the anaesthetic-free operation: "the knives appear somewhat blunt". Afterwards, the Lord sprang - or, more accurately, hopped - into action and exploited the commercial opportunities of his leglessness.

A cottage nearby was turned into a leg shrine, where visitors could pay to join a tour that first displayed the blood-speckled chair where the amputation occurred, and culminated with the grave where the leg was buried. Visitors flocked to this macabre attraction, although one decidedly less impressed tourist decorated the grave with the graffiti message, "here lies the Lord's limb; the Devil will claim the rest of him." Bizarrely, Lord Uxbridge's family were notorious for losing limbs, and especially hands, all over the battlefield of Europe - even his wife succeeding in losing more hands than an inexpert bridge player.

Thankfully, Lord Uxbridge was around to provide Sadler with a hand that day. Sadler lost no limbs in the accident, otherwise escaping with severe bruising to his body and confidence. But his risk taking was bordering on the pathological.

Why did he stop flying? It could have been a combination of this near-death experience, the risky financial model of expensive silk balloons and their destruction, and, most likely, a realisation on Sadler's part that this was an inappropriate profession for someone with a shop, wife and children to support. And very much factored into these plans for all three was his continued survival.

Though if Mrs. Sadler hoped this abstention from balloon activities would help her children, then fate was to intervene later - cruelly. It would be fascinating to know Mrs. Sadler's opinion of her husband: proud supporter, or mystified at his recklessness? His first wife was to die in 1790. But there were still further tragedies ahead for the Sadler family.

A document contained within Christ Church's collection confirms that Sadler had developed a professional interest in designing steam engines by 1786. In 1791 he patented a mobile steam engine, designed with a reaction turbine and condenser. The subsequent patent Sadler took out was described as "tandem single acting compound atmospheric steam carriage".

His steam engines were used by the Royal Navy in Portsmouth, at mining pitheads and also in a mustard factory on London's South Bank where "Sadler's engine keeps a great number of edge stones at work grinding mustard, lint and other feeds. The sieves and other apparatus for preparing their goods together with the pressing machines for extracting the oil and making the oil cake are all worked by the engine," noted John Rennie.

It appears likely that Sadler limited himself to only filing one patent for a steam engine, probably because of his ongoing concerns over an increasingly litigious James Watt. Watt may have successfully garnered the main credit for inventing the mobile steam engine, but this could have been merely a PR battle. There was certainly reported antagonism between Watt and Sadler, yet typically only one side of the story - Watt's side - appears to have been written up.

Sadler had certainly produced a moving steam engine around the same time as Watt. He engineered a rotary engine that provided steam power to a wheeled carriage; or, to give his invented contraption a shorter name: car. Maybe Sadler invented the first car?

Let's pose a question. When did the first car appear on the streets of Britain? The answer is surprisingly early. It occurred in Sadler's time. By 1 June 1803, a private steam carriage was traversing the roads of London. Presumably on 2 June 1803, the first traffic warden appeared, slapping a ticket on the bonnet.

Surprisingly, even by the beginning of the twentieth century, steam cars were superior performers to motor vehicles; the engines were lighter, quieter and capable of travelling at greater speeds. But there was a drawback: vast amounts of water needed to be carried around to feed the insatiable boiler. The steam car's demise was mainly caused by the mass production paradigm of Ford and Morris, rendering the combustion engine vehicle considerably cheaper than before. This was twinned with the technological breakthrough of the electronic starting mechanism. Drivers were rightly suspicious of the old hand-crank starters, which justifiably earned a reputation for unreliability. The invention of the Kettering starter, alongside the mass production pricing model, was key to replacing the steam cars. Yet before the combustion engine had evolved Sadler's prototype design, albeit with considerable modifications, remained in use for over one hundred years.

Throughout the non-balloon decades Sadler retained a continued presence in Oxford. In both 1789 and 1790 posters appeared throughout the city offering an interactive public lecture billed as "Philosophical Fireworks". Taking place in Oxford's Town Hall in St. Aldates, these were more entertainment displays than lectures, though Sadler would have been keen to stress the chemistry involved throughout his indoor fireworks. Nevertheless, his lectures were aptly described as "more fiery than philosophical".

The resulting bangs and flashes were not considered to be for a genteel audience - and apparently contained some fireworks more suited for outdoors than indoors. But one converted critic, an Oxford don, described Sadler's scientific intent: "he is a clever, practical and experimental manipulator in chemistry." He also believed that Sadler was patronised "by a few scientific men then at the University".

By 1792 Sadler had planned to accompany Sir George Staunton to provide engineering assistance to the Macartney Embassy in China, though they only reached Italy. There Sadler was involved in recruiting Chinese interpreters for the mission, aimed at improving trade between Britain and China.

Instead of continuing to the Far East he returned to Britain and, after designing a stationary steam engine put to work in the Coalbrookdale foundries in 1793, he was reunited with his former boss Thomas Beddoes from the laboratory in Oxford's Broad Street.

Beddoes was keen for Sadler to become chief engineer and chemist overseeing his Pneumatic Institution in Bristol. While in Bristol, Sadler remarried, wedding Martha Hancock in the Church of St. Augustine the Less, College Green, on 24 October 1795. The site of Sadler's second wedding no longer stands as the church was damaged in a German air-raid in 1940 and eventually demolished in 1962.

Soon afterwards Sadler relocated to Portsmouth to begin employment as a professional chemist with the Board of Naval Works. Well, cooking is essentially chemistry - so an expert pastry chef is really a talented chemist.

Initially the Navy employed him in Portsmouth in 1795 as a "barracks master", a role which rewarded him with a £300 annual salary. However, by 1796 he was appointed as the Navy's official chemist, primarily based in Woolwich, and had his salary increased to an extremely comfortable £400 a year.

While employed in this role Sadler was responsible for providing the Navy with its very first steam engine, erected at Portsmouth Dockyard "to the design of James Sadler".

Sadler's part as a competitor in steam engine invention was not exactly embraced with a healthy spirit of competition. James Watt is caught fulminating in a letter from Birmingham of September 1786, declaring: "I am extremely sorry that he still busys [sic] himself with the steam carriage. In one of my specifications I have secured it as well as words could do it according to my ideas. In the meantime... let Sadler throw away their time and money hunting shadows."

Sadler did not take out a patent until five years afterwards, and this deferral could well have been due to Watt's antagonism. An illustration of Sadler's design is included in the *Sketch Book of William Reynolds*, which provides an accompanying description: "Small engine as it worked on the hill at the Dale in Coalbrookdale made by James Sadler 1792." The illustration reveals Sadler's design to be a vertical rotary engine most probably used for winding upwards and downwards from a pit. Relying upon steam above atmospheric pressure entering a high-pressure cylinder, the piston is driven forward, while efficiency is maximised by the steam exhausting to a condenser.

J.E. Hodgson observed in his 1928 London lecture coinciding with the centenary of Sadler's death: "It is fairly obvious that these values in Sadler's piston and diaphragm, relying as they do merely upon friction, could not remain satisfactory." Moreover, it seems evident that Sadler realised this, for in his next sketch in May 1793 we find with lettered descriptions "nozzles, values and chests like those of Watt, worked by a tappet on the piston rod". These modifications, and subsequent revisions in both 1793 and 1794 were made with the aid of Beddoes, now "a famous physician in Bristol".

Sadler then built two more engines, including one constructed in 1796 in Garlick Hill and put to work for Sutton, Keen & Company mustard makers. Interestingly, Watt's enthusiastic, and possibly obsequious, younger colleague John Rennie wrote a letter to James Watt reporting in the language of a spy: "Sadler's engine works exceedingly well. I attempted to get a sight of her, but was foiled. Sadler had been endeavouring to pervert the minds of the good citizens and to persuade them that his engine is much better and cheaper than yours, and uses only about half the coal. This man should be looked after."

That appears ominous. James Watt, establishment darling, conversing in language from *The Sopranos*. "Sadler needs looking after" takes on a contemporary air of "taken care of", "sorting out", "snubbed out", "whacked"... Rennie reports to Watt a few days later and confirms, "Sutton & Keen have trumpeted the value of Sadler's invention with great industry." But he admits: "I attempted to get sight of her [the engine] again but was foiled."

John Rennie was then an eager young assistant (and part-time spy) for Watt and Matthew Boulton. Born in the bizarrely named East Lothian hamlet of Phantassie, he later became an engineer in London, and installed stream-driven apparatus in mills, thus industrialising their capacity. Several were subsequently burnt down, almost certainly deliberately by Luddites fearful of their jobs being eradicated. An engineer and specialist in iron foundry techniques, Rennie constructed the first Southwark Bridge.

Of course, the fact that Watt and his engineering accomplice Boulton were so concerned about Sadler simply serves to flatter him. Boulton is moved to observe that "Watt experiences a rumbling of pain in his chest due to the efforts of Sadler's" competing steam engine. That sounds like he's describing indigestion; I wonder if Rennie could have helped with that. (Rennie? See what I did there? Oh, never mind.)

James Watt (1736-1819) is quoted on the £50 banknote: "I can think of nothing else but this machine." Well, there was the spying, and the ridiculously small-minded fight with Sadler, whereas a spirit of co-operation might have brought forth greater rewards for both sides, not to mention scientific advancement for a country at the time terrified of a French invasion.

Inevitably it would have been difficult for Sadler to sever himself completely from aeronautics, given the celebrity status it had earned him during two short years. But the reputation and recognition his ballooning adventures had created for him were now cashed in to obtain high-level appointments. One of these meant he moved to Portsmouth to take on a prestigious new role.

Around this time, Sadler had also branched out into the soft drinks industry. By the 1790s he had established another factory business. Based in Soho, to the east of Regent Street, the firm used a Sadler- designed manufacturing system to produce bottles of "water heavily impregnated with air bubbles" - "soda water", as it is less clumsily referred to today.

However, Sadler had a shrewd marketing ace up his Georgian frockcoat sleeve. The crates filled at the factory all contained bottles astutely labelled with an illustration of a balloon. Cleverly, Sadler saw the potential of his ballooning exploits for marketing his carbonated water.

30 MARCH 1797: WINDHAM

Sadler's second marriage produced a son. Christened Windham Sadler, after his father's early supporter and benefactor William Windham MP, he was baptised on 30 March 1797 at St. George's Church, Hanover Square, London. Both the future President of the United States Theodore Roosevelt and architect John Nash, designer of nearby Regent Street (the layout is said to be modelled on Oxford's High Street with its famous curve, where Sadler's pastry shop was located), were married at St. George's.

6 NOVEMBER 1798: SADLER'S GUN

Diligent testing combined with an instinctive acumen for invention were just two parts of Sadler's recipe for success. He next decided to utilise these twin attributes to improve the Royal Navy's cannons and rifles.

An illustrated pamphlet *Account of Various Improvements in Artillery* was produced in November 1798 bearing Sadler's name as the author, billing himself as Member of the Board of Naval Works at the Admiralty and Barrack Master at Portsmouth. It shows, with detailed engravings, his tested designs for a radically modernised 32-pound cannon.

Lord Nelson was so subsequently impressed that he requested as many of the guns that Sadler could provide.

Strangely, Sadler's report and blueprints for the newly efficient cannons were presented not to the Royal Navy, but to the directors of the East India Company, as the company operated their own private navy!

Sadler made crucial calculations on efficiency: the length of the carriage, the weight and size of ordnance, how many men were required to re-load. But it was not just the boats designed to carry these newly forged guns that were resigned to sailing in storming and choppy waters - Sadler was clearly fighting stormy politicised battles himself too.

Gun advancement experiments overseen by Sadler had been conducted since 1795. There was a specific reason for this: the French. War was seemingly certain, and there was accompanying paranoia around Britain that a French invasion was imminent. Coded warning signals had been adopted in case the French were spotted attempting to land on British soil. Hence the requirement to improve the nation's firepower was paramount, and numerous possible improvements and advances were tested by a demonstrably dedicated Sadler.

Sadler specifically took issue with a report made by Count Rumford in May 1797, stating that this report was stealing the credit for his research. Sadler fulminated: "The descriptions of the improvements mentioned by Count Rumford are precisely the descriptions of the Patent Gun made by James Sadler on which the experiments were made by order of the Board of Ordnance. It is also well known to the Secretary of War and many eminent officers of the Navy that J.S. communicated this improvement to them, and actually constructed guns on the same principle many years before the experiments were made at Woolwich." The use of the third-person James Sadler in the text leads the reader to suspect that these were not his own words.

Sadler had discovered that "much of the gunpowder escapes unfired" from the artillery models then deployed by the Royal Navy and so set about remodelling this part of the guns' design. Crucially he added velocity by striking the correct equilibrium between shot weight and barrel length. He also discovered that the cavity for powder escape was costing vital accuracy, calculating that a quarter of all guns would miss their intended target. Sadler identified and addressed the causes of slow combustion.

Capping this, he also solved another serious problem with the Navy's guns: their tendency to be, as Sadler phrased it, engaged in "the dropping of the muzzle", i.e. the gunpowder blowing the gun itself apart. He asserted: "It is certain that brass guns are sometimes rendered unserviceable by the discharge of less than 200 shot." He therefore set about establishing the optimum amount of gunpowder required for each gun model, too much or too little reducing the velocity and accuracy of the discharge. Quoted in his pamphlet, Sadler states: "It is an important fact that a shot which has just force to pass through one ship's side will produce more mischief than if it's velocity were greater."

Sadler conducted painstaking research, firing cannons with different levels of gunpowder - adding an additional ounce of powder before each separate firing. This must have made him a very annoying neighbour.

He concluded that the Royal Navy's standard insistence that each gun should be loaded with ten pounds and ten ounces of powder was dangerously flawed. Not only did he report that a mere four ounces would retain a full 80% of the same range, but he discovered greater accuracy. Moreover, the guns did not overheat, so rapid repeat firing - rendered impossible by the existing larger powder loads - was now available to gunners. Sadler reported that the current recommended charge "endangers the gun carriage, strains the vessel, and incurs a greater risk of rendering the gun unserviceable... It may therefore be concluded," he states, "that smaller charges of powder than those at present used, might be adopted with the advantage to public service."

The Naval Committee duly published a report, observing that "Sadler's gun is much stronger, the dimensions having been found by repeated experiments to be best adapted to produce sufficient steadiness." Another iron gun created by Sadler of the same calibre "weighs less than half the common gun" and is "already in use in His Majesty's service." The report also notes: "Sadler's gun is little more than half the length of the old one, it takes less room, it is more easily run in and out as well as charged and discharged."

Topping off the improvements, Sadler also designed a rapid fire mechanism that avoided the need for slow priming. He patented the resulting design of his 32-pounder with non-recoil mounting, reviewed as being more accurate, faster loading and crucially only employed three men to operate rather than the twelve required to fire its predecessor.

Sadler then set his sights on smaller rifles, starting with setting the sights on rifles - literally. He redesigned almost every component of the existing rifles issued to the Navy. The ensuing published paper, lengthily titled *Description of a New and Much Improved Rifle Gun by James Sadler, Member of the Board of Inspection at the Admiralty*, laid out the thorough technical details of his gun studies and the blueprint for a superior new model.

Sadler informed readers how he had given a total overhaul to the rifle, testing each aspect of the firing and loading mechanism. During testing he fired 38 continuous shots in the presence of an approving Sir John Cox Hippisley MP - an individual famously described as "that busy man" by King George III - and several high-ranking Naval officers from Swinley Camp. He figured out a method of increasing the compressed air into the cartridge during the firing action, and maximised numerous other efficiencies. Sometimes he injured himself as a consequence; he incurred "an accident with a small piece of ordnance" with his hand "much hurt by the powder catching fire". Yet by experiencing the faults first-hand, Sadler reasoned, he was able to rectify them. Certainly the British Navy's safety record was not impressive, with men routinely injured by cannons and rifles - only some of which belonged to the enemy. Consequently Sadler's labours led to a vastly more efficient, and safer to use, rifle for British military personnel.

This was certainly a task Sadler took seriously, and the establishment was apparently impressed. Sadler's pamphlet observes: "Some professional men in the military service of the East India Company are of the opinion that the improved gun and carriage may be of eminent advantage in the country fortresses. Both gun and carriage are easily manoeuvrable and the rapidity of which it may be moved and fired in all directions in a battery, would enable a trifling garrison to resist with confidence the attacks of a very powerful enemy."

Sadler had encamped himself in Naval testing yards, spending "the course of one summer and most of the following year" meticulously recording data from his repeated firing range experiments, and noting that "officers had never seen so much accuracy produced from any other ordnance". At one experiment at The Warren, the First Lord of the Admiralty was present to see the very first shot fired by Sadler's newly invented gun "cut the bolt in the centre of the target".

Although a frequent visitor to Woolwich and Portsmouth, Sadler was living throughout this period at 10 Stafford Row, Pimlico, and he published his report a mere three weeks after his son, the ill-fated Windham, was born in the same house.

Sadler ended the century on the up and up (even without a balloon) when he was elected in 1799 as a life member of the Royal Institution. But his career was to descend like a punctured balloon at the start of the next century.

Unfortunately Sadler appears to have cultivated a nemesis in the Royal Navy named Sir Samuel Bentham, the brother of Jeremy Bentham, the spiritual founder of University College London. It is unclear why Bentham harboured such a malicious dislike for Sadler. Inconveniently for him, Bentham held high rank, becoming Inspector General of Naval Works. Bentham was appointed to oversee the reform of the Royal Navy's dockyards, a role that would have brought him into close contact, and conflict, with Sadler. They also shared an agenda in that the two men held almost identical remits, including guns, boat building and Naval equipment from rigging to copper-bottoms. It is likely that Bentham sanctioned the revolutionary adoption of Sadler's steam engines into the dockyards in 1796.

During his time with the Navy Sadler undertook a far-reaching range of tasks. He conducted investigations into the properties of copper sheathing and instigated analysis of the docks' fresh water spa and gunpowder combustion. Additionally, he invented an on-board brewing device, oversaw an investigation into the seasoning of timbers used in ship construction and produced plans for "annoying" French enemy vessels in Boulogne harbour. He also found time to invent a more efficient air pump, replaced signal lights with his own more luminous invention and conducted numerous experiments into impurities found in gunpowder and ammonia.

And in addition to all that, Sadler published numerous scientific research papers, including his works on: *The Process for Refining Lead* (1806), *Explanations of a Common Impurity* (1806), *The Distillation Processes of Seawater* (1807), *On Smelting of Lead* (1811), *On the Dislocation of Veins* (1814), etc. Such an output bears a typical hallmark of a polymath, and is likely to be research wholly undertaken by Sadler himself.

Yet towards the end of the nineteenth century's first decade, Sadler and Sir Samuel Bentham seem to have fallen out irredeemably. As a consequence Sadler struggled to retain his position, and in 1809 he was dismissed without receiving compensation for his self-erected experiment apparatus. Furthermore, Sadler had privately built his own research laboratory in 1802 and crucially this appears to have been requisitioned by Bentham without compensation for his own vast expenditure involved. Overnight Sadler was instantly plunged into enormous debt.

8 FLY IN THE APPOINTMENT: COUNSELLING

It has become clear that I need to learn about phobias. Festering ignorance is no longer an option. If I want to tackle my restrictive phobias, this requires educating myself. I need to obtain insights into my anxieties, and discover why part of my brain, unfortunately a very bossy part, is having difficulty distinguishing actual threats from imagined ones. Luckily an Oxford University clinical psychologist and phobia expert agrees to enlighten me.

Sufferers of psychological impairments often report it helps to discover they are not suffering in isolation, so it helps merely to have Dr. Hannah reassure me that I am not alone in enduring my described symptoms.

Dr. Hannah agrees to provide me with insights into the human brain in exchange for a posh frothy coffee, which is a reasonably good deal. Then the hospital café owner pops his head through a serving hatch like an undaunted tortoise and shouts that they're closing. So we relocate to a utilitarian corridor, which looks poorly maintained, and is the sort of corridor where the cops arrive on a TV show to bang on one of the doors only to be told from behind a chain-lock, "he ain't here!" before they kick down the door anyway.

There is a drinks vending machine. Installed by a private company, it advertises lots of choice, though doesn't work and keeps our money anyway. Presumably it is located in the hospital as a visual metaphor for the modern NHS.

Speaking with Dr. Hannah and benefitting from her knowledge is a little like being taken backstage by God for forty minutes, and having the entire workings - and limitations - of our human cognitive functioning explained. She has so many pearls of wisdom in her possession she could make a necklace out of them.

I have an opening question that I really want answered. Always ask questions you want to know the answer to, not to show what you already know. "What is a phobia?"

"What I would define as a phobia is when you perceive something as threatening when it isn't; the volume in our internal threat system is set too high - like being fearful of a cat rather than a lion, which provides no evolutionary advantage." Great, in evolutionary terms my fear of heights is akin to being terrified of a cute kitten pawing a ball of wool. "Because you would spend a lot of your time in this fight-or-flight panic mode and thus not able to do things you need to do."

"What's fascinating within psychology is that if you kept applying the fight-or-flight mechanism to something that was non-threatening, you think you would learn nothing bad happens and next time you adopt and select better responses and the fear would dissipate. But what's interesting is that this doesn't happen. So it is a conundrum how this is maintained. How do people remain fearful about something that causes them no real danger?"

"Do phobias lessen with aging?" I enquire.

"Height phobia is probably fear prompted by a normal evolutional response, but applied too widely. If you sense a threat like a lion, fight-or-flight physiological arousal facilitates you doing something about it. So people who are not fearful around lions don't pass on their genes very effectively - because they've died out."

So being riddled with anxiety is a good thing then. It means I get to pass on my genes. With a lady!

"No," interrupts Dr. Hannah, "it means you're less likely to get eaten by a lion." Oh.

I frequently wonder, why does my idiot brain "know" two contradictory things simultaneously: i.e. registering the dichotomy that I am perfectly safe in this threatless environment whilst my brain is flashing a red warning "evacuate" light. "How do people remain fearful of something that causes them no real danger?" People often have to live in an environment where they face their fears regularly, so why don't they learn it's OK?

"Learning Theory, which is something the early psychological behaviourist theorists developed, was that a physiological response gets paired with a stimulus; like Pavlov's dogs you go through a learning stage phrase of autonomic arousal. Except only about 11% of acrophobics have had a traumatic experience preceding the onset of their phobia. So the learning theory model is insufficient to explain the development of height phobia. With acrophobia there is evidence to suggest it isn't acquired, but is innate because of its evolutionary advantage. As soon as babies and other land animals can crawl, they exhibit anxiety when presented with heights. Maybe most people unlean their fear of heights, rather than phobics acquire it.

"Self-awareness ought to kick in after a number of events when your feared outcome doesn't happen, shouldn't it?" I check.

"Exactly, so you would anticipate that after a while when your feared outcome has not happened you would expect to build up self-awareness over time. There are a couple of things going on in phobia responses. Firstly, there is a tendency for avoidance. Hence sufferers will do anything they need to do to avoid the situation coming up."

I nod excessively at this point. I avoid any possibility where there will be exposure to height. "And the concept of escape if faced with the situation, and in perceiving it as threatening, we unsurprisingly make a very hasty exit and experience extraordinary relief. But over time this reinforces the idea that the situation really is dangerous, and that avoidance and escape is the way to stay safe," Dr. Hannah elaborates.

"Then something fascinating happened in the field," she continues. "We got this model of pure phobias and psychologists thought that if people are avoiding them then we'll do exposure therapy."

"This is used in Obsessive Compulsive Disorder and anxiety management," I clarify.

Dr. Hannah then formulates her own question for her to answer next, causing me to suspect that she would be considerably better left to interview herself as both interviewer and interviewee whilst I went off in search of an unbroken, unclosed coffee outlet.

"So when doesn't it work?" she asks herself. "That's the important thing cognitive therapy brings to the table. It shows there is something even more subtle going on for those people. Even in situations when they look like they're confronting their phobias, there is something going on in the mind that's still telling them they are putting themselves in danger."

Keen to have some input, I add: "They're not engaging, they are somehow remaining aloof so this experience can be disqualified from providing vital learning experience." Dr. Hannah nods: "We call it 'safety behaviour'. It's that person doing everything they can to feel safe in that situation. For example, if you are terrified of heights and although you've done everything you can to avoid them but you can't and you've got to go up your tower you might say 'if I clutch the rail really tightly, or stay a foot back from the edge I won't be caught by the wind, or if I'm with someone I trust as they may be able to help me out,' you have somehow convinced yourself that this cannot be treated as an experiment to learn from, as you don't believe you are truly facing the fear. So when you return to ground, you have a whole handful of reasons why you have come back down safe. It converts a benign experience into a 'near miss' experience."

That is so true. Believe me.

Of course, that's what I've been doing for years. Knowing how my brain has been actively deceiving me, and mis-crediting my achievements to others, deceptively manipulating me, instantly helps me confront my fears - like learning how a trick is done reduces how much the magician impresses you.

Dr. Hannah also cautions: "It may turn into magical thinking."

Magical thinking is when survival or success is attributed to thinking particular thoughts, wearing a lucky item of clothing, performing a ritual, doing something a set number of times, repeating a mantra, praying, counting, ordering or carrying out superstitious acts, etc. I was voluntarily imprisoned by ritualistic magical thinking throughout most of my teenage years, but lacked the foresight to mention it to anyone, and thereby concluded that it was a debilitating yet isolated condition that affected only one person, thereby making them desperately unhappy. I am indebted to learning about magical thinking, and discovering the trick done on my brain immediately confiscated its power. Again, once you know how the trick is performed, the conjurer no longer impresses.

Dr. Hannah extrapolates the damaging, spurious logic of magical thinking on a phobic patient. "Hence their attribution thinking was that 'I was never really in danger because I did these certain things.' A treatment of phobias can occur whilst putting someone in this situation where learning can take place. The crucial contribution of cognitive theory is that phobias are driven by beliefs, which ultimately can be tested."

Hmm. So belief is the hydrogen in Sadler's balloon, keeping the phobia afloat. If I can vent the belief, puncture it, then the phobia should descend rapidly. I am keen to ask: "Can this belief can be stress-tested sufficiently to undermine it?"

"In exposure therapy you would do something over and over again, becoming increasingly challenging," Dr. Hannah answers. "With cognitive intervention, you'd think 'I have to put this thought under the microscope and if I do that effectively the anxiety will come down quite quickly.' It's the key to getting a really nuanced, well-designed experiment. So that you can get up high without gripping, friends, magical thinking, and learn my catastrophic event won't necessarily happen."

This is precisely the insight I require. That we all require. Why don't you get taught this stuff in schools? It would have helped me much more than learning irregular French verbs like... er... I can't remember a single irregular French verb.

"Does that dilute the potential power of psychoanalytical approaches?" I ask.

Without requiring even a fraction of a second's thinking time, Dr. Hannah replies: "A phobia could develop over time from cognitive attributions and behavioural responses (avoidance, escape, safety behaviours) and then it grows. Psychoanalysis looks at phobia by viewing an early experience and, in the broad sense, trauma. Some fear of something else has been diverted or transferred onto something else. My understanding of the psychoanalytic approach isn't the go-to approach for a phobia. Whereas CBT has lots of evidence that it is effective in anxiety."

Twice as a toddler I fell down the stairs. Both were events of such magnitude that, even though they occurred as a three-year-old, I recall vividly my traumatic tumbles today. One fall constitutes my earliest memory. I was so proud of my red wellington boots that I wanted to show them to everyone. And I would only remove them, with immense coaxing and reluctance, to go to bed. Unfortunately, they proved to be impractical footwear for descending stairs, and sure enough I fell down the stairs. This fall downstairs remains my reference point for the worst pain I have ever experienced. And given I am unlikely to experience childbirth, my maximum encounter with pain is likely to have peaked when I was only three years old.

Which prompts me to ask Dr. Hannah: "Does giving a phobia sufferer a name risk entrenching it i.e. a patient or client may say "I am agoraphobic and therefore I am defined as that?"

She pauses. "That is a really, really..."

...Please don't say "shit"...

"Excellent question," she confirms. Phew.

"Yes, it is a double edged sword. It's validating, it's helpful, it's containing, it shows other people have this problem. We know what a fear looks like and we know how to treat it, and it's not you going mad, silly or being selfish."

Such validation would definitely have helped me, had I sought it earlier in my life.

"On the other hand," Dr. Hannah continues, "if people typically equate it with a medical term and condition, then it allows a definition of what this means, so it maybe won't go away. Diabetes cannot go away, but it can be managed. With a phobia there is often scope for both managing it effectively, but also eradication. Then there is a certain amount of personal responsibility that comes into play - an agency to deal with it psychologically. If I have a label that means 'it is not my fault'. It maybe also comes to mean 'there is nothing I can do about it, this is how it is going to be' then that is very limiting."

I ask her: "Why do I encounter physical symptoms with a mental response, when stepping on a ladder? My brain floods with fight-or-flight response triggers. My body's detected a threat."

"Those anxious sensations feel like a threat in themselves," Dr. Hannah concludes. Then what often happens, and this is where panic cycles and panic disorder come into play. In acrophobia and agoraphobia we make catastrophic misinterpretation judgements about normal bodily sensations and feelings. You notice palpitations and dizziness, think 'I'm going to faint and fall off', or we make an inference about the situation based on our feelings. We call that 'emotional reasoning'. Conclude that if I feel fearful then we interpret that as 'I am fearful therefore I am under threat' which equals false reasoning. Therefore the lack of an actual threat is not missed." "I hope you're getting all of this," I silently tell my own brain.

"Vertigo" sufferers and height avoiders like me are terrified of becoming dizzy or fainting at altitude. You can see why the summit of something extraordinarily high is not the best place for an involuntary lie-down. Phobic responses generate a "fight or flight" stimulant. Or in my case, a "flight and flight" reaction, as the prospect of a flight is now predominantly responsible for filling my days with undiluted terror.

"Fight or flight" dispenses an adrenaline shot, increases the heartbeat and pumps oxygen to the brain. In other words, it is nature's way of putting on your best trainers to flee threats, or ensuring that you hang around for the ensuing scrap. Therefore, with the brain insistently ordering the manufacture of adrenaline and oxygen, fainting is the last thing that is going to happen when encountering a triggered response to a phobia. Fainting occurs when blood pressure plummets. So when you're anxious, blood pressure increases and it's nigh on impossible to faint. This means that if a misleadingly titled TV nutritionist should faint when encountering a phobic trigger response during a reality TV programme (no one specifically in mind, M'lord), then the reaction is as fake as it is damaging to the public's awareness of brain functionality.

Then Dr. Hannah serves up an indisputable Top Fact - scientific knowledge to the rescue. "There is one beautiful exception to this rule. With blood and injury phobias you are fearful of bleeding to death. And in that phobia the exact opposite physiological occurrence happens. Your heart beat is lowered, your blood rate drops. Blood phobics are the only people who can faint. Many phobics believe they will faint, but in fact you have so much oxygen in your system that you cannot faint. It is evolutionarily advantageous to lower your blood pressure. Lowering your heart rate stops you bleeding so profusely - even by passing out if you need to. Isn't that a brilliant treatment?"

There, told you my brain was clever. This information is revelatory, portentous on a grand scale. Moreover, it offers enormous practical help with bathmophobia and acrophobia. One of my biggest, although admittedly unrealised fears, until having this conversation with an expert, was that I would become faint and dizzy, and risk falling over on stairs or somewhere else at high altitude. Not only will this be physically impossible, but I now know the opposite will occur, and my brain will provide me with a double espresso shot of adrenaline and oxygen. I just need to avoid cutting myself at altitude!

But I still need to tame my amygdala. The amygdala is the primitive part of the brain with the authority to shut down the clever part of our mind - the sophisticated *Guardian*-reading, latte-sipping frontal cortex that's thinking of booking tickets for the new British Library exhibition. Our amygdala reacts to cars back firing, loud bangs, and any other highly unpleasant noises or pattern matched images, by immediately shutting down all other processing parts of the brain. Dr. Hannah reassures me that there is also a specific part of the brain whose allocated job is to step in and deal with conflict.

It transpires, then, that there is still some hope, if I can get my amygdala to listen to common sense.

"There seems to be emerging data that talking therapies or CBT [Cognitive Behavioural Therapy] can alter brain functioning. So if you're undergoing therapy you can find that neuro-chemical changes occur as a result." At this point Dr. Hannah cites a research article by David Clark and Aaron T. Beck (Beck is regarded as the godfather of CBT) reviewing neuro-chemical changes following CBT. She just happens to have a copy on her - as her downtime out-of-office reading material of choice. I am impressed by her off-duty dedication.

"Cognitive therapy is associated with a reduced activity in the sub cortical regions in which both the hippocampi and amygdala function. So it would reduce activation in those areas and increase activity in the pre-frontal cortex." I am flattered that Dr. Hannah considers she can start to get slightly technical with me now, without losing my attention or comprehension. Hippocampus is the area of my brain where memories are stored. It is the Greek word for 'seahorse' given early anatomists considered it resembled this shape – a fact which, ironically, is now being stored in your hippocampus. Unpleasingly 'hippocampus' is not a university for hippos. Do not store that non-fact in your hippocampus.

I report my experiencing of increased anxiety, driven by trivial things. Sometimes I have intense difficulty getting on a bus or going anywhere- yet I can perform an hour of public speaking to a packed hall. My anxieties seemed to be strangely selected, my brain categorising almost at random potential experiences as "calm" or "panic".

Modern workplace managers have sullied a once decent phrase by over-use and corporate adoption: "Think outside the box." Having worked in an office for decades, I can confidently report that the worst thing anyone could do was to think outside the box. This was viewed as an aggressive challenge to each individual stratum of defined authority. Think outside the box and you risked execution as a dangerous anarchist, challenging the hierarchies clinging to their narrowly defined powers. And yet every team meeting supposedly cherished thinking outside the box as an aspirational value of the organisation.

But now I really do need to start thinking outside the box - the small, dark box of anxiety with just a few air holes allowing me to glimpse parts of the world others take for granted. Instead of being trapped by negative thinking loops and constant catastrophizing. It's time to hit the "refresh" button on my mind. Which means it's time to recruit some counselling.

Proving that youth is fleeting, yet immaturity can last a lifetime, I needed to be 49 years old before I realised that if a phobia or psychological condition remains untreated, it's probably going to either (a) last a very long time before it goes away (b) never go away.

Something has to be done about my festering phobias. Prevalent in many phobias is the contradictory cognitive dissonance needed to sustain them - that a phobia is often not a fear of direct dangers associated with the fear: i.e. darkness is unlikely to attack you. It is the fear of concealed dangers, predictably of the exclusively imagined variety, that cause the problems. If I am going to replicate Sadler's flight, then I am in desperate need of counselling expertise.

There are supposed to be only two certainties in life: death and taxes. Which means Starbucks and Jimmy Carr must be immortal. Since I am not a giant international monster conglomerate, faceless and rapacious (a big hello at this point to Google, Vodaphone and Amazon), I am filling out a tax form online. As a freelance comedy writer it soon becomes clear that, like Jimmy Carr, I too have ingeniously devised an airtight strategy to avoid paying income tax: earn less than £9,000 a year. Who needs specialist tax accountants?

My financial predicament is not good. I know that I need to seek counselling, and also that I can't afford to pay much for it. Which is odd. We're prepared to pay for all sorts of pills, treatments - and prescription charges couldn't rise any faster if they were pumped with hydrogen - but not necessarily for the state of our mental health. After all, our mental health is the ultimate factor in deciding if we're happy or not, content or otherwise - yet is rarely considered worthy of any maintenance expenditure. Mental health MOTs should be compulsory. Emotional intelligence should be on the syllabus. Really, it should.

After much googling, networking, unreturned emails and phone calls, capped-off by dignity-eroding begging, I discover a training course of counsellors who require guinea-pigs. I can be a guinea pig. If the worst case scenarios play out when I'm in the role as the advert has proved to be ambiguous, I can expect carrots, a fresh supply of green leaves and a nice hutch. If so, it already remunerates better than full-time writing.

I am allocated a pair of counsellors who have been, I am assured, fully trained. Although whatever their training incorporates is never voluntarily elaborated. They will conduct a session with me, which will hopefully expand into more sessions. An appointed senior counsellor will observe all or any of the sessions. Like a stalking, looming shadow, the Supervisor will ensure everything is conducted appropriately. That reassures me. With the junior apprentices, who have only counselled role-players before, not proper psychologically damaged real-world inhabitants like me, the Supervisor will surely be very much present. I see her once, mainly so she can reprimand me ("we don't consider the term 'fruitcake' helpful, Richard"). Not to worry, who needs a qualified lifeguard, with me and two brand new counsellors splashing around in the deep end? Sink or swim, they say.

I am offered a date for my first free consultation session.

My twin counsellors are desperate to shed their counselling L-plates, but to achieve this they have to interact with a live client. This surely maximises my chances of getting the job. Sure enough, I receive a phone call from a counselling Supervisor. She asks me a number of questions to ascertain my suitability to receive training from the twin trainees. The interview is going well, until she asks me what sort of counselling I would be expecting. This is a surprisingly difficult question - I assume that answering "the good sort" will risk me not getting the position. "Ideally I would like a Rogerian person-centred empathetic approach, but would be content with any CBT." Thanks, Internet.

Rogerian is the eponymous Carl Rogers, while Cognitive Behaviour Therapy - although I convince myself shortly after replacing the receiver that I may have acronym malfunction and announced that I preferred CPT instead of CBT - CPT being the trade association for bus drivers. I am reminded of this later when given a pile of questionnaires to complete that are so lengthy and ominous that I progressively alter my response to the recurring question "might I consider suicide?" from "Strongly Disagree" to, fifty minutes of questionnaire mental health evaluation later, "Strongly Agree". A few days later I receive a phone call. After his initial consultation they inform me I have been accepted "on the programme".

I am informed that there will be a lot of legal waivers to sign. Fine, I say. Having to sign so many waiver forms, whose numerous pages are equivalent to a Bodleian Library holding stack, can be tidily paraphrased: "if my counsellors are so incompetent that they convince an otherwise healthy client to kill himself within four minutes of the opening session, then it is Definitely Not Their Fault." OK, I consent, choosing to focus entirely on the "I'm a journalist and it's free" part of our agreement.

Don't look at me with that judging face, please. Journalists are often so badly paid that I know several who attend press launches and PR junkets, not because they are interested in some "exciting new shade of nail varnish remover" product launch, but merely to obtain a guaranteed evening meal - albeit usually comprised of Twiglets and Pringles accompanied by heroic amounts of cheap red wine whose painful after sting is eventually numbed by the sixth glass.

Reporting for my counselling session, I ring a doorbell. After enduring a delay so long it can only be explained by someone having to destroy evidence, I am buzzed in. I feel surprisingly nervous. No one checks who I am, or indeed allows me to verify that I have the right address. Ironically, I face two flights of steep stairs. I don't like this, but walk slowly, leaning forward to ensure my centre of gravity remains in front, therefore permitting me to fall safely forward on the carpeted stairs. Since there is no one around I use the handrail. Social convention decrees that only the very young and very old are allowed to use handrails. Passing public often express a "oh, aren't they cute" look at young children deploying a handrail, but a dismissive eye-roll of "coffin-dodger" when seeing the elderly climbing stairs. This is the logical culmination of a society that chooses to fetishize children while ignoring the elderly. Whatever you do in this country, don't get old.

According to Relate's own website, where there is also an opportunity to discover your personality type "as featured in *Cosmopolitan*" by completing an online quiz, and then sending £19.99 to receive the answer in an emailed PDF file (and presumably receiving a one word report back: "gullible"), a counsellor is quoted torpedoing the myth that clients expect to be told what to do. This surprises me, as I predict (wrongly or rightly) that grappling any sort of direct advice out of their tightly closed hands will be well-nigh impossible. Hold a loaded gun to a CBT practitioner's head, and ask them "should I pull the trigger?" and they'll reply "But, what do you think you should do?" So I am intrigued to see whether modern counselling sets exercises, makes practical interventions into destructive behaviour and, crucially, says "you need to stop doing that - and here's how you can stop". Maybe my prejudices are, like so many prejudices, constructed on an uneven base of ignorance. The confirmation bias Dr. Hannah had foretold.

My counsellors are called Steve and Claire (or at least they are for the purposes of this book - the legal profession are rich enough without taking my paltry assets). Are my suppositions and prejudices about to be destroyed or justified?

Claire and Steve are skilful counsellors; good, noble, world-improving people who help me enormously, enabling rational emotional behaviour to occupy parts of my cognitive processes that only anxiety had previously inhabited. That's another point I would like to chalk up early on, to enable any reading lawyers to circle it. The world would be an undeniably better place to hang around in if there were more Steves and Claires populating it. I would dearly like to mention them in the thanks and acknowledgement section of this book, but can't do so as it would palpably reveal their identities. They pointed this out to me, after thanking me for the kind thought. This confirms they are cleverer than their guinea pig client. But my first meeting does not start well. At all.

"So," Steve begins, "you said on the phone you suffer from agoraphobia."

I suspect he said "agoraphobia", but doubt that a professional clinician would make such a fundamental error in the opening sentence of our first session.

"Yeah, it's a rather extreme fear."

"How did you feel about managing to get here today?" he enquires.

"OK. I'm alright with stairs when I'm on my own nowadays, unless they're really steep or exposed or transparent or you can see underneath or... maybe not that OK with stairs just yet. Exposed steep stairs with lots of daylight shining through are the worst."

"It's exposure that triggers a reaction of fear?" asks Steve.

Don't do a flasher joke. That would be crass, unhelpful and misjudge the situation. They'll also confiscate your right not to be considered an instant twat. "Exposure to heights, yes."

"That's interesting," announces Steve, "not just being outdoors or confronted by open spaces, then?"

And a bell rings to signal idiot confirmation. I'm supposed to be the idiot here, and he's the enlightened proper grown-up. And I am an idiot for not correcting him earlier. "No, that's agoraphobia," I correct.

"Isn't that your condition?" asks Claire.

No. No, it is not.

"No," I say in the softest voice I can select. I don't want conflict. I am not very good at conflict.

Frankly this is the worst possible start. It is difficult to comprehend that a health professional is mixing ailments that sound a bit similar to other conditions. "Hello. I'm here because I've discovered lumps," "OK, we'll treat you for mumps."

"I suffer from acrophobia," I announce. This comment prompts exactly the same response in the recipient as if I had just informed a tame bear of the same thing. Clearly this is not self-explanatory. Anxiety is readable on their faces. They are desperately running a "search for file: acrophobia" in their heads and their brains have just returned a "no matches found" message. Pausing any longer would risk callousness, so I impart: "Acrophobia is an irrational fear of heights."

"Right," he says, nodding his head pensively. This can't have been the start he wanted either. "I also suffer from bathmophobia." I allow a slightly cruel wait. "And can you just remind me what that is?" - the word "remind" loaded with a previously unused meaning of "tell me for the very first time ever". At least he didn't then proceed to treat me for siderophobia - that's the fear of stars, which sounds very similar to fear of stairs.

His co-counsellor Claire gets up and treads out a lump in a mat. If she's a counsellor with OCD tendencies then this is decidedly odd. Five minutes later she does it again. "Rug problems?" asks Steve. If he was being translated with subtitles it would read: "Stop fixating on the rug!"

"Bet in a career in psychotherapy you'll see a lot of patients with rug problems," I say with my most non-threatening smile.

"What?" asks Claire.

"You know… rug related problems, lots of rug addicts!" I say to the sound of a windswept, empty plain.

Nothing.

"Tough consultancy room," I say. Claire smiles. Not laughs, but I'll take a slight smile. I'm grateful to her for that.

"Er… you know, rug problems, rug related issues, rug addiction… sounds a lot like, a bit like, nothing like… rug problems. Tough couch," I continue unwisely.

Steve's expression displays unrelenting dour discontentment. It's left to Claire to orchestrate the next key part of the session. In response to her questions, I tell her about all the height restrictions imposed on my life. Discovering I was bathmophobic when eight years old at Tattershall Castle, my infatuation with Charlotte Jones, the girl who always went upstairs on the bus while I could only ever sit on the lower deck. And how a schoolgirl had recently outed me as bathmophobic, revealing that my condition was not as hidden as I formerly hoped. Then I reveal my interest in James Sadler and the intended upcoming balloon trip.

"And you want to tackle your acrophobia?" Claire establishes. "Yeah. I want to rugby tackle it." "Why?" she says, like a personal trainer geeing me up and raising my shouted commitment to overcome an upcoming challenge ahead. "Because I want to send it crashing to the ground." OK, bad metaphor for someone terrified of doing a balloon flight.

"Let's get to work then," promises Claire.

My counsellors conform to an ethical code of practice, so they won't divulge any information about previous clients. Therefore this necessitates having to finesse out subtle anecdotal stories about clients Claire has encountered in training, without naming names, revealing locations or breaching patient confidentiality. "Out of the extreme anxiety cases I've dealt with, you appear to be by far the best-adjusted," she later informs me. Initially I find that a comforting compliment, although it is like pointing out Sneezy is the tallest of the seven dwarves. Then she qualifies the remark by adding the portentous statement: "But that is no indicator of the depth of your anxiety."

I make the observation that the majority of clients here must be female. "And what makes you assume that?" Steve asks. Good, we are yet to start the session properly, but already they are asking open not closed questions. "Because all the magazines in the waiting room are for women," I answer. "Oh, we should get some men's magazines," announces Steve, then realises this may be open to misinterpretation. Don't say anything funny, Richard. "Yeah, that would be nice," I say in the most neutral tone I can muster.

"Richard's right. Counsellors probably see slightly more women than male clients," Claire announces, mainly to stop Steve or me having to verify that we did not mean top shelf men's magazines. "Probably quite a lot more female than male clients, actually." Her unexpressed "that's because women have to put up with a lot" is relayed by tonal implication. But she does this for good-humoured intentions, not spitefully. This turns out to be the first moment in our professional relationship where she allows a chink of comedic light to illuminate her personal life, before quickly drawing the curtains tightly back again after revealing a teasing personal insight. Gravitas is added by the accompanying look she arrows me with her eyes, which is basically screaming: "Men, eh!"

"I didn't mean we get porn mags for the waiting room, obviously," says Steve - unnecessarily. "I did know that," confirms Claire.

My counsellors continue to repeatedly ask open questions. There is certainly a keen agenda to establish how I feel. Those who experience counselling often report a frustration at not receiving direct answers yet alone direct advice - although direct debits are never missed.

This approach can generate feelings of frustration. For example, if a counsellor ever appears on *Mastermind* their approach would be of limited use: "Who won the FA Cup in 2014?" "Who do you think won the FA Cup in 2014?" "I'll repeat the question…" "Why is knowing who won the FA Cup in 2014 important to you?" "How does wanting to know who won the FA Cup make you feel?" Bleep, bleep, bleep. "I've started, but I'll never finish." "At the end of that round you have scored £90 off me, and passed on no actual advice."

They ask if I have any other diagnosed anxieties. "I partially suffer from achluophobia."

"Achlu…" Steve begins to repeat, but stalls half-way through.

"Bless you!" I interject spontaneously.

Claire laughs. Steve fires her an admonishing "I'm very disappointed" look, as though she's been discovered chewing in class.

I explain achluophobia is a fear of darkness. I do not usually admit this to anyone, since the associated embarrassment is a main part of the condition.

But it is a low-level anxiety compared to my main phobias and general state of twitchy perturbation.

"Have you diagnosed yourself on the Internet?" he enquires, in a tone implying he is already sure of the answer, hence his question was for display purposes only.

"No. I've had this condition since the late 1970s, so that might have been difficult to do then." I really didn't mean that to sound sarcastic.

Claire unsuccessfully represses a smirk. For this she receives That Look again from Steve.

These two must be having a work place affair. They must be. No two people of different genders could possess such an irrational dislike for each other unless they were in a permanent relationship. They cannot resist subtly undermining each other's comments, often starting sentences with "thinking has moved forward since then…" to nullify each other's points. They evidently believe their comments are buried underneath sufficient coded subtlety to avoid detection to outsiders, but I might as well have caught them rutting like rabbits on the waiting room sofa, it's so obvious they're a couple.

Suddenly, after spending nearly all the opening session misunderstanding, mishearing and misdiagnosing, the female counsellor leans forward and actively provides me with what I predicted to be that rarest of contributions in psychological clinical consultancies: direct practical advice.

"The best approach to overcome an extreme fear of heights is to focus on what aspect causes you the most restrictions in day-to-day life. I assume stairs must be a strong contender for being addressed first?"

"Yes," I manage to reply from my startled state of something actually happening to help cure me. "Yes, thank you. That would be a good thing to address, to help cure me," I say clumsily.

"We don't like the term 'cure' here. We prefer a less judgemental description of your condition we're currently addressing," corrects the male counsellor loftily.

Claire and I join together as teammates in giving him a deserved "shut up!" look, before she continues. "There are various therapeutic techniques we can draw on to help you manage anxiety. You need to challenge your looped thought processes that incorrectly signal danger. One approach is to gently introduce yourself to an environment that triggers irrational fear responses. So go with a friend, and then allow them to accompany you to some stairs - the steep sort."

"Open-ended ones, with no banister, and you can see daylight underneath the steps?" I suggest. She nods. "God, I hate those." "I know you do," she confirms, in a reassuring, quite maternal way.

"Stand on the first step. Practise breathing mechanisms. It could well be that your breathing rhythms are subconsciously tripped when confronting trauma

127

patterns - reacting to, and pattern matching, the source of your tension and thereby increasing encountered stress. This could cause stress levels to spike, cortisone manufactured, increased heartbeat, which in turn self-sustains irregular or shallow breathing. That alone could be a large contributing factor to the fear. Anxiety can be a self-breeding beast, constantly replicating itself. Your anxieties and phobias could be connected, in that your self-esteem is lessened by knowing you're unable to deal with stairs as an otherwise successful adult."

She called me a "successful adult". Wow, it feels good to have someone pin that medal on me.

"Only do what you are comfortable with at each stage," she counsels, "but remember you can also do this without a friend accompanying you. Be careful not to credit any progress you make to just having someone else present." She is encouraging me to avoid misappropriation. Also she recognises "absolutist thinking", whereby I believe in irremovable external factors that govern the need for my anxiety triggers.

"There are other strategies we can deploy to re-determine problematic emotional responses - other things we can try later. But it may not be necessary. Focus on doing what we suggested in the short-term, and when you have succeeded, make sure that you award yourself the credit for doing it. Not us, not the type of stairs being insufficient angst-causing, but you."

Wow. Just wow. A golden illuminating light shaft just lit up the path ahead that I must take. I am so grateful for their insights. This is clearly top counselling - managing my anxieties with a structured programme, while adding a sense of buoyancy to my confidence by simply reassuring me that just because I struggle with anxieties, I don't necessarily suck at life.

This is graded exposure. In former, less enlightened times, phobias would be addressed by a practice known by mental health professionals as "flooding" (the phrase "mental health professional" being open to ambiguous dual interpretation). Flooding was a prolonged high voltage exposure to whatever caused the phobia.

Someone I interviewed for this book reported being unable to travel on public transport because he became irrationally fearful of vomiting. Cue being shown pictures of vomit from his counsellor, then taken to a room with a pile of vomit which he had to sit next to for several minutes. The approach here was presumably that if you hurl enough people who can't swim into the deep end, eventually a few will learn to swim. Graded exposure has impressive empirically proven results, and is not only far more likely to help shift an invasive phobia, but patients are also less at risk from the phobia being reinforced - an unforeseen side-effect of flooding reported by some clients.

Nowadays flooding is discredited, and this vastly more beneficial approach to the patient has replaced such callousness. Incremental exposure to the phobia in a controlled environment not only helps reduce a phobia but also lessens risked relapse - a far preferable treatment to the morally wonky flooding technique. Nevertheless scientific progress comes from trying then dismissing all the approaches that don't work. One deployed technique to stop patients maintaining damaging OCD rituals was to wear a rubber band around their arm, then painfully snap it on their wrist whenever they complied with a recurrent intrusive thought by performing an OCD task. Eventually this was found to cause more relapses than good. And would have been a particularly unfortunate treatment for any astihophobics.

"Just keep wanting to overcome it, that's the key," advises Steve.

"And keep doing it until you succeed," Claire adds.

"Yeah," Steve adds," you know what they say about 'if at first you don't succeed'?"

Normally, forever the class clown, I would have added a comment like: "Whoever said 'if at first you don't succeed' didn't work in a bomb disposal unit." Then there would have been an awkward silent. A pause before I would add: "Yeah, just remembered the advice about me not needing to be funny here."

"OK, I think that..." begins Steve, but is rather sharply cut off by Claire.

"What do you think, Steve?" in, if not a caustic way, then in a surprising tone nonetheless.

"That it's time to shut up?" I wonder.

"That our hour is well and truly up," he continues, opting to ignore the hardly missable harshness in her tone.

There's something else well and truly up too: a broomstick up his...

"In that case we had better conclude the session. I hope you felt it helpful," he says.

Counselling sessions are notorious for this: ending when a threatened breakthrough moment is finally imminent. Like pulling the plug out of Archimedes' bath before he had a chance to shriek "Eureka!"

"That was really helpful, especially all those marvellous insights at the end. Please can I see you next week?" I enquire in a mildly begging tone.

"We have to ask our Supervisor," he retorts. Apparently all four of us have to agree to the sessions continuing - all four keys are needed to fit the lock. They let slip a professional secret. Counsellors by nature must be discreet. (Er... that's not the secret bit - I already assumed that. At least I hope they are.) People's most private insights, motivations and vulnerable struggles for meaning are hardly pub anecdote material. Yet containing all this exposure to emotional turbulence within is by definition unhealthy. Therefore counsellors do tell someone else your inner secrets, but in a strictly controlled, sealed, airtight environment: to another counsellor appointed as a Supervisor. She is unlikely to post the best bits of your marriage breakdown on Twitter. Although, according to the waiver form I've just signed, it would be my fault if she did.

"I can see you next week," says Claire, charmingly. That means Steve has to see me too.

"Er… right, well I suppose we could extend to a second session, but not commit ourselves any further beyond that stage at, um, for the moment, and dependent, of course, on Supervisor compliance."

"Is next Wednesday OK? Same time?" Claire asks me, hardly acknowledging Steve's continued presence.

Steve responds by issuing a statement: "We will have to approach our Supervisor before committing to even the most preliminary of arrangements."

"6pm is great for me too. Thanks," I confirm.

"Dependent on…" Steve begins, then gives up.

"Oh, put it in your diary, Steve," Claire concludes.

"Thank you," I say. To both of them. And mean it.

In our next session I focus on the words of both counsellors, who have raised their game considerably from the opening few minutes of our first getting-to-know-you session.

Since these are sessions given by trainee counsellors, they feel entitled to adopt a less formal approach. A few times they make constructive comments about each other's approach, effortlessly slipping into impressive psychology jargon.

Jargon helps. Being bombarded with incomprehensive technical jargon seems to reassure my idiot human brain immensely: doctors know this, advertisers know this, IT contractors without a clue why the computer is doing that odd thing know this, but to my shame, it does really work.

For my part, I provide reluctant feedback too, which they strongly encourage me to do. They are trainees after all, and it is a weirdly formal yet simultaneously informal setting. They delve deeply into my mind's psychological constructs, and then we have a friendly chat about it afterwards. Trust is essential in just about any relationship format, but with counsellor and client it is utterly essential.

They apologise for the occasional bickering, and reassure me that when they're qualified they would not work together. "Never!" Claire over-confirms. Which is a shame as I would love to see these two - undeniably lovely and skilful people as they are - counsel couples with relationship issues. I can envision Steve siding with the husband, and Claire pledging unwavering loyalty to any wife or girlfriend on the consulting room settee. I imagine her imparting in a clinician session: "There's a technical explanatory reason in psychology why men behave like that: current progressive diagnosis has concluded it's because they're all twats."

They instigate further useful goal-setting techniques where I have to visit unpleasantly high places and do my set homework. Essentially, they initiate a reporting structure, where we revisit in unpacked detail my conflicting accomplishments and failures encountered with my homework. It's profoundly effective in numerous ways, but perhaps most crucially in ensuring I actually do my set homework. Knowing someone is taking an interest in my progress helps enormously in implementing my goals.

And their cognitive approach helps lessen the certainty in my brain's processors that stimuli prompt an automatic pre-ordained reaction. Instead, a more considered response needs to interject, whereas previously my mind displayed a mechanistic decision to press the bright red panic button straight away. CBT has not yet banished unhelpful intrusive thoughts, but I crucially feel the presence of allies is helping me to reduce my anxieties.

We also revisit abdominal breathing procedures and visualisation techniques that dwell on positive outcomes and imagery. "Rehearsing success rather than persistently rehearsing failure," I say to the general plaudits of Steve and Claire. "That's a great way of putting it," says Steve.

There is also a swelling sense of wanting to please Steve and Claire, to show them that their work is succeeding. Yet there is an abyss of shame that I feel myself sometimes in danger of falling towards, sucked into a pit of guilt, by the fact I am using their vital resources because I am… well… such a massive idiot. Frightened of heights, fazed by stairs, frozen by anxiety and locked out of much social interaction as a consequence.

There is an inexpressible guilt that sits in the room, never mentioned in the conversation, like an elephant seated in the room at a dinner party. Once I try mentioning the elephant in the room, imagining him at our dinner party: "I'm sorry, we didn't know what you'd like so we've just done you some iced buns - hope that's OK." But only in a comedic context, of course - emotional coward as I undoubtedly am.

Leaving, I turn around to re-enter the room as I forgot my gloves. I catch Steve absentmindedly touching her hair. Just a quick pat, but she responds by arching her neck closer towards him, with the desired effect of prompting him into stroking her hair further, like a cat getting a backrub off a settee leg. It's a heartfelt sight of charming spontaneity, unthinking affection and a gesture that pleasingly offsets their earlier coded bickering.

Not all the valuable analysis of my condition arrived in a counselling room. A young blonde Australian model provided me with one of the most perspicacious and genuinely useful counselling tips in a trendy Notting Hill eatery.

Set up on a blind date for a London-based Australian magazine's feature article with a 23-year-old blonde glamour model from Melbourne, I am experiencing understandable anxiety. Given I'm in my late forties. And English. And the magazine is clearing going for comic contrast.

My date is a minor celeb amongst London's antipodean community, and like me can't turn down even slightly paid projects that offer any sort of exposure, though exposure transpires to be a main part of her day job too. My date arrives and is predictably physically perfect. Early on she confides that she has removed a safety barrier deployed for all her dates, blind or otherwise, where she takes "the exit call".

The exit call, she explains, is where a friend makes a pre-arranged phone call culminating in her departing immediately while breathlessly announcing a death in the family. "Why after twenty minutes and not earlier?" I enquire with genuine curiosity. "Ensures I get a drink and the rejectee has to pay for it." Nice. The courtesy has been applied to me of no exit call. "Why?" I wonder out loud. "'Cos you're an author," she replies, "And I thought how bad and untrustworthy can an author be?" "Have you ever read *Mein Kampf*?" I enquire.

Surprisingly, we bond. Obviously I am irredeemably, irretrievably in love with the unattainable 23-year-old blonde before the menus arrive, but unlike most dates, all attraction must be muzzled, hidden and remain unacknowledged forever. Put in a cement-lined box, taken out in a hired boat to the middle of Lake Windermere and then dropped overboard.

We ought to be on our best behaviour, as the magazine has tasked us with writing a review of our date. And, rather awkwardly, awarding each other a mark out of ten based on our date experience. Yet she gorges on her lamb cutlets, succeeding in shocking me out of my bourgeois politeness stick-to-the-rules mentality by picking up her bones. She then gnaws them like a primitive. Even allowing for the fact she's Australian, and hence probably unaccustomed to knives and forks, this succeeds in delivering a surprise.

It is peculiarly, and somehow inexplicably, unfeminine too (as conditioned by a patriarchal society, right sisters?). She the unreformed meat-eater, while I pick sophisticatedly at my limp salad as I'm trying to shed weight. "So," she says, grease on her lips - I don't know her well enough to point it out, yet alone wipe it off - "you happy with that salad?" She knows I'm not. And it's also a transparent sexual metaphor: me the past-it reluctant salad nibbler, her gorging on all the prime juicy flesh available of her choosing. And she can have any flesh she wants, on or off the menu.

"You've got something on your face," I finally raise the courage to point out. "Any advice for going on a blind date?" she asks me between meat-tearing pulls of her teeth. "Yeah, don't apply to the *Guardian* to go on one of their blind dates where they set you up with a fittie and write about it," I advise. "Why not?" she asks. "'Cos it turns out they do check first if you're married," I say jokingly. "Right. Of course they do. Yeah, you should expect that with the moral *Guardian*," she replies. "Er ...I was ...er... joking," I stutter. "Right," she confirms in an unconvinced tone.

"So, are you going to write funny bits about me? Will there be jokes about me being Australian?" she checks. "No, of course not," I lie. "Ridiculing my unsophisticated Australian accent and table manners?" she suggests. "Of course not, no. No," I reply in my best mock how-dare-you wounded tone. That's four pages of material instantly lost.

"What yers working on at the moment?" she asks in her Oz accent, not yet remotely sandpapered down by six months exposed to less abrasive UK vowel sounds. Thereby I tell her about my treatment for height anxiety and fear of stairs.

"Streuth, you're kidding, right?"

"Yes, yes, yeah, yes... no," I reply.

"I've never heard of that!" she remarks.

She crams two cutlet bones into her mouth at once, and sucks noisily. She may be an unfairly attractive impeccable blonde but even she can't get away with this behaviour looking anything but distinctly unappealing.

Then she asks another question: "Is it possible to be scared of..."

Table manners? Polite hesitancy in conversation?

"...stairs?"

"Yip. It's an extreme manifestation of height anxiety termed bathmophobia," I confirm.

"Right," she acknowledges, finally stunned into temporary silence. She looks around for somewhere to wipe her greasy hands. I hand her a serviette moments before she uses the table cloth.

I ask: "What would a typical Aussie think of a guy who's frightened of stairs and heights?"

"Well, he wouldn't be getting much," she acknowledges. Such bluntness is an asset in Australia. That's why I don't live there.

As she picks up another bone, I wonder whether to offer her a lesson on how

133

to use a knife and fork. She's probably only just been picked up from the wild in Oz, and is beginning to adjust to captive living.

"Are you gay?" she enquires between noisy cutlet sucks. "What? Er, no, I mean… no and there's not anything wrong with being gay. I've never been asked that before - well, apart from by my wife, obviously."

"I know there's nothing wrong with being gay. We have lots of gays in Australia. I have loads of gay friends. Just wondered if you were gay, that's all," she clarifies.

"Are you from the 1970s?" I ask.

"What, you don't like my outfit?" she says, going up an octave in the process. "No…"

"Oh, thanks. Your shirt's not brilliant either," she swipes back.

"No. The 'no' was a 'no' that referred to me not liking… oh, your outfit's great," I bleat like a bleeping vehicle making a reversing noise.

"You Brits are so sensitive. I was joking."

"Phew, thought my score had dipped to 1/10 there."

We laugh. This is fun. We appear to be of the same species (*homo sapiens*) but have absolutely nothing in common. And it is so unusual to spend time with people who match this category. We tend to socialise with people who fit our sense-making templates for the world, allow only those who replicate and mirror ourselves. Reflect our own values, views, tastes, opinions - corroborate our confirmation bias. We pick friends and cultural experiences that tend to flatter our existing prejudices.

Although impossible to be sure, given the compromised clarity in her voice caused by shoving two cutlet bones into it while talking, I think she just called me a "whinging Pom." I decide against clarifying this as its outcome will probably shave some serious digits off both our awarded scores.

Must ask about her if I want to be a good date.

"What work are you doing now?" I ask.

"Showing my body for money, pretty much," she replies.

I laugh expecting this to be another joke, which receives a look that ensures I apply the laugh brake instantly. "Really?" I say. "Well, pretty much. Adverts and stuff. Model work. Are you going to put that in the article?"

"Not if you don't want me to," I reply honestly. "Wow, a man with sensitivity. Are you sure you're not gay?" she says.

"You can put it in. I'm not ashamed of what I do. You hire out your brain, typists hire out their fingers, actors hire out their emotions, I hire out my looks whilst I've still got them." It's a good line - one she's probably developed over time, but a good line nevertheless.

The message I'm meant to receive here is: "blonde model does not necessarily equate to thick". I liked to think I knew that already, but I'd never met a blonde model before. Not offline, anyway.

"Journalism pays badly," I announce. "Only getting £100 for this assignment, and I've had to cover my train fare to London before filing the copy." Then I notice a change of mood.

"Oh... er... yeah. Me too. I know the magazine said we're only allowed to spend £50 on a meal for two with drinks in central London. The tight arses."

"Yeah," I say confirming both her points with feeling.

"Well, I'm happy to cover anything we spend above £50. Which we will with the price of these cocktails." At this point she catches the eye of a glass-collecting waitress and mimes two more refills, without asking if I want another cocktail.

"Are you trying to get me drunk on our first date?" I ask.

"No," she responds, leaving me unsure whether she spotted the surely obvious fact I was joking.

"Will you be alright at heights if you've had some drinks. Might make you less of a scaredy." Normally I admire Australian neologisms, but I can't help feeling her newly-minted antipodean noun "scaredy" reflects neither well on me nor my aimed-for masculinity.

"Are you going to include the bit about me being terrified of stairs in your review?" I check. "No," she says, struggling to find an outraged tone of voice and a look of offended sensitivity. She barely locates either. Her attempt at appearing hurt just looks bizarre and out of place, like spotting a koala bear doing a crossword puzzle.

Then she tells me about her phobias and OCD that she struggled with as a teenager, convinced that she was a peculiar case of isolated insanity. It turns out she was trapped by having to perform magical thinking rituals too, counting everything around her repeatedly. So we do have something in common - yet separated by 25 years and 10,000 miles.

Then she gives me a piece of perceptive advice for the balloon flight: "If it gets too much when you're high in the sky, just breathe deeply. And tell yourself 'I don't need to be frightened here, because being frightened ain't going to help me in any way at all.' I used that as a blocking mechanism when I had voices yelling at me, ordering me to count and recount stuff. Remember you are in charge of your brain, so you can relax yourself through it, and block the voices and the anxieties by saying 'being scared isn't going to help, performing a ritual isn't going to help, so I don't have to do either'. And keep breathing deeply." That transpires to be the most succinct and useful counselling I have probably ever received. Dispensed not from an experienced certified CBT practitioner or psychoanalyst, but a young, blonde Australian glamour model now onto her third cocktail.

We walk to the Tube station and begin our departing speeches. She leans forward and kisses me - a proper didn't-see-it-coming on-the-lips smacker. Right on the chops, mutton chops being the distinctly recognisable flavour of the kiss. "One of the questions they ask is 'did you kiss'," she clarifies. "So now we can both put down a 'yes'. They'll like that," she says enthusiastically.

"Can I say we also had a really great…"

"No!" she says, braking hard to stop my sentence mid-flow.

"I was going to say 'time'. I wasn't hoping for some illegitimate credibility by writing that we'd…" This time, when I need her to finish my sentence prematurely for me, she doesn't. Until she adds after an unnecessary delay: "They'd like it even more if we had sex?"

"Yes," I agree with probably too much enthusiasm, "They really, really would." "Well, they know that would never happen in like a trillion years," she says smiling. "Yeah, a trillion zillion years, obviously." I confirm, mirroring her smile. Then we both attempt to speak at the same time, basically saying the identical phrase superimposed over each other's voice: "This has been fun."

"So," she says, "I'm going to give you an 8/10."

"Was it going to be a 9/10 before my last joke?" I clarify.

"Possibly. Well?" she says. "Well?" I reflect. "What score are you going to give me?" she asks impatiently. "9/10," I reply. "Oh, OK," she responds as if that's the lowest score someone could contemplate awarding to anyone for anything.

"Thanks. That's nice of you," she adds, her voice full of disappointment.

"I suppose we'd better depart before we say anything in the last few seconds that will reduce our scores," I suggest. She smiles. "Oh, just one thing," I add as she swivels away. "I just wondered how…" Without needing me to finish the question, she instantly replies: "£200 for doing my half of the article. But I'll give you a good review and a mark of 9/10."

Gender wages disparity is one of the key necessary battles left for feminism to fight. Feminism has mainly won the war against inequality now, with just a few pockets of resistance still left to liberate. So I can't complain too much at this point in history if I'm the victim of a rare inverse of the usual paradigm where the female earns double the male's wages for doing the same job.

Two weeks later the article is published. But not online, so I have to ask a friend in London to pick up a physical copy of the magazine. She gave me a 6/10.

The next week they keep me waiting when I report to Steve and Claire for my continued counselling sessions. I wouldn't normally expect this to be loaded with psychological overtones, but they are psychologists. On entering the room it is conspicuous that they have been having another row. But both gamely put on their professional faces.

My male counsellor is asking me about my school years and formative teenage development. To avoid the stinging emotions that this line of inquiry will probe, I am diverting the questions by deploying comedy as a blocking mechanism. Frustration is readable in my inquisitors' faces. This is not a strategy that I am allowed to get away with for long. They deflect it successfully - by refusing to reward my attempts at comedy with a reaction, only offering their attention as treats when I say something honest and revealing about my schooldays.

"My schooldays weren't great and I don't really want to discuss what an inconsequential scholar and full-time idiot I was, or how horrid most of my contemporaries were," I announce, hoping to move on.

"Were you exhibiting signs of height anxiety then?" Steve asks.

"No, I have always been tall."

They deliberately do not react, and wait for me to continue.

"Yes," I eventually continue, and receive a 'good boy' dog pat look from Claire for giving them a serious answer and resisting the compulsion to entertain.

"How were you with stairs?" enquires Steve.

"Avoided them."

"Why...?"Claire begins, realising instantly that a "why" question risks tarnished association with accusatory rhetoric, and replaces it with a stock open question prefix. "What were the reasons that made your schooldays horrid?" she rephrases.

I answer honestly: "Some of my fellow pupils were horrid bullies. And I did not engage with the work."

I am falling into irreversible regression at this point, slipping down from adulthood back to feeling like I am twelve again. But Claire and Steve are determined to probe me for hidden insecurities.

"How were your contemporaries horrid?" Steve attempts to establish.

"'Cos they said and did horrid things," I reply, more plainly than defensively.

"How many of them did horrid things?" quantifies Claire.

"Not sure. Not all of them, obviously. But quite a lot."

I really am going to need the tissues soon. It is terrifying how weak and prone to manipulation I am. Kind liberal as I consider myself to be, I am so easily led. No doubt I would have done terrible things under the Nazis.

"Why?" asks Claire with uncharacteristic curtness. I allow time in case they want to amend the "why" question. But they appear content to leave their question unaltered.

"Ask them. 'Cos they were immature, I guess."

"Maybe you're being too hard on them and, crucially, yourself. To what extent is that conduct expected among school age children?" Steve counters.

God, they are good, if relentless, with the open questioning technique.

"Immaturity is both a mental and physical condition," I bark back.

They pause to diffuse any gathering tension.

"Are you becoming angry with us?" Claire seeks to verify.

"No. Sorry."

"It's OK, you are entitled to become angry with us," she calms.

"Thanks. But I'm OK for anger at the moment. I'll let you know if that changes and I need any."

"Angry is allowed," she smiles reassuringly.

I don't think I would ever want to be angry with you, Claire. But I'm not going to say that out loud. Instead I say, "If you're bad shrink, good shrink - you're definitely the good shrink."

She likes this comment. Predictably Steve's not so sure.

"Anxiety sabotages rather than empowers my life," I suddenly say. They both nod an understanding empathy.

I decide to tell them a true story, mainly because they won't believe it's true, and when they admonish me for being dishonest I can reveal it's absolutely, genuinely, verifiably true. I realise that under transactional analysis this couldn't be more bull's-eye, hole-in-one, jackpot, one-hundred-and-eighty "child".

But it is also an important story about fostering emotional development, and my desperation to shed childhood as quickly as possible because I neither cared for it nor my peers. Nor myself - especially myself. Back then I was steadfastly aware that these could not possibly be the promised "best years of your life". They definitely were not. And it reveals my capacity for over-developed emotional empathy for someone I haven't seen for thirty years - and to be honest (which I've been encouraged to be by my Buy One Get One Free counsellors), probably only met four or five times in my life, and am unlikely to ever encounter again.

"One of my friends at a rival local school was genuinely nicknamed "Pussylicker". As a teenage boy I was envious of them possessing such a cool nickname. Though, oddly, she never liked it."

See what I did there? A simple inverse-the-expected-gender joke. Or did I?

Steve literally bites his lip to repress a smirk. His co-counsellor discharges a disappointed sigh, as much for his benefit as mine, in order to loudly express her disapproval. She emits a silent "when you've quite finished, boys" with a short shake of her head. Next, she upgrades her communicative weapons of choice, using actual words to chastise us. Though I now instantly regret making my gag, as it has clearly cost me credibility points. Boy, had I misjudged the environment to do material like this - even comics have to learn about the concept of horses for courses - as well as supermarket ready-meal distributors.

"Please tell us the truth," she pleads in an unnatural tone, redolent of someone who is professionally patient rather than actually wanting to be. The implication here is similar to a parent's crumbling patience, forced to concede to their offspring "although we like you, we do not always like the choices you make and therefore the person you choose to be." She deliberately pauses to locate the right words, speaking slowly like she's fumbling for individual coins spilt in the dark: "Remember... we spoke last session... about... how you... don't have to... perform here."

Well, my story is true. Although I didn't go to the same school as her, I did know the unfortunate schoolgirl saddled with the unwelcomed nickname. For all the adulation society places on children, we shouldn't forget teenagers can be callous, horrid little fascists, especially to each other. We also willingly forget that children have at least two nicknames: one they recall as adults, and another one that was so ineffaceably pernicious with targeted cruelty that teams of odious social network trolls have focus-grouped them to forge the most horrid nickname possible in evil smithies. They will subsequently never admit to it as an adult.

Often such nicknames are buried so deep to be beyond accidental excavation. Since you ask, my school nickname was Rastus (because I once owned a reggae album - believe me, that was off-the-scale, awarding-winning radicalness for a South Lincolnshire upbringing. (I only bought it to impress Charlotte Jones on our school bus.) No, I didn't have any other nicknames (actually I did, but I've repressed them deeply as they still retain the probable potency to make me start crying again.) It doesn't matter what colour wire you opt to cut - the red, blue, yellow or green one - none of us has the capacity to defuse the emotional bomb of explosive childhood memories that can suddenly explode without any issued warning in our adult lives. You can step on and activate an emotional landmine years after it's been planted and its location completely forgotten about.

Having said that, these were more innocent times. My friend's unfortunate nickname bridged two separate ages - the end of cultural innocence on one side meeting with the age of mainstream smutty liberalism on the opposite bank. Hence her nickname had the misfortune to span the two ages.

Because her nickname genuinely originated from having kittens - as in owning young cats, not being in a petrified state. It specifically related to a demonstration in a school "show and tell" talk about how a mother cat licked her kittens clean, as felines, like the French, can forgo the requirement to use water when having a wash. Liking her cats perhaps slightly too much, had caused her to lick a kitten for demonstration purposes. Note to today's teenagers: this does not make you high. Nor will licking a toad from a British pond. That just gives you really bad breath.

Licking her kitten was a practical demonstration of natural history, instructional though of questionable hygiene. A stern matriarchal teacher had stopped this unhygienic practice and warned: "It's not a good idea to lick your pussy, Veronica." And that was the exact moment that the teacher smashed the champagne bottle onto the hull that launched an unsinkable nickname. No iceberg of teacher intervention could ever sink that nickname.

From that day forth she was destined to ignore everyone unless they called her by (a) her real name or (b) one of the other nicknames that she actually preferred. ("Zit face" - that was one of mine, I've just remembered. There were far worse ones.)

Unfortunately for Veronica this was the era when benign sitcom *Are You Being Served?* proved a ratings winner with the character Mrs. Slocombe constantly regaling pre-watershed audiences by inviting everyone to laugh at her pussy - three or four times per episode. That joke was speckled with green spots of staleness approaching the half-way point in the opening episode of the first series, yet alone the following ten series (the tills stayed open for business and innuendo until 1985). This was accepted, wholesome mass entertainment at 7.30pm in the late 1970s - acceptable as the word meant 90% cat with slight 10% undertone of female pudendum. This was as innocent as Powergen buying into the Italian market and deciding to name their Italy-based firm PowergenItalia. Because that spells… oh, you've worked it out already.

When actress Mollie Sugden died aged 86 in 2009, the main BBC six o'clock news honoured her with a clip of her creation Mrs. Slocombe doing - well, what else - a trademark pussy joke three hours ahead of the watershed. And boy could she nail them every time. If you wanted innuendo, in her hands it was never hard and she'd always give you one.

One day in my early teens I was at Chess Club. This proved to be a bad choice of society to join in order to meet girls. But one of the few girls there was Veronica, my friend saddled with the unfortunate shifting-meaning nickname. Other boys would insensitively address her by this charmless nickname, in the same way they would probably shoot an air rifle at a dove. Not that this distraction stopped the bullies coming after me, and I couldn't go upstairs to avoid them. Although I always found a way out of going upstairs, which was a painful constraint, as the boys' toilets were upstairs. On several occasions I risked terrible shame if caught using the girls' because it was located on the ground floor. These were scary times. Teenage years are bad enough without being scared of stairs.

Seeing how some bullies taunted my friend with the distressing nickname was hideous. This was confirmed by my preference to hang around with girls, as I found boys of my same age witheringly immature. Once, after Chess Club, an immensely unpleasant boy, a known bully, was spotted loitering outside our Chess Club room in the same way that a fox is attracted to a chicken coop. Hoping to indulge in some traditionally one-sided blood sports and beat up nerdy chess freaks, he spotted Veronica and proceeded to taunt her by incessantly asking, "are you called that name 'cos you is a lezzer?" (I haven't bothered to correct his ugly English.) Veronica's much older sister, who was sufficiently advanced in years above us to drive a car, entered the building at this point. Arriving to pick her up her younger sibling from Chess Club, she duly encountered the taunter and corrected the bully's ugly face by smacking the reprobate right across his bully chops. He was hit with an equivalent force to stepping out in front of an oncoming beer lorry. Seizing our opportunity, we nerdy chess players escaped from our Chess Club siege conditions by nervously tip-toeing over his prostrate bully body.

That was the last time I ever saw Veronica. She moved away from the area soon afterwards, probably to go on the road supporting her elder sister's new career as a travelling prize-fighter. But I do often wonder what happened to her, and her innocently coined nickname tarnished by the shifting sands of cultural expression. I wonder where she is now, and how she answers at bourgeois dinner parties when the cheese course conversation nostalgically turns to school nicknames. "Oh, I didn't have one," will probably be her prepared response. As she stabs the cheese knife menacingly into the Jarlsberg so that it stands upright in the wooden board beneath. "Alright, I was just asking," someone will respond, "there's no need to have kittens…" And which point she'll ring her southpaw sister and ask if she can pop round to take care of a troublesome guest.

"Er… that was actually all true," I enjoy announcing to my twin counsellors.

"Really? You know we can't help you if you're not honest with us, Richard," Claire chastises me.

She used my name for the first time - for what I feared would prove to be the only time in our sessions.

"Sorry," I say. Deciding not to call her by her name, in case that is a strictly one-way street of familiarity that is only legal for her to go down at the moment.

"That's OK," she reassures me, "I feel we are making progress now."

A voice in my chest is screaming: "But it's true. You know it's true. That's not fair. Tell her it's true!" I tell my brain to select "adult mode" and take one for the team.

"I realise it can be difficult for men," she begins, then pauses presumably to allow me to fill in her clearly implied yet unspoken words myself 'because you're

all massive idiots', "but you don't have to constantly peacock with humour."
Wow. Bit sexist.

"I'll endeavour to be a shy peacock," I confirm.

Complimenting me, she says: "You're very lucky to be good with humour."
They both ask me questions about school. I am focused, honest and candid.
Twice I can't help myself saying humorous things - and twice the male counsellor
smiles - on the second occasion the smile escapes into a laugh which he clumsily
disguises as an unnecessary cough. His co-counsellor makes a mark on her pad
at this time - probably another cross against his name.

"Is he in trouble?" I ask.

"We're here to discuss, you, Richard." Wow, she used my name again.

He laughs again. She makes another mark on the pad. That's probably
another two-day extension to the sex ban he's currently serving. "If we could all
focus," she continues.

"Tell us why you would like to be cured of your conditions," asks Steve. It's
a good question, although Claire visibly squirms in her chair at deployment of
the word "cured".

"Because I'm 49," I say. "Really, I'm genuinely 49. Unlike Carol Vorderman
who I calculate has spent at least the last seven years being '49' - and she's
supposed to be good at maths."

Silence. Outside in the far distance I hear a floating autumnal leaf crash to
the ground with a deafening impact. "Tough couch," I add.

"What makes you feel a compulsion to be constantly funny?" asks Claire.

"Er... Sometimes..." I start to answer, until Claire cuts me off by advising:
"Don't feel a compulsion to be funny here."

"You don't have to be under pressure to be funny here," Steve confirms.
"Though you're funny," he says, kindly.

"Do you feel the constant need to express yourself through humour is an
adult, parent or child reaction?" asks Claire.

"Well, it's my job actually. And the correct answer, as you well know, can
be all three."

"Yes. You're completely right," she responds.
Interesting.

"Did you do your homework?" asks Steve.

"Yes. I..."

The guy bursts into giggles, corpsing like an unprofessional actor. "Sorry,"
announces a visibly embarrassed Steve.

"Speaking about school seems to have caused some accompanying regression
in our behaviours," observes Claire.

"That's true," I say, "You should be a psychologist."

142

Steve bites his lip so hard I expect to see a trail of blood trickle down his chin.

"Do you want us to help you?" she asks calmly.

I'm definitely in trouble. She used a closed question. "Yes, I genuinely do. Really. Thank you for helping me," I say quickly.

"That's OK. So if we can all focus, and if you can please stop doing something for me… do you know what I am going to ask you to stop doing?" asks Claire.

"…to stop being the class clown?" I anticipate.

"Exactly," she confirms.

She's good.

9 SINKING IN THE LAST CHANCE BALLOON: SADLER'S COMEBACK

A report in the snappily titled newspaper *The Hull Packet and Original Weekly Commercial Literary and General Advertiser* published in 1810 provides insight into Sadler's precarious financial conditions, his friends' sympathies and how Sadler is now trying to make amends. Again, it casts his personality in a favourable light.

"Mr Sadler the chief and paternal aeronaut has not done badly. His bills have been stuck up on windows and walls stating his much to be regretted misfortune and his ancient patronage. His present friends are active and alert to free him from trouble and satisfy his claimants." Handbills were displayed as a public act of support for Sadler, pledging to clear his debts.

Ruin had only just been averted by his friends and with the support of well-wishers. But how could such an important and famous inventor, engineer, chemist, entrepreneur and celebrity aeronaut have hit the debt buffers so hard and speedily? The answer lies in his unceremonious dismissal from the Royal Navy.

Sadler had invested considered funds of his own into building and equipping a research laboratory in Portsmouth. When suddenly sacked from the Navy, he was left in considerable debt when his numerous creditors came circling him.

Although lacking hard facts, circumstantial evidence is sufficiently strong to allow the assumption that the motivation for Sadler's return to aeronautical career, fully 25 years after he last stepped into a balloon basket, was financial. Saddled with huge debts after his treatment by Bentham, and reliant on a colossal bail-out from his friends and public supporters, Sadler saw exhibition balloon flights as the only obvious way of accessing funds.

7 JULY 1810: OXFORD: THE COMEBACK

In the pre-dawn light, the streets of Oxford were unusually busy with the rumble of carts bringing early risers into the city, all anxious to claim a decent vantage-point to witness Sadler's return to flying. "From a very early hour carriages of all descriptions, from coaches to fours to common carts, saddles horses, mules and asses, and numerous pedestrians, from all parts of the country, many came expressly from London."

By mid-morning the city was reported as "full of visitors" with many excursions organised from London specifically to see Sadler. The flight was supposedly part of the celebrations for Lord Grenville's induction as University

Chancellor, but it is fair to say that Sadler upstaged him. Notably, Lord Grenville was a relative of William Windham - hence the involvement of Sadler in such establishment circles.

The huge crowd bellowed a collective cry when Sadler stepped into the balloon and several of the guy ropes immediately appeared to break. Upon inspection, Sadler diagnosed the problem, apparently claiming the ropes had not been tied by Naval men "and not by those who understood sailors' knots". Eventually the balloon was ready for ascension, although over four hours late, and four large weights each of fifty pounds each were removed from the balloon basket. Sadler had taken a reported one hundred bags of sand ballast with him, alongside sensible provisions of cold beef, bread, four bottles of water and one of brandy (presumably to numb himself against any encountered coldness at altitude), and... in the distinctly not so sensible category... a cat in a wicker carrying basket. Why? Was he hoping to pop into the vets on the way to the balloon launch, found himself running late and then thought. "Oh, I'll do it after the flight"?

One snooty newspaper report elects to open with the remark: "The grand finale to the week's entertainment - in the opinion of the Town at least - occurred this week at Merton Fields when Mr Sadler and his son went up in their car. This exhibition alike excited the attention of the ignorant and vulgar, and of the learned and the great." It again underlines Sadler's fairly unique attraction in appealing to the interests of both Town and Gown. Other press sources estimated the crowd size at 50,000, but this is unlikely to be a scientific figure though it shows the extent of Sadler's surviving celebrity status.

We know that Sadler had to raise money for the cost of the balloon, since he was broke. For most of June 1810 the balloon was exhibited at the Racquet Court - the site of the current Real Tennis complex just off cobbled Merton Street in Oxford. For a chance to view Sadler's flying machine, members of the public paid the hardly piddling sum of one shilling, approximately equivalent to £5 today. Yet there was no shortage of shillings, and queues formed along Merton Street to see the essential apparatus for the magic of flight. Balloonomania had not yet been pricked by over-familiarity or the extended absence of its leading man.

With such a fan following, it is worth considering again why Sadler waited for nearly two and half decades to return. The most plausible explanation must remain that he realised ballooning was... well... bloody dangerous. Yet Sadler's co-pilot for his first comeback flight was none other than Windham, his fourteen-year-old son. Whatever Mrs. Sadler had said about her husband's aeronautical career, it would be intriguing to hear her views on this latest family venture.

The audience was certainly prepared to be kept waiting. Although the placards declared a 10am flight, Sadler surprisingly miscalculated the amount of time taken to pump hydrogen into the envelope, to such an extent that "it was not until a quarter past two precisely that the aerial machine ascended. The spectacle was very fine. Merton Fields and Christ Church walks were thronged, Cherwell and Folly bridges crowded and every other place from which a view could be caught." The top of every house was crowded with onlookers, with some spectators - clearly not acrophobia sufferers - clinging precariously to the steeple of Christ Church cathedral.

The Chancellor of Oxford University had a safer vantage-point, viewing proceedings from the garden of Corpus Christi College. "Many ladies in gay attire sat watching from the Corpus roof." Sadler had inscribed the following words around the globe's entire 36-foot circumference: "Right Hon. Wm. Wyndham Grenville, Baron of Wooton, Chanc. Univer. of Oxon." The balloon's dimensions were large, with an impressive 24,429 cubic feet capacity.

When the balloon ascended, freed from its mooring ropes facing the railings of Corpus Christi in Merton Field, the overwhelming majority of the crowd was able to spot it for the first time. They reportedly emitted a collective purr upon seeing its colour scheme of "green, red, yellow and black margins above, then an inscription with the style of Lord Grenville and the date of Chancellerian election, underneath stripes of red and yellow, and below all a beautifully shaped and decorated car".

The balloon's dimensions were enthusiastically reported by the press, *The Leeds Mercury* revealing that Sadler had built a sphere of nearly thirty feet in diameter, containing 86,721 gallons of air. Whereas today the standard comparable measures offered by the press for illustrative purposes are football pitches, double-decker buses or Wales, in 1810 the media used haystacks to provide their readers with an easy visual measurement. "The size was considerably larger than a two tonne hay stack," the paper confirmed - helpfully.

Fortunately for a pre-planned flight date, the weather was kinder to Sadler than on his previous flight a quarter of a century earlier, and a slight south-westerly floated Sadler and his son over Merton College and then Magdalen Tower. Father and son were waving flags with such alacrity that Sadler junior dropped his white flag, thankfully causing no injuries to the admiring multitude below. Sadler senior threw several handkerchiefs overboard, like a rock star tossing a sweat band or drum stick into a baying crowd to be fought over.

Ever the enthusiastic flag waver, Sadler had brought several on board to acknowledge the supportive crowd beneath them, including a colossal blue flag bearing the inscription "Protected by the conqueror of Napoleon Bonaparte, The hero of Acre, Rear Admiral Sir Sidney Smith". Once they had drifted in the light wind towards Headington and Marston and were over open fields and clear of the crowds below, Sadler deliberately tossed this blue tribute flag to the earth. This provides an all too rare insight into Sadler's preoccupations outside engineering. Sidney Smith (1764-1840) was a naval officer, whose epitaph was provided by Napoleon's remark: "that man cost me my destiny". He saw action in the American Revolutionary War, and although his name was prefixed with "Sir", he was often mockingly known as "the Swedish knight" because the title came from the King of Sweden after he had served in, and masterminded, the successful Swedish naval campaign against the Russian fleet at the Battle of Svenskund in 1790. As a naval man he was a frequent visitor to Woolwich and Portsmouth, and would most likely have encountered Sadler there in the first years of the nineteenth century. Admiral Smith's naval vessels would have been improved by Sadler's scientific modifications and carried his re-designed artillery - so praised by Lord Nelson. Smith was recorded as being present that day in Oxford to witness Sadler's comeback.

Sadler ensured that scientific instruments accompanied him on the voyage, including two barometers, an electrometer, a dipping needle and two bottles for collecting air samples at altitude - science having yet to establish if there were different properties to air at significant altitude.

Descending at 4.30pm, Sadler's balloon landed near Newport Pagnell, close to modern-day Milton Keynes, in a barley field owned by a well-known local Quaker Mr. Marshall. Sadler had started to exhaust gas twelve miles north-east of Oxford. Throwing out ballast bags to avoid tree tops, he then lobbed his grappling iron overboard to commence the landing process. Skimming a wheat field, the balloon was suddenly propelled upwards again, rebounding fully forty feet airwards after the field labourers below refused to follow Sadler's shouted directive and grab his landing ropes, preferring to flee. As one contemporary report explained: "The hay makers were much terrified by the phenomenon to lend the adventurous travellers any assistance", instead preferring to run away or cower in a hedgerow.

Mirroring the misfortunes of the very first hydrogen balloon ascent all those years previously in France, Sadler also encountered alarmed agricultural workers who mistook the balloon for something quite different - although this time they were not inclined to attack it. However, one newspaper elaborates on the Oxfordshire labourers' concerns: "Sadler observed people loading hay that mistook the balloon for a kite in the shape of a tea urn and were hesitant to come near it."

Eventually the haymakers were persuaded to help, after Sadler senior and Sadler junior had ended their flight with customary recklessness and crashed into a hedge. Some reports claim the balloon ended up in Buckinghamshire, with the basket in Bedfordshire, strewn either side of the dividing hedgerow forming the county border. Workers from three adjoining fields - or at least those convinced it was not a giant teapot - quickly squeezed the air out of the balloon, rolled it up and deposited it in the back of a cart in a farmer's field - a tradition that has continued almost exactly the same way to this day - albeit hopefully without the crashing into a hedge bit.

Mr. Marshall turned out to be friendly, and provided the Sadlers with bread, cheese and brandy. And more brandy. So much brandy that both generations of Sadler spend the night in Newport Pagnell and returned to Oxford the next morning. (At times one wonders how much of Sadler's incredible courage was of the Dutch variety, given he never flew without a bottle of brandy.)

And if you're wondering what happened to the flying cat, he landed with all nine lives fully intact. Sadler managed to touchdown the feline aeronaut safely by using a small parachute self-manufactured to his own design. The cat landed gently in what was then the rural outpost of Headington, long since swallowed up by advancing urban sprawl into the city of Oxford. The cat, christened Puss by the press of the age, became quite a celebrity as an early nineteenth-century example of cats in the news.

The cat in the basket was picked up "by a countryman in a village called Headington, about two miles from Oxford, with a red collar and directions to Miss Roberts, daughter of the coachman proprietor in High Street, Oxford. The countryman took the cat home as directed. On his way home he made an exhibition of Puss, at a premium, to see the cat that had been up in a balloon," reported the local newspaper, showing the countryman's gift for indulging in a bit of opportunistic capitalism. One local newspaper in the Bodleian Library's archives, published in July 1810, specifically states: "Miss Roberts had most attention we are told afterwards, when she was offered more than a sixpence on many occasions to view her famous Pussy." The reporter was obviously the great, great, great, great grandfather of Mrs. Slocombe.

24 SEPTEMBER 1810: BRISTOL

Say what you want about the constellations of modern stars, but it is doubtful whether any contemporary celebrity would have the power to visit Bristol one day and expect every school, shop and factory to close as well as have the day formally decreed as a public holiday by the Council. Yet that is exactly what occurred when James Sadler decided to conduct a balloon ascent in Bristol in September 1810.

Reported to be Sadler's sixteenth flight, and his second after his Oxford comeback, he used the same multi-coloured balloon flown for Lord Grenville's installation as Chancellor.

"The city was all bustle the whole of the morning, and every house that could command a view of the ascension was crowded. The shops were all shuttered-up, and all business were stood down during the whole of the forenoon. The schools were all out, the day made a holiday, and young and old, rich and poor, all came to watch," trumpeted *The Morning Post*. "There was not a house in Bristol that did not boast its party of visitors."

The venture certainly made some much needed money for Sadler, who was publicly known to be settling his earlier debts. This is the likely motivation for inflating the admission price, as he charged the public a hefty 3s 6d each to access the gardens. Noticeably this time, security was employed to collect the admission, with the Bristol Volunteers employed for this specific purpose. In his comeback years Sadler would always hire a militia to collect revenue and guard the venue's perimeter fencing to stop ticketless entrants - in contrast to his earlier 1784-85 ascents.

There was a problem, however. With the 1pm take-off time approaching, a persistent breeze was blowing directly from the east. This meant that any ascent would see the balloon inevitably drift due westwards and straight over the perilous Bristol Channel. Also, it was reported the next day that Sadler had intended to take his daughter up with him, but such was the threat of being blown over the sea that he steadfastly resisted his daughter's entreaties. Her place was willingly taken by a Mr. Clayfield of Bristol who, if considered more expendable than Sadler's daughter, nevertheless reasoned that Sadler himself planned to continue with the flight.

News of a potential postponement had filtered through to the 10,000 crowd, and history had shown that postponing balloon flights often resulted in disorder or, more likely, a full-blown riot. "Mr Sadler declared that if he should veer to the West then we would not venture, from an apprehension that he might drop in the sea." This is a perfectly reasonably apprehension in most people's books, but "great fears of a disappointment generally prevailed".

Then at 1.35pm, only five minutes after the intended take-off, Sadler noticed a distinct change in the wind direction now blowing from the north-east. Hence Sadler "accompanied by a gentleman amateur", the distinguished chemist William Clayfield, lifted off, passing over Bristol (where he repeated his crowd-pleasing though not RSPCA-pleasing trick of parachuting a cat, this time whilst over Redcliffe) en route to Exeter. The parachuting moggy narrowly missed being impaled on the sharp spire of St. Mary's Parish Church.

After travelling just over a mile, Sadler performed his customary and popular act of throwing some letters overboard - the earliest form of airmail - and then continued on a south-western route. But Exeter was never to be reached, because a problem struck the intrepid duo. The wind, as quickly as it had changed direction earlier, suddenly blew back from the east, ensuring that the balloon was now full steam ahead for the Bristol Channel - hardly a safe landing place. Rather than initiating an immediate landing Sadler threw out ballast and raised the balloon even higher. Although a somewhat reckless tactic, it averted disaster as Sadler discovered another current, which now blew him directly northwards towards Wales.

However, the change of wind direction was short-lived, and travelling at a disturbing velocity, Sadler was blown back onto a south-western course. By about 4.15pm he was observed six miles off the North Devon coast at Lynmouth, losing altitude quickly.

The Caledonian Mercury of 1 October 1810 mentioned: "a favourite barometer given to Mr Sadler by the famous Dr Johnson for which he [Sadler] had been offered 200 guineas." That was the last, and thus we can comfortably deduce, most cherished object Sadler jettisoned on this watery flight. Even parts of the balloon's cart were ripped off and hurled into the sea. With the towering cliffs of Combe Martin approaching, they were certainly provided with a motive to restore height as quickly as possible. First they scraped the cliff tops. Then, sure enough, they plopped into the Bristol Channel.

Sadler and companion remained in the water for nearly an hour, with the partially inflated balloon acting as both a marker buoy for the boat that eventually rescued them, but also as a sail blowing them along the Bristol Channel. "A boat was launched instantly, and the voyagers were brought ashore in a state of extreme fatigue and Mr Sadler was unable to stand for having been in the water for some time before the boat was able to reach him." The paper added: "it was by mere accident that the balloon was observed to fall into the sea, and had it not been a remarkably serene evening, the parties must have inevitably perished." In panic, a shivering Sadler and Clayfield had dispensed with everything they could find to regain altitude, even lobbing their great coats overboard. Sure enough, Sadler confirmed that the treasured barometer had been the last item to be discarded.

2 JULY 1811: CAMBRIDGE

Sadler seemingly had no trouble securing the best venues for his ascents, as evidenced by Cambridge University's decision to allow him to mark the installation of Lord Gloucester as the University's Chancellor by taking off from the grandest of college courts: the Great Court at Trinity College.

Lord Byron had left Trinity only four years previously, and often used the fountain in the centre of the court to provide his pet bear with a daily wash. When asked why he kept a live bear in his college room, Byron replied that he intended to have the bear elected as a Fellow of the college. Later Byron, dressed only in a full-size bear skin complete with head, went to fight in the Greek Civil

War. Unsurprisingly, that did not work out well.

Arguably putting himself in equal danger, Sadler attempted to fly from Trinity's Great Court in a stiff afternoon breeze. His publicly stated intention had been to fly with his daughter, described by one newspaper as "an interesting little girl, only fourteen years of age". Yet an increasing wind ensured he had to play the role of a protective father and again forbid her ascent. This was the second occasion that her planned debut as an aeronaut suffered a weather postponement. The press do not note any resultant teenage tantrums. Instead, he offered a vacant seat to the highest bidder - Lieutenant Paget of the Royal Navy offering the colossal sum of 100 guineas to ascend in conditions considered far too dangerous for Sadler's family members. Paget was spared too, however, his corpulent frame making the balloon too heavy to achieve lift-off, and the pathological pork-pie eater had to heave his wide-girthed frame back out of the basket "with some reluctance at 20 minutes past 2 o'clock". Sensing worsening weather conditions with light rain and winds increasing from the north-east, Sadler opted to fly solo.

With the twenty restraining ropes removed, Sadler quickly gained the required height to clear the college buildings and soared above King's College Chapel, enthusiastically waving his hat to acknowledge the crowd's acclamations. Unfortunately, the weather being overcast with light rain, Sadler soon disappeared into dark grey cloud, remaining in view for less than two minutes to his immense ground-dwelling audience, and withdrew "from view of the spectators with as much quickness as the curtain falls upon an interesting scene of a play," as one contemporary observer chose to phrase it.

Dr. Johnson's precious barometer having been lost to the sea in his previous flight, Sadler consulted his replacement to calculate that the cloud was nearly a mile thick. Eventually emerging at high altitude on a splendid sunlit day above the cloud, he surmised that his velocity in a high wind was precariously fast, and that soon he would be over open sea. He started to valve the balloon, and plan a descent.

His navigational instincts were correct, and he attempted to land in Essex a few miles from the coast. Throwing out his grappling iron was unsuccessful, and the balloon bounced back off a copse, dragging the basket across a barley field. A thick hedge served to catch the balloon basket, giving Sadler some rough treatment in the process. The envelope became caught in a tree, causing substantial damage to the balloon - the same one that had crashed into the Bristol Channel on his previous outing. Again, Sadler was extremely fortune to have escaped with relatively minor injuries. His decision to spare his daughter from the experience could well have saved her life.

It is almost impossible to differentiate between Sadler and his sons in reports of the age, so no one is categorically sure how many flights Sadler senior accomplished. *The Bury and Norwich Post* reported that he had accompanied fifteen fights prior to Cambridge, but others report it as the sixteenth or eighteenth. We do know that Sadler exhibited the balloon at Cambridge Town Hall for several days before his Trinity College ascent, raising money towards its construction by charging one shilling admission. Posters and leaflets were distributed around East Anglia, and advertisements printed in the local press, all proclaiming: "Mr Sadler respectfully informs the nobility and gentry, and the public in general that HIS SUPERB BALLOON and GRAND CART are now exhibiting at the Town Hall."

Clearly with debts to pay, Sadler appeared to be running a more financially efficient operation on his return, as proven by his decision to charge a hefty five shillings to gain entrance to the Grand Court to witness the ascent - and risk a mauling from Byron's bear.

12 AUGUST 1811: HACKNEY

Somehow Sadler managed to repair the balloon after its violent, tree-tangled crash landing following the Cambridge ascent. One suspects his balloon was more patches than original envelope. But the cart was irreparable, having splintered into sawdust.

Therefore, with a brand-new wooden cart aboard, Sadler next organised a London launch - the first balloon flight in the capital for several years. Taking off from the garden of the Mermaid Tavern, "so well known as the scene of political meetings", in East London, his strikingly ornate basket made its flight debut. The cart, it is fair to say, was a hit - at least according to contemporary newspaper reports: "Its beauty and brilliance drew forth an involuntary burst of applause." In retrospect, this could just have been an outpouring of relief after a four-hour wait.

Draped with bright yellow silk and matching cushions, crimson velvet and azure blue cloth festooned with satin and gold braid spelt out a message to celebrate the Prince Regent's birthday, alongside an emblem of the Prince of Wales' emblematic feathers "in a triple plume in gold". It was "one of the most superb objects it is possible for ingenuity of man to devise, or which the fancy of the spectator could hope to see realised!" stated *The Morning Post* the next day, with a diminishing grip on perspective.

It was presumably a cart of lighter construction than its predecessor because this time Lieutenant Paget was able to be raised by the considerable pulling power of several tons of hydrogen. But the funnelling of the hydrogen into the balloon stretched the patience of the crowd long before it stretched the balloon frame. Commencing at 9am, the balloon was not sufficiently inflated to be airborne

The first Hackney ascent, 12 August 1811, Sadler on left (Wikipedia Commons)

until 2.30pm. Soon afterwards the pair ascended. "The airy travellers were in sight for about a quarter of an hour." Packing life jackets, ballast and grappling irons for landing, they also had on board two huge bright purple flags: "Bearing the coats of arms of his Highness of the Duke of Gloucester and the Earl of Hardwicke which they continued to wave as they pursued their trackless path, in grateful testimony to the reiterated shouts and plaudits of the innumerable spectators," gushed *The Times*.

Sadler's appeal was undimmed, with the public showing no signs of rejecting ballooning as a fad. Roads to Hackney were thronged with people and carriages representative of all classes. By mid-morning some of the main access roads were reportedly as completely blocked.

Proving that Sadler meant business these days, he had organised a perimeter fence, and admission was controlled by the Tower Hamlets Militia. Three thousand paying customers patiently waited the four hours for the balloon to fill with barrelled hydrogen.

The performance was certainly showbiz by this stage of Sadler's comeback career. When the balloon was fully inflated, and ballast had been placed in the cart by his crew, Sadler emerged from the corner of the gardens dressed sveltely all in black. He then proceeded to walk to the roped cart like a boxer approaching the ring, soaking up the audience's affection and spontaneous applause. Once installed, he gave the signal for all thirty rope-bearers to release their grip, and Sadler climbed clear above the surrounding trees to widening applause.

Not for the first time, however, Sadler had chosen a date with deteriorating weather conditions. With a breeze picking up strongly, he was blown back and forth over the Thames, crossing the East India Docks twice. After an hour and a quarter in the air, the balloon hit the ground at Tilbury Fort in Essex close to the Thames estuary. Attempting to land in what had become a gale was predictably fraught, and after bouncing along the ground Sadler's flying companion Paget was thrown out of the balloon. Fortunately he grasped the side, and remarkably only sustained minor injuries. But once again, the injuries to the balloon envelope were anything but minor.

29 AUGUST 1811: MERMAID TAVERN II

Nietzsche once suggested that doing something exactly the same as before, but expecting a different outcome each time, is a definition of insanity. Quite how mentally unstable Sadler was becoming after far too many bumpy landings is a matter for speculation, but after his latest crash he decided two weeks later to... that's right - take another flight from the same location. This may have been organised as a consequence of the scramble for places a fortnight earlier, with huge numbers struggling to see the first flight. Although 3,000 spectators

"Prime Bang up at Hackney" (Ashmolean Museum, Oxford)

were reported present at the first fight from the Mermaid's gardens, this was a relatively small-scale audience by Sadler's standards. Thus more money was to be taken at the box office by adding a sequel.

A popular cartoonish image in the style of Hogarth was circulated soon after Sadler's first Mermaid Tavern flight. Titled "Prime Bang up at Hackney or a Peep at the Balloon", it depicts the riotous chaos that ensued when a plebeian crowd assembled, smitten with balloonomania and shoving for a glimpse of Sadler's elevation.

One of William Hogarth's paintings - indeed, arguably the artist's most famous work - was to profoundly influence the life of Sadler's co-pilot for his flight on 29 August 1811. Presumably stumping up a huge asking price to accompany Sadler in the basket - likely to have been over 100 guineas - was Henry Benjamin Hanbury Beaufoy.

He was the local MP, representing the constituency of Hackney Wick, and owned a vinegar distillery in South Lambeth after reportedly seeing Hogarth's notorious print *Gin Lane* and deciding to switch from distilling ruinous gin to vinegar. Beaufoy was charitably minded, founding no fewer than four Cambridge University scholarships. He donated considerable sums to education - £10,000 to the City of London School alone, and £14,000 to established "ragged schools" in Lambeth. He compiled a personal library with over 25,000 titles including four copies of Shakespeare's *First Folio*. But the probable reason why Sadler and Beaufoy were brought together was a shared interest in the advancement of rifle barrels - both had undertaken published research on the subject. During his ascent with Sadler, Beaufoy maintained a log recording his observations, thoughts and physical sensations during every minute of the flight.

This time the prevailing wind blew in the same direction as a fortnight previously, although mercifully with no gale, and it took Sadler to Essex again. The pair landed safely at Easthorpe a few miles west of Colchester.

7 OCTOBER 1811: BIRMINGHAM TO ASGARBY

In a precursor to a stunt from *Jackass the Movie*, Sadler took off from Vauxhall Gardens in Birmingham in a force 6 gale. This enabled him to travel to south-east Lincolnshire at an average speed of around 84mph - thereby making him probably the fastest human being in history up to this point - at least the fastest to have survived mainly intact. Such recklessness was shared with his unfortunate co-traveller, a young gentleman John Burcham of Dereham, Norfolk, described as "polite and intelligent" - though not sufficiently intelligent to avoid flying in a hydrogen balloon during a howling gale.

The launch site attracted the customary crowds genuflecting to Sadler's celebrity status. "An irresistible point of attraction to all ranks of people," was how the *Birmingham Gazette* neatly defined his appeal in 1811. Sadler's ascent was greeted by cheering multitudes with several spectators firing guns. Not that small arms fire was anything like as dangerous as what Sadler was about to face: a blowing gale.

Waving both his flags to salute the crowd as he took off, the wind soon snatched them from his hands and they fell to earth. The balloon was presently whipped away by the winds and soared like a comet towards the east coast of Britain, passing above Lichfield, Coventry, Tamworth and Leicester before reaching Lincolnshire almost within an hour of departing Birmingham at 2pm that afternoon. Burcham later stated that they were at their highest point of elevation above Market Deeping, with Sadler's instruments showing an altitude of 2.5 miles, which enabled them to see Peterborough, Wisbech and Crowland from their basket's vantage-point.

With 200lbs of ballast aboard, the foolhardy duo were able to lose height quickly, as Sadler realised that the Wash was looming ominously into view on the horizon. They duly reduced altitude as quickly as possible to avoid the cold waters of the North Sea, but their speed was still worrisome.

It was Sadler's unfortunate passenger Burcham who provided a practical experiment of Newtonian physics (appropriate, as Lincolnshire was Isaac Newton's home county). He ably proved the theory of moving forces by piloting his balloon straight into an ash tree. Narrowly missing a tall church spire in Asgarby, the balloon hit the tree at speed, upturning the basket and returning Burcham roughly to earth. Completing his journey of 112 miles in just over an hour, Sadler was thrown from the basket separately, in the Lincolnshire hamlet of Burton Pedwardine, located a few miles further south. Although he sustained inevitable injuries in the process, this arboreal encounter undisputedly saved his life as the impact shook him clear of the basket seconds before the hydrogen-filled balloon surged upwards again to be last seen heading for the North Sea.

Today Asgarby is barely a hamlet, a scattered handful of buildings. There is a sole building on one side of the "main" street, the out-of-context, splendidly tall-towered Church of St. Andrew. This thirteenth-century parish church, restored in 1870, is a Grade One listed building. There is still an ash tree in the hamlet today, perhaps a direct descendant of the tree that saved Burcham's life by temporarily entangling the balloon, allowing him to jump out. Such was the violence of the storm that "the silk of the balloon hung around an ash tree in the most extraordinary way, tearing itself amongst the branches and tearing itself into a thousand pieces." (Quite a descriptive account, although the thousand pieces managed to re-ascend immediately in the strong winds and soar across the Wash and into the North Sea…)

Burcham and Sadler were both confirmed as concussed, each convinced that the other had died. Eventually, though, they caught sight of one other in Heckington, allowing for an emotional reunion described by a correspondent from Boston, Lincolnshire in a lengthy letter to a local paper: "they flew into each other's arms with such enraptured expressions of joy, as cannot be conceived by those who have not been in circumstances nearly similar!"

The *London Chronicle* confirmed: "Mr Sadler then went to Heckington, and in the street there first saw again his lost companion, each the moment before fancying the other killed." They were taken to the Crown Inn where they stayed until 3am. The next morning a crowd arrived from the nearby town of Sleaford to see the balloon. Several farm workers who had observed the balloon soar above their field earlier, described how they had considered it to be either "a comet or a giant tulip". Obviously.

1 OCTOBER 1812: SADLER ATTEMPTS THE IRISH SEA

A Dublin newspaper reported on Sadler's historic attempt to be the first to fly across the Irish Sea: "The day was particularly favourable to it. The morning was fine, the sky generally clear but slightly interspersed with light fleecy clouds and a brisk gale blew in the direction which the aeronaut wished to steer his flight." A brisk gale? Once again, Sadler had suffered from the ludicrous practice of advertising a flight date in advance.

Suspended between two vast poles, the balloon inflation commenced through a silk pipe at Belvedere House, Drumcondra. After residing nobility Lady Mary Lennox and the Duchess of Richmond had inspected Sadler's balloon, each member of the organising committee paraded from the house to the lawn, carrying aloft Sadler's cart.

Launched into the gale, Sadler's giant balloon rose rapidly, zooming upwards at a disconcerting pace in spite of the eleven hundredweight of ballast in the cart. One observer compared its speed to the champion racehorse of the era, Flying Childers.

Progress in the gale was fast. Sadler commented: "I found myself to the north-west of Holyhead when still being resolved to make the coast of Lancashire, and judging this to be the most favourable opportunity, I opened the valve and by permitting some of the gas to escape, passed to the south of Skerry Light House over Anglesey at an altitude of 3 miles 652 yards." A decision at this point to commence a simple landing above Anglesey would have provided him with the record as the first Irish Sea aviator.

"Had I continued in this direction, a very short period would have brought me over the Coast of Cumberland but my principal object was to terminate the voyage at Liverpool," Sadler stated, "I was however disappointed for the wind shifted more to the southward. I found myself driven in a contrary direction to that which I wished to proceed. In a short time I lost sight of land. The evening was fast closing in."

Obliged by stern necessity, Sadler lobbed the remaining ballast overboard and took his chances at a higher altitude. No favourable wind was found, so he desperately scanned the horizon for potential rescue ships. Darkness was falling rapidly, cloaking the sea in blackness. In the deteriorating light, Sadler spotted approaching shipping. He expelled gas so quickly that he splashed down into the sea like a returning space capsule from an Apollo mission. Sadler recollected: "I observed vessels beating down the Channel and entertained the confident hope that I would meet with prompt assistance that my circumstances would require. I opened the valve and in a few minutes was precipitated into the sea. But to my great mortification I found that the vessels continued their course without paying the least attention to my situation, although there can be little doubt of me being observed – thus deserted." Remarkably, the boats ignored his plight.

This version of events was later confirmed by a correspondent J. Fellows, an agent of Her Majesty's Packets based at Holyhead. He speculated: "The extraordinary circumstances of not receiving assistance from the first vehicle Sadler encountered when he first descended can only be accounted for by the terror his appearance must have occasioned to such people not used to or expecting such a sight. One could hardly conceive it could be from any other cause, or the want of humanity in their crews."

Sadler was left grasping a rapidly deflating balloon in freezing waters. "I was clinging to the netting as a last resource, and in this situation was frequently plunged underwater," he confirmed. Mercifully, another vessel flying the Manx flag came into view and, unlike its predecessor, rescued the stranded aeronaut forty miles north off Great Orme.

A rope was hurled to Sadler. Even then, he was still not out of the water - literally. He disappeared under the surface, before being eventually winched into the boat. "After being dragged through the waves, I eventually got on board with much difficulty, after being in the water for at least half an hour, being quite exhausted, nearly insensible, and almost lifeless - a state in which I remained for a considerable time."

The vessel that saved Sadler was named *Victory*, out from Douglas fishing for herring. Captain John Lee took Sadler to Liverpool where a crowd had assembled at the dockside expecting to spot him. But Sadler was described as too shocked and fatigued to greet his public. Accordingly he was immediately taken aboard a Royal Navy boat *Princess* to Holyhead where he informed locals of his intention to cross the Irish Sea again.

The *Morning Chronicle* reported on 14 October 1812: "We have to inform the numerous friends of Mr Sadler that he has arrived safely back in Dublin a few days since undergoing many hair breath scrapes."

Several earlier Irish Sea attempts had ended in ignominy, including that of Wicklow-born Richard Crosbie, the first Irish aeronaut. A humiliating change of wind direction led him to touch down in Powerstock, over ten miles further west of the Irish Sea than his launch site. Later Crosbie was fined for vandalising Dublin's most popular eighteenth-century brothel – not, it seems, on moral grounds, but in a dispute over pricing.

10 STAIRWAY TO HEAVEN: TO THE NEXT LEVEL

At our next session we make significant progress, and I am beginning to be won over by counselling. My pick-and-mix approach to the talking therapies may have been journalistically-based in origin, but Cognitive Behavioural Theory is a winner. Psychoanalysis provides me with better gag-making opportunities, yet conversely renders me rather sad, locked into an introspective mood after each session. The rusty locks have been forced open to reveal memory banks inaccessible for decades storing forgotten humiliations, rejections and disappointments. Do not underestimate the kick-back when you force open the lock on these emotions, as potent as striking minor chords to evoke instant sadness.

In preparation for my balloon flight, I am ratcheting up my exposure theory. Several studies have shown that prolonged periods of exposure to the cause of an abstract fear is better for re-training my brain's anxiety mechanism than short but frequent sessions. Gradually I am getting the faulty warning light to stop flickering on in my brain when I am really in no physical danger.

The therapy revolves around exposing me to my fear, until the anxiety gradually dissipates. Hence I go with a friend and stand as close as I can to the edge of a banister with a drop of one floor below - only one floor, but it triggers acute panic in me. As close as I can get constitutes me hugging the wall. Discomfort does not diminish as I millimetre nearer to the edge.

Then I try again. Reaching the edge of the banister repels me like a magnet, shooting me back to the nearest wall with a potent invisible force. Determined to persevere until I can do this, I discover that fear of public embarrassment is a strong motivator. John Cleese once remarked that Englishmen are determined to reach their graves unembarrassed, and if avoiding embarrassment means I have to accomplish something genuinely terrifying that my brain has miscoded, then given it's an English brain it will always choose avoidance over potential embarrassment.

I ask my counsellors if they have any visualisation techniques that may work, instead of me having to go to the edge. Quite correctly, Steve recognises me trying to initiate an avoidance technique for my homework.

My behavioural intervention strategy is not that pleasant, but like most medicine I make myself swallow it. I need to get better with heights, because at the moment an hour in a balloon floating 3,000 feet over Oxfordshire will not only ensure I scream with terror, but my behaviour will also rather ruin the experience of my fellow passengers who will have paid around £125 each.

"How was your anxiety-eliciting stimulus affected?" asks Claire. I like the fact she doesn't need to de-jargonise for me anymore. I interpret it as the compliment it's meant to be. Her unspoken subtext I interpret as: "We know you're smart enough to understand our technical psychological language. Just because you're frightened of heights and experience manifested difficulties in going upstairs doesn't mean we think you're an idiot."

"How would life be better for you if you had no trouble negotiating stairs?" Claire asks me, signalling with a tonal change that we are back into the session. She's wearing her counsellor's game face again. I need to answer honestly, truthfully if this is going to help me. "I would feel less like a failed adult." It would certainly be a start to gluing back together my shattered sense of masculinity. Claire and Steve continue incentivising me, regularly topping up my desire to reduce restrictive anxiety.

Throughout my teenage years I suffered from OCD. Maybe I should save that revelation until I am world famous and I can sell the obligatory misery memoir to a publisher for the Christmas hardback biography market. Because that's what people in this country appear to want for Christmas: overpriced, ghost written autobiographies about the rich and famous having an unpleasant time.

Nowadays, in an increasingly psychologically literate nation, the acronym OCD doesn't usually require explanation that it stands for: Obsessive Compulsive Disorder. But I think it is only courteous to explain acronyms as otherwise it is an aggressive barrier to clear communication.

There is a responsive prevention technique for sufferers. For example, an OCD sufferer imprisoned by perpetual hand washing rituals is told to touch the inside of a bin. Normally this would trigger acute anxiety and continued involuntarily ritualistic hand scrubbing. However, in a controlled environment, sufferers are told they cannot wash their hands.

At the beginning this is only for a few minutes, but in later sessions it can be much longer. Initially sufferers will become so agitated they will sometimes cry. Yet, like the determination often required for physical improvement, there is no gain without pain. And sometimes no sane without pain either.

After a while the substantial majority of acute OCD sufferers realise, no matter how unwillingly, that not washing their hands for twenty minutes after touching the inside of a dirty bin does not kill them. In fact, it has virtually no effect at all on their physical well-being. By repeatedly proving that the physical self is unharmed, the malfunctioning anxiety reluctantly learns to dissipate.

It can be a slow learner, the amygdala, and frankly my amygdala, like most people's, is a bit thick. The point is that germs in bins don't tend to kill you.

Cancer, heart attacks, high cholesterol, speeding cars and girlfriends who check your text messages tend to kill you. Yet having an abject anxiety-inducing phobia towards beer, burgers, fags and cars is surprisingly uncommon - given these represent actual sensible life-threatening factors.

Behavioural intervention does help with stairs. If you avoid something, it is unlikely to get better - I'm pretty sure that works for most other things too. Avoiding the kitchen doesn't mean the washing-up will get done.

"I think we should encourage self-exposure," says Steve. They ask me to log my exposure, and call it a "living with fear manual". They set targets and we review them. I genuinely want to make progress as I feel a strong compulsion not to waste their time. I feel ridiculous standing at the bottom of steep, backless stairs and then making myself go up them repeatedly, edging closer to first- then second-floor landings with sheer drops below. But I know this has to be done to be cured, for me to become self-judged as "normal" - whatever that is - is a justifiable outcome whatever the methodology.

Yet in situ on a stairwell the frightened panic does not wholly subside, although the volume level of anxiety becomes progressively turned-down after repeated exposure.

One of the most useful insights counselling, and especially CBT, provided me with was the inoculation against awarding false credit for my successes. This was a destructive behaviour I had unwillingly and unknowingly been engaged in for years. Whenever I scooted up stairs with the pace and confidence of a teenager trying to reach their bedroom to slam the door after an argument with their parents, I was incorrectly attributing my successes to false circumstance: it wasn't the scary type of stairs; it was because no one else was around; it was because they were wide, or shallow, or familiar, etc.; and an extra thousand etcs.

So I do something that in the last decade has come to the rescue of everyone who is terrified of stairs or heights, that lets them stand around for no apparent reason without revealing they are temporarily paralysed by fear. I get out my phone. People seem to tolerate phone checking as acceptable behaviour wherever you are standing (well, with some exceptions: No Man's Land next to an Israeli border being one example I learnt the hard way. Oh, and during sex, it turns out, is also frowned upon. Who knew?).

Like a Victorian canal owner threatened by the arriving speedier railways, a psychoanalyst dismissed CBT in *The Guardian* in 2008 as "a quick fix for the soul". Personally, my soul would be delighted with any quick fixes - the sooner anything sheds my anxieties and repressive irrational terrors, the better. Where the canals-superseded-by-railways analogy also works is with the comparison of past versus future in the two adopted counselling approaches I experienced. Psychoanalysis, by definition, conducts an autopsy on the past, promulgating that the past therefore informs the present. Yes, to an extent, it does - history may have already happened, but it does rather set our current circumstances. However, CBT focuses on where we spend all out time: the present. CBT focuses on current thinking models. Change the thinking, change the response, change the behaviour. Like the railways replacing the canals, CBT gets us to the same destination a lot quicker than going via the psychoanalytical route.

Typically a handful of CBT sessions will suffice, whilst it is possible to die of natural causes before a psychoanalytic counsellor completes their theory. Cynics may argue that CBT's inclusion on NHS treatment spreadsheets, and official recognition in the NICE guidelines, is because of its cheapness. But cost-effectiveness is measured in the NHS not only by the patients seen, but also by the ones they don't see because of mental health problems eradicated further upstream. NICE, the National Institute for Health and Clinical Excellence, officially endorses CBT, as well as the policy that words beginning with "H" should be omitted from acronyms.

Counselling requires inevitable adjustment for a shy and relatively retiring individual like me, neither experienced nor comfortable with discussing myself continuously. Callous experience of Jean-Paul Sartre's hellish other people has shaped my belief that anyone speaking should be capped at thirty seconds. After thirty seconds, sometime else has a turn to speak, or signals you may continue. This avoids directionless, tedious monologues and conversation-hoggers scoring highly on the I-ometer (an imaginary machine I've invented for determining the ratio of I's peppering an individual's conversation). It also encourages an efficiency of language, and the pressure of thirty seconds should ensure that points are made quicker - rather than encouraging conversation monopolisers who prefer to take slow connecting trains to reach the point.

Early on in my sessions I discovered that "so, what about you…" is not a permitted conversational direction in counselling. These questions are trumped by the higher suited cards that a counsellor can play, the ones which supersede my question about them, out-ranking me with a "and how do you feel about that?" Constant exposure to this sort of question is alien, though does not risk disenchantment or disenfranchisement with the medium as I desperately want to neutralise and shed anxiety from my life. That is always my focused motivation.

Claire and Steve remind me of that, but crucially allow me to respond to the question: "what areas would you most like to deal with in this time?" Of course, some people love the indulgence of discussing the only subject that matters: themselves. But I don't.

Although it's an accidental career choice, I have gigged many times as a stand-up comedian. Victoria Wood is a stand-up comedian too, only less accidental than me. Both of us, however, are equally shy people off stage. She told *The Guardian* in 2010: "But I think it's not a paradox. Often these children who feel they don't quite fit in, they're not part of the group - I think a lot of very seemingly shy people have got this ability to connect with a group, rather than one-on-one."

Steve and Claire understand such self-contradictory cognitive dissonance. Most people, believe me, don't.

Soon any subconscious dissent towards counselling culture dissipates, and I slowly release the brakes on discussing my personal innermost feelings. After several sessions I discover this new-found freedom to articulate feelings and thoughts that I would previously ensure remained tightly sealed within my own head - inexpressible to anyone. Claire and Steve are equipped at getting these comments out of me, and after a while I no longer pretend that these raw personal insights can be dismissed as set-up for an inevitable punch line.

As the jokes decline, the insights increase. Paramount in the process is the trust I feel in Steve and Claire's presence, enabling me to express the formerly inexpressible. Rather than never inform another human being of my shaming inability to undergo the most basic of tasks without harbouring prickly anxiety, now my resistance to communicating these truths has evaporated.

I continue to undergo various homework exercises designed to dissect my emotional responses. Eventually it becomes apparent to me, that Steve and Claire's presence and questioning are designed to re-examine my reported experiences from an entirely different perspective, freeing me to evaluate and process recurrent experiences and anxieties. Once my thought processes are projected onto another person, the irrationality becomes far easier to spot, like an image under ultra-violet light.

We all project an image of ourselves to the world - often if we're honest (which we rarely are, especially to ourselves) containing considerable photo-shopping embellishment. Then it clicks. A piercing realisation of what the talking therapies and CBT can achieve. Counselling provides a rare opportunity to flip over that photograph and read what's written on the back. The information contained there is vital to establish who you are, and what others are really looking at when they encounter that image.

Anyone going to Thailand to "find themselves" or contemplating justifying a twelve-month holiday after university (twelve months off from what? Texting your friends, playing *Grand Theft Auto* and two for one cocktail promotions?) is seeking enlightenment in the wrong place. CBT can provide insights. The counsellors lead you to the truth, but you're the one who still has do the actual picking it up. Relearning key areas of my phobic fight-or-flight activation is crucial to re-programming my brain. Perhaps counselling is akin to downloading an anti-virus software package for the brain.

Intellectual processing responses are exercised, and the more muscle they've got, the less they can be bullied and ordered around by unhelpful emotions. A primitive emotional response can be dismantled at source by better thought processing - that's CBT's mission, and also Claire and Steve's mission.

At its best CBT confronts irrational belief. Responding to non-verbal cues, CBT's approach interrupts destructive thought loops, challenges them. My negative catastrophizing thoughts have been getting their own way, unchallenged for far too long. Thoughts need to engage with emotions to produce a considered, rather than irrational, response. In its purest form, CBT aims to change how a person thinks, in order to change how they feel.

I am encouraged to spot the false danger signals. Counselling helps me identify and label my thoughts, tagging each response to my fears. My counsellors help me sort my thoughts, allocating them into either helpful or destructive responses. Recognising this is important and interpreting them as false alarms is crucial. This is what my counsellors term "image restructuring" - I have to interpret the difference between image and reality. My brain can do this in front of a TV screen, but is apparently not so good at interpreting live action. Yes, I will jump if watching a scary scene in a thriller, so my brain is being suckered in by the experience, but thankfully the mature, grown-up, on-duty part of my brain is aware that I am in a safe environment and that this is just a telly programme. It's just not so good dealing with live images, where my external perception apparently competes for resources with my brain's memory store of internal images.

Pattern matching is only going to reinforce my terror. My counsellor calls this "time for some cranial photo-shopping", meaning that my scary images stored in my internal memory have to be edited - and re-shot to reflect life more accurately - to replace my brain's stock library footage of terrors.

It is as if my brain has been asked to draw a picture of a landscape or a still life bowl of fruit, and instead of reflecting reality, has covered the Wiltshire landscape with threatening lions or added grenades to the fruit bowl. Once armed with this knowledge of how the brain is tricking itself into becoming more fearful than is necessary for given situations, it is surprisingly helpful. It soon becomes possible to catch yourself falling into these deep troughs of worry, and become better at recognising the trigger signs and, conversely, avoiding the dangers.

In a way I am disappointed with myself that such a simple fix can help. Part of me wants to reject such simplicity, stating that surely my brain is so advanced and smart that it requires prolonged exposure to complex theories - probably involving equations - than merely what I've described above. But then I've known since an early age that I was an idiot. "You're not an idiot," my counsellor

Claire reassures me. Which was very nice of her, though I hadn't mentioned the subject of idiots out loud. Or assumed, frankly, I was one until she took pains to dissuade me of my idiot status.

My counsellors continue encouraging me to examine my fears, and by so doing defuse the potency of those thoughts' tagged emotions. If my thoughts are sheep, then I am being encouraged to place them into pens. "What are the listed advantages and disadvantages of my current behaviour?" "What are the failings and benefits of my desired behaviour?"

These are then further sifted into short-, medium- and long-term benefits. Indisputably the lesson I learn - and I hope my brain is also paying attention and not doing what it usually does in classrooms, trying to order Prog Rock bands into order of which one had the most facial hair - is to accept that the bad thoughts my anxiety triggers are not based on reality. This separation of real and imagined danger sounds obvious, but so does anorexia. In the latter case the absolute necessity of nutrition to survive is distortedly re-imagined and reinterpreted by the brain as damaging to the body. It's so obviously wrong. So just eat something, right? Well, the majority of people who contract anorexia fail to recover. Over half literally starve themselves to death - often, though not exclusively, young girls - blessed with healthy, youthful bodies. But the brain can be this wrong, and this destructive, that it kills its owner.

Unusually for an artist, he doesn't have a fulltime job in a call centre. I know successful comedy writers who regularly have their work aired on BBC Radio 4 who still can't afford to escape the tyranny of the call centre job; one recently calculated that their rate of pay was £6.84 an hour, which equates to roughly £1.14 per "fuck off".

But a fellow comedy writer supervises my confrontation with stairs. They are nasty stairs. Not the worst possible stairs - those protruding bars from the side of a wall with no backs or handrails are the worst. But bad enough.

I complete the task, my practical exercise, but cannot banish feelings of embarrassment. Also I am aware the stairs were shallow, wide and easy. Then I remember Claire telling me specifically to award myself the credit, not delegate it to spurious circumstance.

If my ambition to succeed remains undimmed, so do my feelings of guilt. There are numerous elderly people in this country who cannot afford to fall over, as it will mean serious - possibly permanent - injury. They have a real rationalising reason to be terrified of stairs, and an understandable justification to adopt avoidance techniques. While I am not as young as I once was - nor is anyone, since that seems to be how time works - my bones will not shatter if I fall over. My dignity and limbs may be bruised, but that's about it. Hence, as per usual, I am flooded with guilt for being frightened of stairs, and wobbling in anxiety. Frankly, I do not consider myself a justifiable burden on the over -stretched, creaking NHS. That is why many anxiety and phobia sufferers never address their debilitating conditions. And yes, there may well be recognisable self-esteem issues in play here.

Mine was not the happiest of childhoods due to low self-esteem. In fact my self-esteem was more subterranean than low. But I did have a best friend and a girlfriend - although they were both imaginary. I think I could have coped with that fact, had not the stinging rejection occurred when my imaginary best friend had an affair with my imaginary girlfriend and they ran off together. That's the sort of self-esteem issue it's hard to rebound back from straight away. Okay, so I'm joking to disguise a truth, yet by so doing expose a truth. Low self-esteem and leaking confidence are inevitable when you suffer from phobias and multiple anxieties.

This is something picked up by Steve and Claire. My counselling sessions have added a sense of buoyancy to my self-esteem. In addition to this, my sessions have also made me develop a sense of wanting do well for Claire and Steve because they must also be wondering if they can shape a difference in their clients. If I, their first client in the wild, end up continuing as a spectacular failure after the hours of indulgence they have afforded me, this will potentially not reflect well on their confidence - nor the Supervisor's opinion of them.

Steve and Claire both feel it is their destiny to be counsellors, a focused assumption that I genuinely envy them for possessing, an assured realisation of unbreakable confidence that there is something in the world they fit and want to do. There are many people who I can imagine working on the tills at Tesco - myself included - but I cannot image Claire doing that job. "Have you got a Reward Card? How does not having a Reward Card make you feel? Were there any traumatic occurrences in your childhood involving not having a Reward Card that you'd like to share? You're a marvellous, wonderful human being with so much to offer, so how fair is it to define yourself purely as a person who does not have a Reward Card?" At which stage Claire would be sacked after the tills supervisor noticed the disproportionately long queue constantly formed at her till: "How does sacking me make you feel?" (By the way, I currently hold so-called "loyalty cards" for five separate supermarkets, so it is clear I am a disloyal serial non-monogamous supermarket infidelity practitioner). I like Claire and Steve. They have a genuine attribute of wanting to do good for people, wishing to release them from imprisoning worry loops. It's a borderline angelic quality.

Actually this is getting stressful, but I do not want to let them down. Myself I have never had a problem with letting down. This is an aspect to counselling that no doubt contributes to its success - the feeling of connected responsibility to your counsellor. We have moved from awkward small talk to a sense of emotional investment in each other, something that would be unlikely to be formed in any other relationship with someone you never see socially, and only meet for one hour a week.

After a while I realise that a key component of counselling is the act of establishing an unavoidable reporting structure. Someone to inform of your progress and setbacks that drives you forward, motivating the bolder push of collected fears up an incline to reach a summit with higher views of yourself where it can be rolled away. I am here for the psychological insights that will enable me to roll away my restrictive foibles that rob life of its multiple flavours.

Counsellors are fearless truth tellers. At least good ones are. They are the critics who encourage you to write your own reviews, plot your own constructive improvement. And I want to tell Claire and Steve the truth in my next scheduled session: that I went upstairs on a bus. They have set me this frankly enormous task - something I have failed to do in my entire life. Unlike school homework - and if you're a school kid, prepare to experience a pang of envy here - my homework has to be done "whenever I feel ready".

My ambition to go upstairs on a bus remains undiminished, but is bolstered by receiving a supportive shove up those bus stairs. In my desperation to escape the swarm of morons seemingly resulting from unchecked idiot breeding programmes throughout the UK, I receive the extra impetus I require to go upstairs on a bus for the first time.

What most other people do unthinkingly, often on a daily basis, I am now going to attempt for the first time in my entire life. That's a long time to avoid something. Previously I was locked out of this place by phobic anxiety, but now I am going inside.

I am waiting in a bus queue and two young guys, probably students, stand behind me. One is freakishly tall and thin with a Beatles-like haircut, the other short and stodgy. Viewed from a distance, they resemble a mop and bucket.

Then two undergraduate girls join the queue, and I become increasingly aware that I am the only person here who is not a student. This appears to render me invisible as students continue their conversations around me. The more brunette of the two girls is wearing a short pink jacket the colour of strawberry ice cream. Noticeably, she is also wearing a pair of shorts so tiny that she evidently sourced them from a doll, then washed them at a high temperature to ensure they shrank a bit more. Her friend has struggled into a miniskirt and low sleeveless top. Between them they are wearing just about enough clothes to dress one person.

The tall and short guys start peacocking behind me. "Yeah, so I was out wearing my best pulling jacket - £300 of hand-stitched material, worth every penny for the action that's brought me." Annoyingly, he continues: "I went to this new place. I was only there two minutes when this fit bird wisely starts to gives me the eye…" I assume he's talking about a visit to an owl sanctuary.

Only he's not. I've never hoped more for an imminent bus arrival. "Problem being, and not for the first time, her equally fit mate is also giving me the eye, you get me, bro?" Stop talking with a Jamaican accent: I know you're from Buckinghamshire.

After only ten seconds of enforced listening I conclude that it is because of guys like him that many women end up settling for a life with cats.

"Oh yeah, that is so totally me too - I always get fit birds and their mates both wanting me," boasts Loud Tall Guy's short stodgy mate. Unconvincingly.

What are the remarkable statistical chances of this occurrence? Being in the same place at the same time with both Britain's biggest and second biggest idiot? Really, what are the odds?

Boarding the bus, I take my customarily lifelong position on the lower deck. Britain's two leading idiots come and sit behind me carrying on their conversation at window-rattling volume. "So I thought, why not ask them both if they want a drink and get myself double the action?" bellows the tall one. "That's just what I would have done," confirms the Deputy Idiot, struggling to see through his ridiculously low fringe that blows upwards when he speaks.

"Did I tell you I made two grand on selling that piece of crap motor? Used it for my golf holiday in my brother's Portuguese place… got my handicap of nine down." What's "a handicap of nine"? Does that refer to your reading age? Its certainly way too old for your emotional age.

Then the two undergraduate girls occupy the bus seat directly in front of me and proceed to start a conversation at a volume more appropriate to making yourself heard between rescue boats in a storm.

"Do you like my latest impulse piercing? I've just had it, so there's still a lot of pus," announces Tiny Shorts. The man next to me stops his coffee cup lift midway to his mouth, places it back down on his laptop bag, reapplies the lid and pushes it away. It will be a while before any of us will feel like eating and drinking.

Then a scream of feral schoolgirls get on and take up the remaining seats around us.

That's it. Like a man working at McDonalds after three days of missed beverage accessory deliveries, I finally announce, "right, that's the last straw". I have to escape these "people". I have to go upstairs, on a double-decker bus. The bus is stationary, so now is a good time to start the ascent. A small child gets on and bounces up the steps; feelings of intense inadequacy start to flower within. But I can do this. After all, I am physically fit, over six feet tall and able bodied. I am incredibly fortunate - a lot of people are physically unable to ascend stairs.

I grasp the handrail more gratefully than an out-reached hand offered from a cliff top. Instead of pacing steps one at a time, I deliberately put my right foot down, and then bring the left one up to rest on the same step. Slowly I reach the top. So, this is what the top deck of the bus looks like. My first observation is that there is no driver on the top.

People reported to me that in previous decades all I missed out on was a fog of tobacco smoke so thick that no one could see when their stop arrived, so would randomly guess when they needed to ring the bell and go downstairs.

But I've made the top deck. There are good views into people's front gardens. My school friend Patrick Allen told me that he could see a naked woman through her curtain-less bedroom window every day from the top deck on the bus home from school, but I did not believe him. There would have been too much smoke. Bedsides, who's naked at 4pm?

Descending the stairs on buses is never easy. Mail bags are allowed more time to depart a moving train than upstairs passengers are allowed to alight from a bus. I take such an unnecessarily long time to descend the stairs, deliberately ensuring my left foot joins my right, before my right foot takes the next step, and holding the rail tighter than a Yorkshireman holds his wallet. Disembarking from the bus, I actually pretend to limp as I leave the bus stop environment to justify the time I've taken. But I've done it. And feel proud of the accomplishment. Perhaps more for Claire and Steve than myself.

At the next counselling session it dawns on me that, as an ex-journalist, my big story that I am proudly reporting is basically: Man Goes Upstairs On Bus. They are not going to drop the dead donkey - or even dead hamster story - for that on the news. Yet Claire is so impressed with me, she looks like being the first one to require the tissue box.

Counselling rooms always provide an immediate visual clue as to the likelihood of emotions clients can reasonably expect to encounter within, in the same way that betting shops always provide multiple "Bet Here" windows, contrasting astringently with a lone "Pay Out" window. Sure enough, as a signaller of the turbulent sentimentality ahead, a tissue box is provided as standard in all consultation rooms. It is always on the side of the table nearest to the client. Claire is so overcome that her voice audibly wobbles. She disguises a preliminary blubber as an elongated sniff. I have done them proud. I am more pleased for them than me, and carefully share the proportioned credit, ensuring all three of us receive exactly one-third each.

Cleverly Steve steps in, realising that Claire has temporarily benched herself by losing a fight with emotion. An occupational hazard I guess. Actors risk corpsing at inappropriate moments, counsellors risk the opposite: spontaneous crying they cannot stop. "So sorry," she says. "It's more than alright, Claire," I say, assuming a newly found authority to use her name. I guess new policemen and detectives routinely throw up when they see their first gruesome murder. It takes repeated exposure over time to build up an emotionally indifferent response. Not unlike the graded exposure that I'm going through, albeit without the grisly murder scenes.

Claire and Steve smile. It's a nice, warm smile. Then Steve unzips a metaphorical tracksuit and comes off the sub's bench onto the field of play. While Claire is momentarily incapacitated on the sidelines working her way through a box of Kleenex's finest man-size try-ply, he proceeds to play a blinder. Carefully constructing through unimpeachable logic that I deserve all the plaudits for my actions, his questions smartly ensure I do not distribute false credit to erroneous factors such as magical thinking scenarios.

After five minutes, and sixteen tissues, Claire announces herself back in the game. Unaware what her opening question will be, I know with unshakeable certainty that it will be an open not closed question. Lovely as she is, Claire routinely answers any question you ask her with another. They embolden my confidence with height anxiety, skilfully asking questions that prompt me into an increasing realisation that I can now handle altitude. Dangers are imagined, not real.

Claire is keen to do more psychological archaeology, and digs a test trench over my formative years to see if she can unearth anything valuable. When I report my terrible falls downstairs aged three and four, she looks like someone whose metal detector's bleep has just uncovered a haul of priceless coins.

"There isn't much to recall, other than I fell hopelessly head over heels. Not in love, but literally head over heels down the stairs. Looking back, it was amazing I was not seriously injured," I reveal. "I was evidently bouncy and resilient, like a cartoon character. I'm ashamed of myself for not being sensitive to my parents' feelings as it must have been heart-stopping terror for them too."

"How much can you remember the physical pain?" Steve asks.

"I can't, but it terrified me for years. Better make that decades. OK, let's upgrade that to until this time last week," I reply.

"Hmm. What are you frightened of most?" Steve enquires.

"Doing it again I suppose," I answer.

"How likely is that?" he wonders. (The subtext being: "You're a healthy strong adult now.")

That was a good move on their part. It might have been a checkmate move, but there is one square where I can still move my king of anxieties to escape. The terror of the incident is too easily recalled. "Well, I distinctly remember falling all the way down the stairs, like a human slinky," I announce, "and just being terrified of that ever happening again."

"When did that happen? And if it was a very long time ago, why should that still be threat now to the adult you?" enquires Claire.

"OK, I was about three or possibly four years old. But it happened twice," I clarify.

She throws me a "my last point still stands". She's good at this non-verbal communication Counsellors are demonstrably attuned to speaking without verbal dialogue.

They ask me establishing questions, designed for me to conclude that my abject restrictive terror of heights is unlikely to be a genuine warning signalled by my amygdala.

Claire asks me how likely it is that I will die falling down the stairs, now I have proved my capability to negotiate bus stairs safely. I interpret her logic and agree it is unlikely.

However, according to actuarial mortality tables, two people died in the UK in 2008 in tea-cosy related incidents and more people were killed by confrontations with drink vending machines.

In reality an average of 644 people die each year in the UK from falling downstairs. You may check that the front door is securely locked, or several times if you have OCDs like me, in order to necessitate a good night's snug sleep, but one of the biggest domestic killers is already inside your house: the stairs. Around sixty people a year in Britain die falling from ladders, and over another hundred are killed from accidental falls from high places.

Those much-maligned keepers of a safe Britain, The Health & Safety Executive - stalked prey of Middle England and the right-wing press - reported that 2,522 employees suffered "major injury" after falling from height in 2013. Tragically 25 workers suffered fatal falls from a high altitude in one year alone.

The Health and Safety Laboratory's Falls on Stairways Literature Review by Anita Scott (2005) remains the definitive monograph on the subject in the UK.

(Skip the next few paragraphs if you don't want to know what happens in the monograph and are awaiting the blockbuster movie version of the book instead.)

The report neatly encapsulates the scenario of falling down stairs with the Templer quote: "To fall down stairs is not only to fall off a cliff, but to fall on rocks below, for the nosings of steps presents a succession of sharp edges."

The research produced some terrifying findings. Be prepared to be scared, very scared, of that killing machine in your hall and landing.

Scott's paper on stair safety reports: "Most stair injuries occur in the home. In the UK there are nearly as many deaths each year from accidents in the home as from traffic accidents. Falls account for over half of these accidental deaths, and half of the deaths from falls relate to stairs. There are an estimated further one quarter of a million non-fatal accidents on stairs in the home each year, which are serious enough to cause the victim to visit their GP or hospital Accident and Emergency department. It has been calculated that this rate of falls is equivalent to a domestic accident on stairs every 2.5 minutes." Before correctly concluding: "Most stair accidents occur in domestic settings."

This compounds the theory that as a society we are encouraged to fear the things most that provide the least threat. Parents ferry their offspring to the school gates in 4x4 vehicles to avoid the bogey man abducting them - yet while there are one or two horrendous examples in the news of UK abductions each year, several thousand youngsters are injured - a few fatally - in vehicle-related accidents. It's the ones we willingly welcome into our homes and driveways to live amongst our families that are the real danger: cars and stairs.

It's no safer overseas. "In Japan during 1976 almost as many people died from falling on steps on stairs (541) as from fires (865). In Canada in 1985, injuries and fatalities on stairs greatly outnumber (by about one order of magnitude) those from all natural disasters."

Thankfully, in the UK at least, someone is on the case - the stair case - to improve safety. And muzzle this domestic killer. "The building regulations have controlled stairway design since 1944, however, they are not retrospective. As a result, there are many buildings in existence which do not meet the current required standards. Building regulations control aspects such as handrail and balustrade heights; step widths, goings and risers, and the step materials and lighting requirements for stairs."

Nowadays legislative Building Regulations decree: "Stairs and landings should be provided with protection against falling over the edge of the treads. Guarding height should be no less than 900mm above the pitch line of the stairs and not less than 1100mm above landings. In addition to guarding, every step with two or more rises should have a continuous handrail to provide guidance and support to those using the stair. Handrails are required to be beside the bottom two steps in a stairway if the stairway is in a public building or is intended for use by disabled people. Handrails should help an individual to regain balance in the event of a fall, and thus reduce the severity of injuries that may result," Scott confirms.

Scott's monograph utilised videotape research: "Videotape has been used to analyse stair fall." Presumably some poor out-of-work actor had to spend several days constantly falling downstairs. He must have felt like a detainee in a South African police station (oh, bit of - hopefully outdated- politics). They must have been tempted to gain additional research funding by posting some of the footage to *You've Been Framed!* to win £250.

The trend is improving; it used to be in excess of 10,000 workers a year (2009) who incurred major injuries after falling from height or downstairs, yet alone domestic carnage described above.

On this evidence bathmophobia and acrophobia are undeserving of that "ir" prefix in "irrational".

Celebrities ranging from 31-year-old Sandy Denny, lead singer with folk rockers Fairport Convention, to boxing commentator Harry Carpenter, died tumbling downstairs. In August 2013 a 46-year-old man died falling down the stairs of a double-decker bus.

And a true horror scene greeted early risers leaving their luxury New York apartments in August 2012 when they discovered the body of 29-year-old socialite Carlisle Brigham, daughter of one of the city's leading investment bankers. She was described by the *Daily Mail* as "dressed all in white and lying in a pool of blood on the stairwell". She had fatally tripped on stairs in high heels. If even the young, rich, famous and beautiful can die falling downstairs, then that proved my fear was legitimate. Plus in today's culture, a celebrity indulging in any activity surely legitimises it.

I decide not to recount these incidents or thoughts to Steve and Claire. Not that they would consider my thoughts off-subject, but I don't want to introduce rain clouds to our celebratory parade.

Claire continues to be careful to avoid any "why" questions. I guess the trick - Claire would no doubt prefer the word "skill" - is to prise open the client's reluctance to speak, without them feeling fired at by a relentless shelling of questions.

"So the worst thing that can possibly happen on stairs occurred, and you weren't even injured?"

"I take your point, Claire, but I was injured badly."

"Sorry," she apologises, "I guess what I meant to ask was even though you were injured a lot you weren't... Well... you know... not permanently injured or killed, well, sort of... you know what I mean?" she states, rather unconvincingly, by her usual slick standards.

"True," I agree.

"How much did you display a tendency to avoid stairs at school?" asks Steve.

"A lot," I admit. "Plus I was infatuated with a girl called Charlotte Jones who only ever travelled on the top deck of the bus."

"Perhaps the shame and pain came from there, not the physical pain of falling down stairs," Claire proffers, before remembering she has to phrase every comment as a question. "Can you recall when was the last time you fell down stairs?"

"Yes. Four years old, I guess. I take your point." I reply.

"How do you remember your primary school times?" she asks, clearly relieved I don't have another inappropriate nickname anecdote.

"Schooldays can be a petri dish of potent emotions," I respond.

"That's true. Was Charlotte's ability to climb stairs damaging to your developing masculinity?" she asks, difficultly.

"That's a hard question. We're getting a bit Freudian now - or is it Jungian? I don't know enough to call the difference," I continue, addressing Steve. "She's not going to suddenly ask me when I first noticed my mother was attractive, is she?" I say to returning smiles from Claire and Steve.

"A lot of Freudian psychology is now discredited," she beams.

"Oh, so it's Freudian then. You were after discovering my persona," I say friendlily.

Actually, persona is Jungian. He adopted the phrase and imported it into psychology. It is the Latin word for "mask". Pure psychoanalytical counselling can be ineffective at worse and extremely time consuming at best. And always, whatever the outcome, objectionably expensive. So I will not be taking that route. CBT on this evidence appears a much more effective way to go. This is a relief to know. Not just because I don't want to discover my buried id probably really fancies Claire - or Steve - when my super ego's not around, but because I was concerned about taking deep sea dives into the murk of my past to discover, examine and search major wrecks in my life.

The only way I can compete with this is to be funny. Their method is better than mine.

"I was completely ginger throughout primary school," I inform them. Which is absolutely true. I even had a full set of freckles, attracting approximately 40% of every "oi, do you sunbathe under a tea strainer" remarks uttered in 1970s South Lincolnshire.

"Were you teased then?" Claire asks with a concerned sadness.

"Yes," I acknowledge truthfully.

"Why?" asks Steve incredulously. It's a kind and instinctive question, rather than a counsellor's reflective response.

"Probably because I was ginger and 'out'. By that I mean not living a closeted strawberry blonde lie. Oh, how 'my people' have suffered historical prejudice. I'm not a gingerest but… Some of my best friends are ginger'… Two tell-tale lines used by the casual gingerest," I say.

They both laugh. This encourages me to continue.

"Prepare to be horrified," I say, "when you learn the names my people have historically suffered. Like at school I was expected to answer to 'Ginger Minger', 'Carrot Top', 'Swan Vesta', 'Thermometer Head', 'Rusty Nuts', 'Ginger Puss', 'Fries With Ketchup On Top', 'Fanta Pubes', 'Ronald McDonald', 'Hair Lice on Fire', 'Muff on Fire', 'Orangutan Features', 'Freckletits' and 'Tampon Head'."

"That's awful," says Claire.

"Yeah, the teachers could be very cruel when doing the register," I say, nailing the topper.

This actually makes Claire laugh when she didn't want to. This shows how our relationship has grown through the counselling process - there's room for personal jokes now, and a bringing-in-games end of term feel. It accentuates their decision to conclude our counselling. We've come as far as we can, and we have definitely arrived somewhere better - and higher - than our departure place a few weeks earlier.

Steve can't speak for laughing, and so it is his turn to be temporarily benched. "After our little comedy interlude," she continues, then pauses, without finishing the sentence. But she's basically saying, "And we're back after the break." Then she says: "OK, time to put on my serious counsellor face."

"Your persona?" I suggest.

"Yes. We need you to do some more homework."

"Oh, Miss… do I have to?" I mock whine.

"Yes you do. If we're going to maintain your progress and enable you to go up in a balloon."

"I did a media thing with a blonde Australian model the other day and…"

"Is this going to be a funny anecdote?" cautions Claire.

"Probably, but that's not my reason for recounting it. OK, I understand why you're both making those faces, but it isn't."

"How helpful to do you think telling us this anecdote will be in helping you reduce your acrophobia and anxieties?" asks Claire neutrally.

"Not sure. I suppose it's helping me get material," I answer.

"Are you here to get material or help confront anxieties?" asks Claire. And resists adding the word "check!" at the end of her sentence.

I inform them of what the Australian model said. Claire and Steve approve. They are also careful to praise me throughout for reaching the top deck on the bus.

"That is a very good line to remember. If that helps you, and I can see why it should be helpful, then you should remember it, and play the line back to yourself when you feel anxious," Claire counsels. "You were right to tell us the anecdote," she adds kindly.

Then it finally hits home. If counselling is anxiety management, then the breakthrough moment occurs when I realise that a lot of what our brains think they know is chronically out of date. Like someone still using Windows 1.1 and ignoring every upgrade or advancement in technology since, my brain is still clinging to pattern matching responses it hasn't altered or upgraded since it was three years old after several nasty falls on the stairs.

Part of the counsellor's art, underrated and underreported, is the ability to decide when the client need no longer continue with the sessions, and when they are ready to be released back into the wild - free and untagged. Of course, less scrupulous counsellors may decide to keep their client, known in their notes as Mrs. X, Mr. Y or My New Kitchen Extension, on their books indefinitely. But most are, like Claire and Steve, hopefully honest and credible healers. Unusually for counselling, they do insist that I come back to see them socially and report on my flight. I certainly will, as I would welcome seeing them again.

They terminate my sessions, which in itself provides me with a confidence booster shot, as they evidently deem me ready to fly. Though I'm not so sure myself. But they have given me their honest appraisal that I am as close to ready as I am likely to achieve.

In turn, I have to be honest. I don't feel that I am ready to stand at the cliff edge just yet, half the soles of my shoes on land, half over the abyss. I have not become suddenly comfortable with heights. But I can at least see myself being somewhere high now. Before I would only have chosen avoidance. Even if avoidance was not an offered option, then I would have made it one - like someone in an examination attempting a multiple choice paper and adding their own fifth answer option in pencil "(e) avoidance techniques" to the existing four choices.

Since I am as ready as I am ever likely to be to do a balloon flight, I book myself onto a flight online. In the last few days ahead of my schedule flight, I head north to undergo a pilgrimage to a Sadler site.

11 SADLERS' ROYAL ASCENT: CELEBRITY AND FAMILY FORTUNES

7 SEPTEMBER 1813: WINDHAM SADLER'S DEBUT SOLO FLIGHT

Windham had not expected to fly solo when James Sadler planned another exhibition flight from Cheltenham in the late summer of 1813.

In spite of deploying almost three tons of vitriolic acid and iron filings, James and Windham were clearly struggling with a porous balloon leaking more than an undetected spy at GCHQ.

The balloon and basket were paraded from the Pump Room to the launch site, with the members of the flight committee striding alongside: "comprised of twelve gentlemen of the town, distinguished by wearing upon their breasts large silver medals that were presented to Mr Sadler by the inhabitants of Birmingham after his last ascension in that place. On one side is an excellent likeness of this celebrated character, with an inscription stating it to be James Sadler the first English aeronaut. On the other side Mr Sadler is represented seated in his elegant car, under a balloon and stating it to be his 21st ascent on 7 October 1811 and that he traversed 112 miles in one hour and twenty minutes." The silver medal's inscription neglects to mention that Sadler crashed violently on that flight and was feared dead.

Although the pomp and ceremony went to plan in Cheltenham, the launch did not. During the inflation "the wind blew extremely boisterous" and toppled over the poles acting as the tethered balloon supports. Again, seemingly forgetting

Sadler's Birmingham Medal (Smithsonian Institution)

the Birmingham flight from 1811 - even though he was currently wearing a huge silver medal specifically as a reminder of that ill-fated endeavour around his neck - Sadler was once again preparing to take off in a gathering gale.

The *Morning Chronicle* observed: "it is to be greatly lamented that out of the concourse so few had paid an admission to see the ingenious and enterprising artist Mr James Sadler, the first English aeronaut, will be the loser of several hundred pounds rather than the gainer."

He was reported as having given up a prestigious engagement in Ireland to be lured to Cheltenham, and the town had responded by closing every bank, shop and school for a half-day holiday to see Sadler's ascent. But now the ascension was running late due to problems with pumping hydrogen into the envelope. These problems were blamed on the silk supplier, whose crimson and white material was smaller than the amount Sadler had ordered, and the quality was branded 'insufficiently strong and prepared".

After three hours of attempted balloon filling and mindful of the capacity for frustrated crowds to riot, Sadler concluded it could not take his weight. Cometh the hour, cometh the man - or rather, the man's son. Windham Sadler stepped forth into the basket. The local press reported: "an interesting youth, the son of Mr Sadler, only 16 or 17 years of age, entered the car with all composure, fortitude, courage and indifference that his veteran father possesses." Windham may not have possessed much aeronautical piloting experience, but he held one key attribute for ballooning over his father: his weight. The teenager was likely to have been considerably lighter than his father; James Sadler was used to munching his way through numerous banquets held in his honour.

Windham flew out of the county with his father pursuing on horseback. At one stage Windham flew through a snow storm, which was so violent that he had difficulty operating the vent to lose necessary altitude. Showing that he had learnt piloting skills from observing his father, he calculated correctly the amount of ballast to jettison, particularly where he feared entanglement with trees when the balloon commenced a fast descent.

Finally he landed just outside Chipping Norton where he was greeted by locals approaching with a raised pitchfork and demanding, "Lord, Sir, where have you come from?" Fortunately the local vicar, Rev. G.D. Davies, then appeared, and presumably took less persuading from the youthful debutant that he was not an alien visitor intent on enslaving all earthlings.

Windham then returned to Oxford, where locals paraded him around the city in celebration - a tribute Oxford citizens had bestowed upon his father many years previously. Both Sadlers returned to Cheltenham the next day with their trophy balloon pulled by four horses resplendent in "shining silver breast plates". Here they indulged in several laps of honour and the townspeople took turns to pull the aeronauts' cart by hand, parading them before numerous impressed and bowing locals.

It is easy to see how endorphins can be created by celebrity, and this perhaps explains Sadler's willingness to continue making perilous ascents.

OCTOBER 1813: DERBY DEBACLE

In October 1813 James and his son Windham took the unusual step of placing an announcement in the *Derby Chronicle*, stating "that he [Sadler senior] has received injustice" and issuing a stern proclamation about "his feelings to decline entering into any future arrangements with the Derby Committee".

It was the culmination of a highly public spat between James Sadler and a committee formed in Derby for the main purpose of placating a town that had rioted when a previous aeronaut, Mr. Wilkes, literally failed to get off the ground.

The *Derby Chronicle* lauded "Mr Sadler the celebrated aeronaut who gave up his arrangements for exhibiting balloons in Bristol on the solicitations of some gentlemen at Derby to go there ahead to ascend with his balloon as a consequence of the disturbed state of the public mind as a consequence of the failure of Mr Wilkes."

Mr. Wilkes, a would-be balloonist, had failed to launch in Derby on 20 September 1813. "After incurring insurmountable difficulties inflating his envelope, Mr Wilkes had abandoned his Derby flight" in front of an audience who were in apparently no mood to disperse without seeing a balloon launch. This led to "a very alarming riot that was principally quelled by the gentlemen who had supported him in his attempt, assuring the populace that they would apply to Mr Sadler the celebrated aeronaut to ascend from Derby with his balloon."

The Derby committee then "sent an express to London to apply to Mr Sadler, but not finding him there, the application followed him to Bristol where Mr Sadler was making arrangements for the exhibition of the balloon, which his son Sadler ascended with, and a new balloon, the largest that was ever made, the size of which is so enormous that no place in London could be found sufficiently large to make it in. The nearest place that could be procured was Reading Town Hall, where several first rate artists were employed to ornate it at the expense of several thousand pounds."

It was widely reported in the press on 2 October that Sadler intended to move his balloon to Bristol, and then attempt to fly across the Irish Sea. But, being given a better offer by the burghers of Derby, he apparently intercepted the coaches carrying his balloon and equipment to Bristol and issued instructions for the convoy to turn around immediately and head for Derby.

An organising committee was set up, and agreed "to pay Sadler 500 guineas" for the ascent, with the strict proviso that he was responsible for all other expenses associated with the fight, including filling the balloon with gas.

Unfortunately, Sadler arrived in Derby to be greeted with the news that the town's authorities no longer intended to honour such a deal. "They declined giving this and refused to pay his expenses. He in consequence left Derby in disgust."

This prompted an increasingly irritated correspondence between the Derby committee, led by Dr. Forester, and James Sadler himself. All of the letters were given to a Nottingham newspaper, which gleefully published the entire correspondence, duplicated shortly afterwards in the *Derby Mercury*.

The Derby committee started by sending Sadler an illustrative copy of their local paper "announcing the great disappointment the town and neighbours of Derby have recently suffered". Explaining how outraged the local population had become after not seeing a promised flight, the committee asked Sadler to do the job properly. Unfortunately they wrote to Sadler's then address: 41 Brewer Street, Golden Square, London. Since Sadler was in Bristol at the time, the letter took several days to find him, mainly because he was then travelling to Nottingham to stage another flight. When the letter did eventually reach him, he replied immediately accepting the job, and travelled to Derby post haste in post chaise.

Post haste was precisely the Derby committee's problem. The bid to organise a flight at such short notice meant that the committee had only just started a public fund-raising subscription to cover its costs. If it was not obvious before, after a few days the committee members realised that it would take several months, not days, to raise the necessary 500 guineas of capital.

Hence Dr. Forester wrote to declare that Sadler's terms were "inadmissible". Sadler fired back: "I regret that my propositions should have been inadmissible" - implying "because they're not" with a sarcasm garnish. He also reasonably pointed out to Dr. Forester the short notice given to make provision for the Derby ascent.

Sadler thundered: "In regard to the offer contained in the resolutions of the Committee to set on foot an immediate general Subscription for my ascent at some future period, I must beg leave to decline giving the Committee any such trouble upon my account. Reflecting upon the very unexpected kind of reception I have been so unfortunate as to experience from the Committee from the first moment of my coming here and, in particular, my personal reception by yourself on my first arrival, make it a duty to my own feelings to decline accepting any future offer whatever from the Committee or from yourself for the ascent of my balloon." Sadler continues: "I should not have come to Derby."

But for the very pressing terms of your letter alluded to, and in which it appears, that you had a wish that I should have ascended even so early as the 5th of the month, together with other resolutions of the Committee contained in the Derby newspaper transmitted to me by you with your letter. It was from these combined circumstances that I became induced to give the fullest credit to you and to the Committee for the sincerity of your intentions to fulfil the promise you had made to the public that I should be engaged to ascend from this place, thereby making a compensation for the money the Committee had already received from the public and to recompense them if possible for the mortifying disappointment they had experienced from the inability of the Committee to fulfil the engagements they had made with the public, and which they had so unluckily made manifest in their unfortunate attempt in attempting to send up a linen balloon.

So there! Although it is immensely possible that the letter was drafted with considerable input from a secretary or clerk, it does challenge an expressed view that Sadler was incapable of using enough grammar to string together even one sentence. Nevertheless, it remains an extremely rare example of a Sadler letter, there being very few in existence laced with any personality insights. And it captures him in no mood to hold back in admonishing the Derby committee.

There is also no escaping the unpalatable conclusion that Sadler could evidently be a tad querulous. Was he by now so used to being a celebrity that his behaviour was affected by the backstage tantrums we associated with the famous?

The Derby committee thought so. Determined to escalate the spat further, the committee's Secretary W.H. Bailes returned fire in the *Derby Chronicle* a few days later: "Mr Sadler is under a great mistake in insinuating that the Committee had made an absolute engagement." They then inflated the agreed sum by one hundred guineas from their earlier account, describing it "as no less a sum as an advance of six hundred guineas".

In consequence of the pointed manner in which Mr Sadler has chosen to speak of the unexpected kind of reception, as he calls it, from Dr Forester in particular (as appears in Mr Sadler's printed statement of the correspondence between him and the Committee), Dr Forester feels himself called upon to declare he is perfectly unconscious of having given any just cause for such an imputation. So far from meaning to show either disrespect or inattention towards Mr Sadler, whose celebrity he was not unacquainted, Dr Forester was most desirous to see the aeronaut in Derby. His intentions to treat him on the footing of a gentleman and man of science.

After expressing disappointment at Sadler's decision to go public with their correspondence, and still reeling at the hurtful remarks it contains, the committee member's correspondence continues. Having claimed to have had two meetings with Sadler, he brands him "as having arrived in Derby with perhaps rather extravagant expectations of various kinds, as there is now reason to think, and finding them not realised, has thought proper in a moment of disappointment to complain of his reception, and insinuate pretty plainly that he has not been sincerely dealt with."

8 NOVEMBER 1813: NOTTINGHAM

Taking off from Nottingham in his latest escapade - a location possibly picked for its longstanding rivalry with Derby? - Sadler landed in the middle of the Cottesmore hunt. This should have provided sufficient distraction for the quarry to escape the hounds, as Sadler's massive striped bauble crashed nosily to the ground just outside the village of Pickford in Rutland. "The balloon appeared the size and shape of a round haystack inverted ten yards high it was composed of broad segments of crimson and yellow silk, over which was a net, and to that was the appended the basket about four feet high covered with ornamented leather and velvet," declared one impressed newspaper.

Venting the balloon a few miles earlier to avoid the turrets of Belvoir Castle, he continued into Rutland's airspace. Coming into land at Thistleton Gap, the breeze placed the balloon on a direct collision course with a windmill, necessitating substantial ballast release to regain height. It had not been the calmest of flights, and Sadler had traversed a patch of low cloud that showered freezing drizzle on the aeronaut. A female fan had tossed a knitted shawl into the basket as Sadler took off from Nottingham, and he discovered it frosted with icicles upon landing.

A report, credited to Sadler, was circulated to the *Liverpool Mercury* and other newspapers. Whether or not it is ghost written can only be guessed at, but it seems likely. He describes passing over the Great North Road, then "at this moment I was highly gratified with a second view of the aerial regions of Exton Park and its beautiful sheets of water having before passed over it on my excursion from Birmingham in October 1811." He had travelled thirty miles in an hour's flying time.

Certainly Sadler's appeal was showing no signs of waning by 1813. A crowd of 30,000 people were kept waiting for seven hours before the delayed launch. This flight is commemorated by a distinctive green circular plaque placed above the front entrance of the Fellows, Morton and Clayton public house located on Canal Street, considered to be the site of Sadler's ascent that day. Erected by Nottingham Civic Society, the plaque was fittingly unveiled in November

2013 exactly two hundred years after Sadler made the first ever flight from Nottingham.

27 MAY 1814: FIRST BURLINGTON HOUSE ASCENT

James and Windham flew together as a duo from the gardens of Burlington House in honour of the Duke of Wellington. For once they had chosen a calm day without a blowing gale. As if to prove that the pair were incapable, either separately or together of undergoing a routine, uneventful flight, this time they created more trouble for themselves by recklessly ascending to a dangerous altitude.

Being a stickler for carrying scientific equipment on board, Sadler senior would have appreciated the danger involved - and yet he rose to a height calculated at five miles.

Needless to say, the extreme cold bit fiercely into their capacity to function. It also froze the vent shut, which meant the balloon continued to rise in the thinning air. Eventually it was opened, and the balloon then started its protracted descent towards South Ockendon, five miles north of Grays in Essex. Once again, Sadler had narrowly avoided another landing in the sea.

15 JULY 1814: BURLINGTON HOUSE SECOND ASCENT: WHAT MAN DARE, I DARE

Deciding to conduct a balloon flight from a take-off point in Central London generally comes under the heading "to be discouraged". One problem is that there are few wide open spaces to offer safe landings in the heart of the metropolis. Deciding to fly in the middle of the capital during a raging gale comes under the heading "death wish".

Like father, like son, Windham Sadler mirrored James Sadler's exploits by taking off in a storm. So concerned were the massed spectators that many held onto the balloon basket and guy ropes, refusing to let the balloon fly. This behaviour contrasts markedly with previous ascents where crowds rioted if a balloon did not launch within minutes of the advertised take-off, regardless of life-threatening gales.

The reason for such a U-turn in the crowd's attitude at this particular launch was the presence of a female aeronaut who accompanied Windham in the basket.

Due to the "strength of the wind, spectators who clung to the car were very loath to let either of the two voyagers, especially a Lady, to the uncertain air," remarked the *London Chronicle*. Another newspaper revealed that: "Aerostation is not such a subject of such admiration as it was some years since" before going on to confirm that "the appearance of a lady flying on the wings of the wind is now a novelty in England."

Hence the way to regain public interest was to innovate, and now Britain had a female aeronaut to get excited about. "There is a disposition amongst the British public to support and sanction every woman of spirit," reasoned the *Exeter Flying Post*.

Windham's co-flyer was Miss Mary Thompson, an actress described as being "intimate with the Sadler family" and "renowned in the dramatic corps". She had flown with the Sadlers in Dublin a few weeks earlier in a short flight, and was now launching from Burlington House for her debut English flight - gale or not.

And she was certainly a figure that the nation found easy to take to its collective heart. The *Cornish Advertiser*, which it is fair to assume may not have had its reporter on the ground as an eye witness, nevertheless observed that Miss Thompson refused to acknowledge the concerns of the crowd not to fly in gale force winds, and in so doing was described by one contemporary newspaper as "not before excelled in any example of female courage". Replying to the question "can you go up?" Miss Thompson is recorded as saying: "Certainly. What man dare, I dare."

Ladies and gentlemen - or gentlemen and ladies - British feminism had a heroine several decades before Emmeline Pankhurst.

Windham may not have learnt from his father that flying in gales was to be avoided, but he appears to have developed a greater sense of making money as a ballooning professional. Viewing the balloon at Burlington House was a paid-for-only privilege, and huge fabric screens were erected to block any interloper's view. Only those with a valid ticket passing through security stations manned by armed guards could see the globe.

Dissatisfied with merely viewing "the ladies of status sitting in windows outside with much promenading", several ticketless spectators tried scaling the walls to gain access to the balloon. The hired heavies pulled most of the freeloaders from the wall mid-climb, dissuading "several courageous fellows from mounting the parapets". A daring few managed to avoid security, and "when out of reach of the guards thought it proper to laugh and express their contempt which afforded the mob no small share of mirth".

In common with many of both Sadler senior and junior flights, the hydrogen inflation took longer than anticipated. The *Lancashire Gazette* published a full statistical table of the balloon's proportions and capacity, declaring it to be 236 feet in diameter, manufactured from 2,950 yards of silk and requiring a disconcertingly specific 2074½ pounds of hydrogen to render it airborne.

Eventually "they ascended in a style of magnificent violence," as the *London Chronicle* described it. They quickly rose to such a height that "the water trickling down the gas pipe froze immediately". Shivering with cold, whilst the frozen vapour and condensation threatened to block the vent, Windham succeeded in relieving the obviously over-pressured balloon of some of its hydrogen. The orb then descended at an alarming rate, necessitating ballast jettisoning to regain a steady altitude. Miss Thompson, writing observations, recorded that at one stage the ballast was not sinking as fast as the balloon - which is probably a good time to start panicking. Hurling everything they could overboard slowed the descent.

Very soon afterwards they broke through the low cloud cover to discover they were eight miles from the North Sea coastline. Had the balloon not been over-vented by Windham, their destiny would have been a wet one. Such was the strength of the gale that they had flown 49 miles in only 40 minutes. Navigation charting their position was rendered almost impossible by unbroken low cloud. The cloud was by now so low, and the declining light so murky, that Sadler later admitted he could hear the mooing of cattle in the fields beneath him before he could see land.

Hitting the ground at speed, the balloon bounced back airwards from the first cornfield where the duo attempted to land, before a grappling hook finally caught in a hedgerow's roots. This anchored the basket, though the resultant pullback and violent trajectory into the fierce wind inevitably tore the balloon. A nearby surgeon Mr. Willsher, out on horseback, came to the pair's aid and informed them they had landed at Great Tey four miles north-east of Coggeshall in Essex.

Miss Thompson was travelling back to London at 3am the next day when she was involved in a crash - the post boy fell asleep and the cart came off the road into a shallow ditch. The discrepancy between safety in the two transport modes - balloon and coach - was much discussed by playful supporters of aeronautics.

1 AUGUST 1814: JOHN SADLER'S ASCENT

Another Sadler flight occurred in August 1814, with another Sadler ascending. Confused? So are some of the press reports at the time, and subsequent books of the period written on aerostation, but a third Sadler was now also undertaking public balloon flights.

James Sadler's eldest son John Sadler launched from St. James' Park near Buckingham Palace to mark the twin celebrations of Lord Nelson's victory in the Nile, and the centenary of the House of Brunswick's' accession to the English throne.

Although it was announced that Mrs. H. Johnston would accompany Sadler's oldest son, the pre-flight balloon inspection found some alarming problems with the valve and netting, with only a single dangling string left to secure it to the top of the balloon hoop. The Duke of Wellington was quoted in some newspaper reports as strongly advising the party against flying. A compromise deal was cut, where Mrs. Johnston stepped out of the balloon, but Sadler - another clear inheritor of the family gene for fearless flight bordering upon recklessness - took off alone for a solo flight. A Japanese kamikaze pilot would have refused to fly on safety grounds. A rational, or more accurately, irrational, explanation was provided by one newspaper correspondent present: "Feeling for the disappointment of the public, and for his own honour, Mr Sadler was determined to go up."

Flying over the massed spectators below attending the day's festivities to mark the joint celebrations, John Sadler dropped two bags of tiny paper parachutes bearing a jubilee message. Continuing in an easterly direction he reached Woolwich, where disaster, as rather predicted, occurred.

The rope that secured the envelope within the netting broke. It slipped violently, and Sadler had to grasp at the dangling rope to stop the balloon parting ways with the basket.

A separation of balloon and basket at an altitude other than on terra firma does not make for a successful ballooning experience. All the time Sadler had been gaining altitude, and lacking the experience of his father and younger brother, had dispensed with too much ballast overboard.

Faced with a frozen vent, a balloon continuing to ascend and a slipped net barely keeping balloon and basket together, John Sadler used a knife and stabbed the balloon. This was the part of the trip where he got lucky, as he managed - presumably without any former experience of stabbing a balloon - to release hydrogen at the correct rate to ensure a safe landing.

Then his luck turned to bad again, as he was about to land in the middle of the Thames estuary. The breeze, like his luck, changed direction once again. He finally landed with only a sprained ankle incurred in the process on the Essex side of the estuary. A passing fisherman retrieved his balloon from the water's edge, and acted as a river taxi by taking John Sadler several miles upstream to Gravesend, where he summoned a post chaise back to Burlington House to recount his averted catastrophe.

Unlike his brother and father, this scare was sufficient to end John Sadler's aeronautical career and he reportedly never flew again.

15 AUGUST 1814: YORK

A few days later, James Sadler senior, Windham and Miss Thomson all headed to York to undertake another flight - though it is likely that only Windham (still seventeen years old) and the new female star of ballooning - credited with revitalising the public's appetite for the medium - occupied the basket.

The balloon took off from Kettwell's Orchard near York Minster. After the windswept horrors of their Burlington House ascent, the twosome were finally paid back with some good weather fortune. Their globe remained visible in the unblemished blue sky for the entire flight duration of around 45 minutes until they landed in Easingwold, twelve miles due north of York. Following normal practice, the promoters had exhibited the balloon for several days before the ascent, this time charging a hefty, pocket-emptying whole shilling just to see it on display in York's Assembly Rooms.

17 SEPTEMBER 1814: PONTEFRACT

Linking their York flight to their next aerial venture on 17 September 1814 at Pontefract was horse racing. During the race meetings at York and Pontefract, large holidaying crowds would provide a festival air and a source of customers requiring entertainment.

Both Yorkshire ascents featured Windham and Miss Thompson as a double act. Huge crowds were attracted in Pontefract, where several years earlier James Sadler had experienced an extremely harsh landing that could easily have proved fatal.

26 NOVEMBER 1814: PLYMOUTH

After ascending from Exeter in a flight described by the press at the time as his "seventh ascent", Windham Sadler stayed in the West Country for his next aerial excursion in late November 1814. Late November was a decidedly risky time of year to stage a flight on a date advertised in advance, and this was confirmed when he was caught in strong winds and icy conditions after taking off from a frosty Plymouth.

Trapped in an inescapable descent, Windham sustained several injuries jumping out of the basket as it collided with the Devon earth at considerable speed. Lightened by the absence of a pilot, the basket instantly took off again only to be found later wrecked in Tavistock on the edge of Dartmoor, with the wooden cart fragmented.

Even though the once fashionable practice of aeronauts parachuting cats had long since stopped, Windham was using up a worrying amount of his nine lives.

I am at a wedding. This means I have accepted an invite (especially since I am not the gate-crashing type). Though, truthfully, this has been mainly motivated by the opportunity to travel somewhere connected with Sadler: Manchester.

Since I briefly worked with the bride, I am relegated to the lowest possible status among the wedding guests. I am allocated a place at a reception table so far from the head table that I struggle to see the bride, groom and best man - due to the earth's natural curvature - until they stand-up to make a speech. Everyone keeps asking me who I am. I evolve my reply from "I'm Richard, I used to write with the bride" to "I'm not a gate-crasher - look, here's my invitation card".

By some considerable margin, I am the oldest person on my table. This statistic would remain true if I was thirty years younger. I'm seated next to Ryan. He is eight, and after making small talk about football, he concludes it necessary to start talking down to me. His slightly older sister silently observes our conversation for a few minutes before joining in, selecting an entrance level where she clearly feels compelled to talk down to me from an even greater height. "So," I ask Ryan and his sister Sasha, "how come you're 'out alone' as opposed to 'home alone'?" "Our parents are on the top table," replies Ryan.

Being placed on the children's table does at least mean that the complimentary yet frugally quantified one bottle of red and white utilitarian Romanian house wine/sink unblocker, provides a fortuitously increased glass-per-adult share ratio. "Have you got a wife?" asks Sasha with a bluntness thankfully usually lacking in adult conversations. "Yes." "Where is she?" enquiries Ryan with clear suspicion implied in his choice of tone. I tell Ryan that she's invisible. He rightly points out that he is eight and not three. Fair enough. "Where is she?" they ask again. I explain that she just couldn't come. "Doesn't she like you anymore?" he presses. "What? Er, I hope so, I don't know. She just couldn't come."

"How does that make you feel?" asks Sasha. "Well, I feel that… hang on, do you work for Relate?"

Then a sudden jolting reminder, like an unexpected breeze that arrives out of nowhere, causing you to adjust your footing to avoid being blown over. "Sasha's boyfriend dumped her!" "He wasn't my boyfriend and besides I dumped him, you …", and she whacks him with disturbing violence. Frozen in shock, I sit with my mouth open.

Then I realise I'm the adult here; the seemingly responsible one. "Er… that was… you shouldn't do that… why did you…?" But the narrowly opened window of opportunity to intervene has gone, and it's already been slammed shut on my fingers. The time for intervention is over, the deadline for any UN appeasement policy expired. A huge blob of chocolate fudge cake is lobbed straight into Sasha's face, the "Alpine glazed triple chocolate sauce with pomegranate trace" - why do you need a creative writing degree to compile a menu these days? - dribbling down her posh lemon dress.

Instantly we're surrounded by proper adults. Unlike pretend adults such as me, they know what to say and do. Ryan is led away for routine questioning, and a furious uncle appears and drags Sasha off. Sasha manages a convincing "(sob)… he just flung it at me… there's something wrong with him… I didn't do anything," neatly omitting the obviously irrelevant detail that she landed a slap on him that would have floored most professional boxers.

It was indubitably a serious incident - the wine could easily have got knocked over. Ten minutes later, and the two protagonists reappear. Sasha is wearing a strategically placed cardigan to cover the chocolate splat, and Ryan has a red swelling on the side of his face which has evidently been deemed ice-pack-worthy. They both act like the incident has not happened, and go back to talking down to me. "Do you want a new wife?" asks Ryan. "Um… no I wouldn't. I'd prefer the one I have to start liking me again," I reply. "Mum doesn't like daddy anymore, so maybe you could have his wife one day." offers Ryan. "Er, thanks, Ryan." My brain cannot resist projecting this image in front of my eyes: "Hi Ryan's mum, we've never met, but your son says we must have an affair. So, um, shall we book a cheap motel room for some purely recreational sex? Do you mind going halfsies - £29.50 each?"

It seems paradoxically inappropriate, yet simultaneously highly appropriate, to be discussing the merits of spouse retention at a wedding. "Pass me that bottle," commands Sasha. Instinctively I comply with the request, and pass over a bottle while maintaining my gaze on Ryan. Both my brain and my hand have joint responsibility for passing the bottle, assuming it was a soft drink - otherwise, why (a) would Sasha ask for it (bad reason) and (b) why would they leave a wine bottle on the children's table? (Probably for the same reason they left an adult there.) I don't avert eye contact with Ryan as I want to continue my conversation and try to be a responsible adult with an opportunity to maybe teach a youngster something i.e. you can't change a spouse once they go out of fashion like a pair of trainers.

"What are you doing?" shouts Ryan. "Sorry, wasn't thinking!" Like a patient snapped out of hypnotherapy, I'm suddenly conscious of what I've just done - namely pass a bottle of white wine to a twelve-year-old. "She only drinks red," says Ryan, the colour being the cause of his outrage. "You'll get in trouble," he warns, somewhat prophetically. I feel like I'm their supplier, and decide I have to finally act like a responsible adult, and make a parental intervention to reclaim the wine.

Looking after children properly doesn't necessary reward you with popularity. That's a given. But I am newly charged with a strong desire to do the right thing so ask firmly for the bottle back, counselling "you're too young to drink. Please give me the wine back." "Relax," Sasha begins in her calmest, most grown-up, most - it later transpires - manipulative voice. "I drink wine with meals at home - we started in our French house. Mum and dad wanted to introduce us to responsible alcohol consumption, so we only drink one glass of red wine and always with a meal." "Er… that's very modern. Er… but I don't know if you should drink here in public, it's different from at home." "Oh, you're not going to be a boring adult are you?" Clever. Much cleverer than me. And she's twelve. Who wants to willingly subscribe to being a boring adult? Normally, I'd say "no". So "no"! "You're not going to start fighting if you get boozed up are you?" I check. Like a politician on the *Today* programme, she avoids answering the question by changing the subject, whilst glugging her glass full to the brim.

"Did you marry the wrong woman?" Ryan continues. This is the sort of cut-to-the-chase honesty that kids do well. Or, more accurately, do horribly. "No, I don't think that at all." "Then you should try harder to make it work," adds Ryan, the eight-year old agony uncle. "Er… I don't know if it's redeemable." "Then get a new wife," Sasha adds, simply. "There's lots of women here." I pick up her wine glass and say that we will all get in trouble if she drinks any. Needless to say, she does not respond to this opinion with nodding supine agreement. "Oi, give me that back!" So I drink her wine. In one. "God that was horrid," I say. I was not acting.

Twenty minutes later and Sasha approaches me, and introduces Emily like she's a postman with a package to sign for. "This is Emily. She works…" Sasha has clearly forgotten where Emily works in the twenty seconds since she asked her. "…she works… er… somewhere." Emily wears glasses, is clearly fifteen years younger than me, and doesn't look like she is enthused about receiving any male attention today. She has a look of the librarian about her. But she is just what I want - a potentially intelligent adult human being whom I can interact with. "Shall we go upstairs?" she says. Part of me wants to say in mock protest, "but we've only just met", but thankfully I realise that would be a potentially crass and damaging remark. "But we've only just met," I hear myself saying, promoting an internal dialogue between my brain which says to my mouth in angry tones "I thought we agreed NOT to say that." "Well," replies my mouth to my brain, "you were the one who put the thought there, so what do you expect? And you couldn't come up with any other line."

"Sasha said you're a comedian," says Emily, before causing me to seriously question her judgement at evaluating other humans by remarking: "Sasha is very grown-up." "Yeah, she's great," I say, agreeing to something that was the exact opposite of my own experience. "Think they wish her brother could catch some of the maturity off his sister - apparently he lobbed a chocolate cake at her in an entirely unprovoked attack," she adds. "About that… Sasha told you?" I check. "Yes," she confirms. "Nothing," I say.

"Have you got any children?" she enquires. "No," I reply, "and I think I may have missed the boat. In fact, I'm still nowhere near reaching the dockside."

"Well, unlike us, you can still have plenty of time," she counsels, "and now you're divorced you can meet someone else." My brain thinks about saying "What? Divorced? How come you've heard before me?", then my brain offers me a stupid joke but tells my mouth not to say it out loud. This time my mouth pays attention, and the words remain unspoken. "So, would you like to go upstairs?" she asks again. "What? These really steep spiral stairs with no backs?" I check. "Yes, the ones that lead to the balcony. I'm told you get a good view from the top," Emily replies. "Er... probably not," I say shamefully, although I want to continue talking to her. "Oh, I er... oh..." she stammers, understandably taken aback. Just as I am ordering my brain to allocate all departments immediately onto finding the right thing to say to her next, we are suddenly distracted.

Ryan runs past us. There is a massive smear of wedding cake across his face, and he is busily combing currents from his hair. "Sasha!" bellows a military-type man, who is attending the wedding in an army uniform. What is it about military people that make them want to attend weddings in their work clothes? Painters and decorators don't get married in their overalls.

"Sasha!" hollers the military guy. "Yes?" Sasha answers calmly and matter-of-factly, as if she's been asked to confirm if she prefers milk or lemon in her tea. Her father's mood is the polar opposite and yet Sasha continues to check her phone. "YOU KNOW THIS BEHAVIOUR HAS TO STOP - AND YOU ALSO KNOW, DON'T YOU, THAT YOUR BROTHER'S SUIT IS HIRED?" "Yes," she replies again, as insouciantly as if confirming she will also take sugar with that tea.

"PUT DOWN YOUR PHONE. YOU'RE LEAVING!" the uniformed man bellows like a Sergeant Major. Which, it is quite possible, may be his actual day job.

Ryan is standing beside his father, enjoying this opportunity to see his sister about to be court-martialed. I note for the first time that wedding cake icing has been scrawled into both the back and front of his expensive looking, and recently revealed as hired, jacket.

Sasha gives a "nothing to do with me" look to both of them that fails to win over any neutrals.

Their army officer, who may well be called Corporal Punishment since this looks distinctly likely, glances at the table where his two delinquent offspring had been sitting either side of me. "HAVE YOU BEEN DRINKING RED WINE AGAIN? YOU KNOW YOU'RE NEVER ALLOWED WINE!" - another addition to Sasha's charge sheet. "That man gave it to me." I shake my head. "He's frightened of stairs!" I adopt a she-just-says-silly-random-things expression followed by a 'kids, eh?' skywards roll of the eyes. This last remark backfires, as the likelihood of an adult male being scared of stairs is so unlikely that it renders

Sasha's previous fact equally discreditable - the one about a responsible adult giving her wine. As if. Talk about unlikely.

Ryan and Sasha are frog marched out of the reception, and are presumably looking at a long spell in the cooler. Great. The two people seated either side of me may have only been kids, but even they vandalised their afternoon to get out of talking to me. This leaves me to endure coffee course on my own, with wedding cake and champagne. I say champagne, but closer inspection would almost certainly reveal "sparkling wine flavoured blended product of Moldova". I don't begrudge them that - money is tight. Not that it's easy to get the attention of the coffee and champagne waiters when you're annexed on the children's table.

A tall elegant woman in her very early fifties appears, attired in a shapely blue dress and large Royal Ascot-type hat with a brim so large it's unlikely she could fit into any conventionally sized bathroom. It is so over the top it resembles one of the eighteenth-century balloon hats that Sadler would recognise. She has clearly been a head-swivelling beauty in her time, but the multiple stress fractures produced by parenting and married life relentlessly lapping against her inner sea wall of tolerance, are beginning to show. Her resistance is visibly beginning to crumble into the sea.

Her spirit is being replaced by another sort of spirit - almost certainly gin. "What is it this time? You promised you'd both behave today!" she imparts to the two arrested children being marched past her. Significantly, neither Ryan nor Sasha turn their heads to acknowledge her, nor their father. Red wine stains are all over the front of Ryan's shirt, noticeable as soon as he unbuttons his jacket. This war must have escalated. Sasha also has red wine on the back of her lemon-coloured dress, and mint sauce in her hair. This is quite an achievement, not least because the main course was fish. Did she bring her own mint sauce in case the food fight arms race escalated?

The parents are making the decision to remove them before the food war escalates even further, sensibly before the nuclear option arrives: aerodynamically perfect profiteroles with a gooey sticky chocolate sauce. Logic decrees if they're out of the room when the later teatime buffet is unveiled, then that constitutes disarmament.

Then the librarian lady Emily approaches me. "Why didn't you say you were frightened of stairs? I'd have understood. I thought you didn't want to talk to me because I was boring." She has been drinking. A lot.

Having launched her missive missile, she turns away and is gone, leaving my floundering response mostly unheard: "I'm not... OK maybe a bit... I do want to talk to you... really..." She's now quite some distance from me, so I shout sufficiently loudly for most people to turn around and look at me: "... I do."

My life officially sucks. Two hours later, I see Massive Hat Lady again. I discover she is Sasha's mother and that her best friend Emily is upset because another guest was rude to her. She is extremely drunk. She's dancing, or rather being held upright, by another man who's come to a wedding in his work clothes - another soldier. No longer bothering to keep up the pretence of sipping daintily from a flute, Sasha's mother is sucking on the end of a Cava bottle. "Do you have children?" she asks me. "Alas no, I fear I've left it…" "You f***** lucky bastard," she confirms. She then hugs me. I get smothered in curly chestnut hair and assaulted with lots of sharp hat brim, but it's nice to hold and literally feel the warmth of another human being for a few seconds after you've spent all day on your own being ostracised by a wedding group who mainly think you are a gate-crasher.

After several seconds, however, the hug becomes progressively awkward, and I realise that since she's showing no inclination of letting go - and using me in the same way that a clematis would use a fence. I attempt rebalancing a drunken woman upright. This turns out to be notoriously difficult. Replacing her in a position where she won't topple over is akin to balancing a coin on its edge. Having succeeded, I tip-toe gently away from the table in case I cause a vibration that sends her tumbling towards the floor with a loud crash. At no time does she let go of the Cava bottle. "Perhaps if you let go of the bottle, you could steady yourself with the other hand - no, you're not going to do that, are you?"

Then her husband arrives, wrestles the bottle from her - although not without a spirited defence and greater resistance than he has probably ever seen in the day job - and she is carried off like a drunken real-life enactment of that scene from *An Officer and A Gentleman*. Disappointingly no one hums "Up Where You Belong".

After eight hours at the wedding I speak to the bride for the first time. "Sorry we haven't spoken before. And sorry you were on the kids' table. Suppose that must have been really boring for you." "Er… yes. Nothing much happened."

Eventually I leave the wedding guests and retire to bed, after first leaving my stained shirt - caught in the chocolate cross-fire - to soak overnight in a hotel bathroom sink.

I am in Manchester to see Sadler's plaque, located where appreciative Mancunians have named a street after his achievements - more than his hometown of Oxford ever did. It's late and I am lying in bed in an aggressively expensive hotel room, imploring sleep to arrive as I have a busy schedule planned for tomorrow. Instead of successfully falling asleep, I am a 49-year-old man currently having an argument with his penis.

"That brunette was nice at the table opposite just now," my penis feels compelled to point out.

"Yeah, I thought you'd notice her," I reply. To my penis. Even though I want to go to sleep, our conversation continues.

My Penis: You should have asked for her phone number.

Me: What? No, of course I shouldn't.

MP: She was up for it.

Me: She was not up for it. You always conclude that. She was friendly and pleasant - and it was nice to have a chat with her. Just because a woman is friendly doesn't mean her congeniality should be rewarded by being hit on. Sometimes you repel me.

MP: Well, you should have at least asked her if she wanted to come up for a drink.

Me: No, that would have appeared creepy. Now go to sleep.

MP: Can we watch the porn channel.

Me: No! You know we never watch the porn channels. Why? So we can depress ourselves by watching footage of people having a far better time in a hotel room than we're currently having.

MP: Typical - you never spend any money on me.

Me: What's that supposed to mean?

MP: Other guys spend money on the porn channel.

Me: Stop it. Why would you want to see some poor girls with false breasts and dead eyes regretting not persevering with their GCSEs?

MP: Who said anything about going to Tesco?

Me: I'll do the jokes. You're always such a dick.

MP: Good joke.

Me: Thanks

MP: Are you still awake?

Me: Thanks to you, yes.

MP: Can we think about my favourite weather girl now?

Me: No.

[I have a request that will ensure I have a fulfilled life if granted. If this scene is ever dramatised for Radio 4's *Book of the Week*, please could the role of my penis be voiced by Charlotte Green. Thank you. Believe me, it's only a small part.]

In the morning I wonder why I am increasingly experiencing a growing libido, and harbouring a secret unexpressed longing to mate with most of the women I see around Manchester later that day. The answer turns out to be unsurprisingly

Freudian. Just when you think Freud has been discredited to make way on the couch for more empirically proven psychological theorists, he still proves capable of relating some insights that remain undissolved by the incoming tide of progress.

I'm not weird - it's just that I'm convinced that my death is imminent and have an instinctive desire to pass on my genes. OK, maybe mildly weird. Thus every woman I see has heightened, exaggerated attractiveness to render her a potential mate ripe for insemination. See, there's definitely nothing weird about me.

My body is starting to prepare itself for what it believes is inevitable death. It is starting to close down. The urge to pass on genes is paramount in this process. Military personnel were supposedly banned from keeping journals in both world wars, yet of course many logged their innermost private thoughts. This rising urge to pass on oneself, preserve an aspect of your being, some tangible material part of you inhabiting the future, burns with a primal power when your body truly believes it is under mortal threat. My body is going into premature mourning mode, closing itself down, grieving for its nearby loss - its unavoidable demise. Like a man in a war.

It recognises its last chance to pass on a bit of me into the world before I disappear for ever. A physical symptom manifested in a human form.

My brain lies to my body that I am in such abject fear when I am not. This is the power of a phobia. I recall the advice of Steve to focus away from negative anxiety, and the tip from my Australian magazine blind date to stop thinking thoughts that offer me no help whatsoever. It does help. And it reinforces my inclination to do this balloon flight, no matter how terrified I remain of heights. I am not going to be an avoider for the rest of my life, though the rest of life, my brain keeps wanting to point out, may not be that long if I go through with the flight.

I travel into Manchester as I am keen to see a park, a street and a plaque, all with Sadler associations, and conveniently next to each other. Escaping the swarm of rush hour Manchester traffic, which appears to be present even on a Sunday, I start to head toward the newest part of the city to find the street named in Sadler's honour: fittingly called Balloon Street. I anticipate the wealth of Sadler memorials to be here, but unfortunately, the Haworth Gardens where Sadler took off, both in 1785 and 25 years later, has no visible signs of him. No statue stands in his honour. The mansion house that he flew from was finally knocked down in 1980.

Fortunately a proven treatment for anxieties is exercise, and I obtain much more exercise than I expected walking around central Manchester and its aggressively urban retail developments. Significant regeneration of Manchester's commercial centre has occurred in the last two decades, mainly thanks to investment projects and the IRA.

Sadler's blue plaque is surprisingly difficult to find, as is Balloon Street.

More walking than I expected is necessary, as Balloon Street appears to have become elusive. Manchester's authorities seem to have taken the street signs down - do they still think there's a war on? Ironically, Google makes the experience even more taxing (yeah, mean that one). Google Map offers no returns whatsoever if typing "Balloon Street".

Ascending from the recreational gardens adjacent to a large house in the Long Millgate area of the city in 1785, Sadler was honoured by a thoroughfare behind the field being christened Balloon Street soon afterwards. The house then became a pub, and continued dispensing beer as the Manchester Arms for nearly two centuries. Until its eventual demolition in 1980, when it was destroyed with a wrecking ball - a more route one method of forcing reluctant drinkers to leave after last orders than flicking the light switch on and off a few times. Ask locals, as I did, whether the area is associated today with Sadler, and it appears that the Manchester Arms is much better known - and more fondly remembered - than Sadler. Especially by one older Mancunian gentleman who enthusiastically informed me that it was the first pub in Manchester to introduce lunchtime strippers in the 1970s. See, Manchester does have a cultural history!

Eventually I find what remains of Balloon Street: a street incongruously compiled of faded Victorian buildings alongside the gleaming newness of a shiny modern headquarters for the Cooperative Bank. Stepping over tramlines to get a better view, I find the plaque near Manchester Cathedral on the corner of Corporation Street. Cautiously checking for trams constantly swooping past, I cross the street and get as close as I can. A circular plaque, topped with Manchester's coat-of-arms, proudly proclaims: "From a garden on this site James Sadler pioneer English aeronaut made the first manned balloon ascent in Manchester 12 May 1785." Appropriately marking the 200th anniversary of Sadler's first historical English flight, the plaque was erected by Manchester City Council in 1974. A statue of Robert Owen, the founder of the Cooperative movement, stands guard over it.

Barry Worthington's *Discovering Manchester: A Walking Guide* at least credits Sadler's noteworthy achievements in the city. The book confirms that the Manchester Arms was indeed the first pub in the city to introduce strippers, before bemoaning the fact that it was demolished to make way for a road that was never built. "We must be mad," he concludes. This tragic double loss - a pub and lunchtime strippers - is a clearly a difficult bereavement for any true Northern man to accept.

It is at times a lonely pilgrimage. No one else stops to read the plaque all the time I stand there paying tribute with head bowed, clasping my lowered hands together to subconsciously adopt the body language of a solemn churchgoer.

Yet viewing this Sadler memorial increases my motivation - adds an extra cylinder to my ambition - to fly like Sadler. Nearly two and a half centuries later, in the most relentlessly modern of contemporary shopping areas, Sadler is still considered worthy of acknowledgement to the occupiers of this most urban temple of modernity.

Most historical biographers eventually reach a stage where they crave a meeting with their subject. This is after trawling through endless boxes of library papers, pursuing false leads, panning bowl after bowl of gravel in the occasional hope of spotting a flashing glint of real golden insight. In my case the longing is exacerbated by Sadler's lack of letter-writing proclivities or perhaps even abilities, for it is possible that he was barely literate.

Just twenty minutes in a coffee shop with Sadler is what I crave most - ideally at the Lemon House Refreshment Hall.

Speak quickly, time is precious. These are the questions I want to ask James Sadler: why did you do it? Where did you learn so much about engineering, chemistry, invention, design and gases? Why wasn't collecting the money due to you important in your first years of flying? What did your wife think of your exposure to such risk? Why, when everyone else was getting killed, did you persevere? Why did you stop then return to flying after a 25-year gap? Why did the Royal Navy sack you and leave you bankrupt? How surprised were you that your friends collected money to re-establish your financial and physical wellbeing? Why did you fall out so violently with Oxford University? How mendaciously do you think the University treated you? Can you really barely read or write? What do you think of the quality of the pastries available in Oxford's High Street today? Why did you include both "Hall" and "House" in the name of your refreshment hall (and house)?

Unlike most biographers of long departed historical figures, I can actually go and sit next to Sadler, which I do on the eve of my maiden balloon flight. I have earned the right to do this, and we have something in common - tomorrow morning I will join the club he started as the inaugural member: those who have

199

risen above Oxford in a hot air balloon and looked down at the Dreaming Spires below. When I say I sit with him, I genuinely do - and not in any metaphorical sense either. I sit down with the great man James Sadler, pioneering aeronaut and pastry cook of this parish.

That's because I am sitting next to his grave. Sadler was buried in the hushed grounds of an Oxford college -or rather he is now. He was initially interred in the churchyard of St. Peter-in-the-East, and the church's core remains relatively intact today from the twelfth century, with its origins even earlier (it is referenced in the Doomsday Book, the publishing sensation of 1086). I wonder how many publishers turned down the pitch: "So you want to create a tax inventory by listing every town and village's property? And you think there'll be interest in this after 1086?"

Having existed as a place of worship for Oxonians since the tenth century, St. Peter-in-the-East closed to public access in 1965 when it was deconsecrated, and it re-opened its now pew-less space in 1970 when it became the library of St. Edmund Hall - one of the current 38 colleges and six Permanent Private Halls that form the collective whole of Oxford University along with the institution's faculties and libraries. Books are stored on a spiral staircase ascending the church tower - so it must really annoy the librarian if you ask for a book near the top of the tower. Then, having patiently waited for the librarian to descend with the requested book, ask for "volume two as well, please". Timing is important in comedy.

Sadler was what is termed by some contemporary vicars as "a four-wheeler". This means he used the same church for being christened, married and buried - a christening, wedding and funeral nowadays ensuring that the service's top billed protagonists arrive by car - hence the terminology. Though the expression usually implies that it is the only time they set foot inside the church, this seems unlikely in Sadler's case. Certainly his family had continued involvement with what was their parish church. Sadler's younger brother Thomas was baptised there in July 1756. Indeed, the church/library continues its connection with Sadler today by displaying a plaque to mark his historic achievement of being the first Englishman to fly. Erected by the Royal Aeronautical Society, it was unveiled in 1928. It bills him as "James Sadler of this city", avoiding any ambiguity as to which side, Town or Gown, claims his legacy. Located in the west wall of the church, unflatteringly hidden behind a bookcase, it nonetheless accurately depicts the type of balloon Sadler built, encapsulating his spirit by depicting him waving his trademark pair of flags, and is clearly well maintained by its current owner Teddy Hall.

Sadler, like most successful pioneers in history, possessed the required good fortune to be around at the right time. Had Alexander Graham Bell been born

Intimations of mortality before the flight (Richard O. Smith) a hundred years later, his "I have invented a new wired speaking device" would have merely prompted pitying sighs and the common response, "pretty sure we've already got one of those, mate - plus mine does email and Angry Birds". Instead, he's a household name. Likewise, had Churchill delivered "we shall fight them [the Germans] on the beaches" in the present rather than twentieth century, then people would assume he was talking about obtaining the best sunbathing spots or winning the beach volleyball. Undoubted visionary and committed polymath as Sadler was, he would have realised that the age had provided him with his opportunity - but the grasping was very much down to him.

There is a paucity of personal information available about Sadler. Archives hint that he was successful at keeping his emotions hidden from public scrutiny nearly one hundred years before the Victorians made such a choice popular - though Sadler clearly antagonised several powerful people. There is little of the man seeping into the papers left behind. Letters are merely written in work mode, devoid of any insight into the internal workings of the man - with the exception of one angry exchange. The exception is the querulous letter fired off to the Derby committee. Otherwise there is infuriatingly little of the man in all the papers left behind.

Even accounts allegedly written by Sadler are most likely pieces of sanctioned ghost-writing. Other early balloonists had form in this area too; Lunardi's ostensibly self-written account of his flights was widely dismissed as a fraud at the time, though that didn't stop healthy sales figures. It fed an insatiable public requirement for anything balloon-related. A popular item during the height of balloonomania was a doorknob bearing Sadler's miniature colour portrait. The range was even extended to include a smaller desk draw knob featuring an even more miniature Sadler likeness. Lunardi now appeared in the format of an actual knob - one for irony fans everywhere to enjoy.

Press reports of the age jostle each other in a race towards hagiography, with Sadler consistently portrayed as a Great Briton in an age of great British wonder. And yet it is through such trivial details, the everyday miniature - the bonding mortar of the trivial that holds the elaborate decorative tiles in place - that causes the pattern to emerge to the viewer. Away from the grandiloquence and deepest purple of prose that many newspapers of the age advanced, small observations about Sadler's personality can be deduced. He is often reported as coming out to wave to crowds, even greeting them in walkabouts. One evening in Cheltenham, he appears at his hotel balcony "although already fatigued from the day" many times to appease the crowd, reported as a gesture of appreciation rather than feeding diva tendencies.

Elsewhere he is reported as calmly accepting that hardly anyone has bothered to pay the advance admission fee to see him fly. And this latter point is significant, as ballooning was extremely expensive - without an aristocratic patron, the only source of funding would be public subscription and admission - and Sadler does not appear to have pursued the fortune that many commentators suggest could have been his for the banking. Only when he reappears as an aeronaut in the second decade of the nineteenth century is he correctly more cautious with collecting admissions fees. This change can only be accountable to his earlier bankruptcy.

Despite the late eighteenth century's perceived embrace of hedonism, eventually prompting revolution in France and intense fear of copycat revolt in Britain, Sadler appears aloof from any distinct stratifications of class. He is claimed as a utilitarian man of the people, uneducated yet undisputedly brilliant. Meanwhile he is also comfortable in exalted company, interacting with the noblemen and titled gentlemen of his age, and - at least initially - claimed by the University of Oxford as one of their adopted own.

Sportsman, musician, actor and TV presenter were not yet career routes to celebrity for those born outside the nobility, so a meritocratic rise to the top was a rare and cherished opportunity. This may partly explain the public's affection for Sadler, proven by countless letters to contemporary magazines. It was easy for the public to believe he was one of them. Yet teasingly we know hardly anything of the man's emotional make-up. This is hard to accept from our vantage-point. Today we expect out celebrities to be emotionally incontinent.

So I sit down next to Sadler. His gravestone was renovated by the Royal Aeronautical Society in 1928 to mark the centenary of his death. The crumbling headstone, which was then further restored in 1984 - yes, the year is significant as the restoration deliberately coincided with the bicentenary of Sadler's first historical launch nearby.

A brief, one-line obituary is chiselled into a well-maintained gravestone, rightly pronouncing him as the first Englishman to fly. Next to it lie the fragments of the original gravestone. Across the path from Sadler's grave stands another headstone, marking the final resting place of Sarah Hounslow. Bizarrely, the engraved date of death is given as "31st February". No one knows why. I hope Sarah's family got a substantial discount from the stonemason responsible for that.

Stepping out of the graveyard, I walk twenty yards towards the High Street. The location of Sadler's cake shop and bakery is a mere scone's throw from his final resting place. Behind the Examination Schools which now occupy the site of Sadler's café, just beyond Merton Street to the south, lay the expansive fields leading to the Isis (or River Thames to anyone not from Oxford). Here an ancient path, clinging to the walls of Merton College, is known as Dead Man's Walk. This sinister name recalls the Jewish funereal route, when the city's

203

Jews were forbidden from burying their dead within the city wall. The ancient Jewish cemetery where the path concluded became the Physic Garden, now the Botanic Garden, but Dead Man's Walk survives in both route and name. In 1984 a plaque was erected marking the bicentenary of the flight. Illustrated with a balloon, the small shrine to Sadler declares him: "The first English aeronaut who in a fire balloon made a successful ascent from near this place 4 October 1784 to land near Woodeaton."

Unsurprisingly, Sadler doesn't reply to my questions. And seeing his grave intensifies my feelings that he did not receive a proper obituary when he died. Incredibly, Oxford University's official newspaper deemed him worth only a one line death notice - and took up most of the space in that one line mentioning his brother!

Maybe this book will provide Sadler with the lengthy obituary he deserves. After all, I am eligible to write his obituary. My first professional writing job was compiling obituaries for a local newspaper. By my calculations, I must have written about 500 obituaries. And yet, did any of the subjects ever thank me? No!

But in spite of Sadler's unwillingness - OK, mainly his inability - to answer my questions, there is still one big question that will have to be answered tomorrow. Will I be able to fly?

12 HIGH NOON IN A BALLOON: CAN I FLY?

Getting a balloon ride organised is unlikely to be a straightforward exercise. Here's how it works. You book onto a flight and then check with your balloon operator a few hours before launch time if the intention is still to go ahead. Changing climatic conditions decree if you fly or not. One fellow balloon passenger told me that they had booked onto eighteen flights: all were cancelled.

Moreover, it is extremely unusual to ever see a balloon crossing the skyline other than at dawn or dusk, when the atmospheric conditions governing air temperature are most favourable. Such optimum flying conditions are sought, and any threat of forecast wind or rain will result in another cancellation. If flying in the morning, which can often mean 5.30am or earlier take-off times, booked passengers have to phone a weather advice line at around 11pm the night before to hear whether their adventure is likely to go ahead and determine how early they have to set their alarm clock.

Quite what Sadler would make of this is intriguing, since he routinely flew in the middle of the day, which we now acknowledge as the worst possible time for ballooning. Mind you, he also took off in strong gales and driving rain. Maybe he would consider us modern beings to be unadulterated sissies, but I suspect he would just marvel at our scientific knowledge.

My first flight was cancelled. Having spent at least 72 hours with pre-flight anxiety, vibrating like someone who has just drunk eight double espressos, the flight was cancelled at five hours' notice. This surprised me, as it was a calm day with an unblemished blue sky. Yet a rising breeze from the east was forecast, so the launch was postponed.

Flushed with pride after completing my counselling course, and being released back into the wild by Claire and Steve better adjusted - if not completely cured - to deal with height anxiety, I wanted to accomplish the balloon flight.

Ostensibly, I am ready for my balloon flight. OK, more accurately my balloon trip is ready for me. It's time.

Flight day omens are hardly positive. I take a number 13 bus towards the launch site. Upon arrival I immediately spot a solitary magpie. Earlier that same morning my wife dropped a make-up mirror - she doesn't explain how, but I suspect it may have been while walking under a ladder. By now my planned balloon trip has been cancelled on twelve occasions. My brain helpfully works out that this means that when I actually take to the skies today it will be number thirteen. That's lucky.

As I arrive at Cutteslowe Park in North Oxford the weather is doing its best to replicate one of those old fashioned summer days that we don't seem to get any more - the sort you remember from childhood, when it was warmer, sunnier and the sandwiches tasted better. Once everything is cocooned in the safety of the past, it's immediately better. There is a miniature railway in the park, though, lamentably, there is a height restriction forbidding me from riding the train. How heightist is that! But there is no height restriction on the balloon ride I am about to take. Unfortunately.

Then the meeting time arrives, as do my fellow passengers (or "daredevils" as I refer to them). But the launch hour comes and passes. Meanwhile a balloon, which I consider a fairly essential piece of kit for the experience of taking a balloon flight, remains mysteriously absent. Eventually, nearly an hour after the arranged take-off time, a Land Rover arrives, impatiently squealing into the car park at speed before braking noisily.

But it only just arrives. The front windscreen is smashed. The passenger door is missing. The bumper is crudely tied on with string. The driver's side, where the window used to be, is now mainly fragmented glass. Presumably the damaged vehicle has shed parts of itself en route like a clown's car. The ground crew explain that they have been involved in a serious road accident, and the police only reluctantly allowed them to continue. I ask if the balloon may have been damaged. They reassure me it is still airworthy - far too quickly for my amygdala's liking.

They set about uncoupling the trailer, and unpacking the balloon - all 3,300 cubic feet capacity of it.

My friend Rebecca, sensitive to my on-going height anxiety, had kindly bought me a pre-flight Good Luck card and gift. She presents me with *Enduring Love* - the book by Ian McEwan, not the concept. After encountering those twelve flight postponements due to unfavourable weather conditions, I have plenty of time to start reading the kind present she had given me ahead of my next scheduled flight attempt. The book opens with a hot air balloon crash. Very funny, Rebecca.

Reading a few pages changes my feelings from laughter at Rebecca's clever joke to sudden fear. It is probably a good decision to read the rest of the book after my flight has been accomplished, should I ever have an emotional reunion with terra firm.

I know that stepping into that basket shortly is one of the hardest things I will ever do. Conversely I know it is an event so appealing to most of the population that they have willingly paid over £100 each to enjoy the experience. But to me it is as hard as beating acute shyness or a stutter. Or standing up to a bully - and in a way, overcoming a phobia is standing up to a bully. And that's not easy. Why is always doing the right thing constantly the hardest available option? Sometimes, why can't doing the right thing involve having a nice sit down with a latte and a chocolate fudge cake?

But this is one of the hardest things I've done - harder than asking Charlotte Jones out at the bus stop years ago and receiving a burning rejection. Harder than going up the steps of Tattershall Castle when I was eight.

Here are two consecutive entries from my diary, recorded nearly a year before my upcoming flight:

25 Feb. Spend evening with veteran balloon flyer. Begin to feel glimmer of reassurance for first time about the safety of being up in a balloon. They tell me that the drive home from the balloon landing site is statistically more dangerous than the preceding balloon flight.

26 Feb 7am. The main item on this morning's *Today* programme is a balloon crash in Luxor, Egypt. At least 19 people dead.

A few months later and another balloon crash headline appears. This time in the Netherlands when a balloon crashes into a lake. Then, shortly afterwards, news breaks of a balloon crash in England. A balloon comes down in a children's play area in Shropshire.

Hot on the heels of the cataclysmic crash in Egypt the BBC broke the story to a perturbed nation that a... er... lamp post was slightly damaged by a hot air balloon landing in Shrewsbury. No one is injured. The balloon apparently landed into a playground to avoid being stuck over the town centre when the breeze suddenly dropped.

This rams home a perennial problem with balloons: they only go where the wind is blowing. Should the wind suddenly change direction, then so do you. Don't expect a steering wheel on a balloon. And if the wind ceases to blow and the breeze knocks off early, then you are basically stuck levitating in one place, which is, with any luck, a suitable place to land. Hopefully this is not above somewhere unsuitable for landing a balloon - like an active volcano, or worse:

Swindon.

Oddly, my pre-flight feeling of acute anxiety is mixed with relief. Relief because I have endured so many cancellations that I now want to get the experience achieved and behind me. Whenever the flights were postponed previously, I initially felt a rush of relief flooding my brain, as my being emitted an audible sigh of "phew, that was a close one" and I instantly felt happy that I had cheated having to go through the fear. But the effects were inevitably short-lived; the relief was like a temporary sugar high that only lasts a short while before an inevitable dip. Then feelings of guilt set in - like someone who has just consumed a whole packet of chocolate biscuits in a sugar binge. My guilt was a realisation that I am rejecting and running away from life experiences.

Other phobia suffers must experience this too - the instant yet unsustainable high provided by the relief of avoiding whatever activity would have brought you into contact with the anxiety. Then a sudden drop into guilt at the realisation of having avoided something that would have forced you to confront your irrational fear. This behaviour fortifies rather than reduces the phobia, as your spirit plummets towards the understanding that you have lost out on yet another worthwhile life experience.

But not today. There is a Radio 4 crew with me. People have come from London. There's a magazine photo shoot with models. This helps galvanise me into going through with it.

It takes a while to get a balloon off the ground. Before the envelope is attached I am asked to sit in the basket for a pre-flight safety briefing. In doing so, just by climbing inside a wicker basket, I am aware that I am about to entrust my life to an oversized picnic basket - the sort of thing that Yogi Bear would attempt to steal from the park where we are due to take off.

Climbing into the hamper is not for the elderly or infirm. Fortunately my fellow flyers are very much of the youthful and physically fit variety. For the photo shoot two tall yet incredibly slim young blondes, *Vogue* model-types who probably ate a blueberry two days ago and are consequently still full, vault into the hamper with agility, though they're so light they float in. If we need to jettison ballast later (significantly you only jettison ballast on a hydrogen not hot air balloon) then throwing these two models overboard would make no difference whatsoever to our altitude. And I trust there will be no shortage of normal-sized women who would be willing volunteers to toss the models overboard if required.

My inaugural balloon ride has started. It is a much noisier experience than I was expecting, the propane burner constantly roared into life by our pilot. We are off the ground, and already I fear we are far too high for me to feel comfortable. I look for the altimeter, only to be told "we haven't got an altimeter". It's OK, these days a laptop screen is the pilot's altimeter. And it informs me that we're only five feet off the ground. The basket suddenly judders from side to side. Up, up and a sway - rather than away.

When sufficient levitation has been achieved, it rises surprisingly quickly. At about twelve feet off the ground, I announce that this is quite high enough for me, and that if we can maintain current altitude for the flight duration, I will be absolutely fine with that, thank you very much. But the on-board computer - no, Sadler would not have had that - spins the numbers upwards on the computer's altimeter. Oh, you have a computer now that does everything, including calculating our speed, height, pressure, etc.

Even at several hundred feet, I can clearly make out my wife waving, then holding a piece of paper, probably checking the insurance documentation and how soon after my demise it's possible to submit a claim.

After only a few seconds we are high enough to look down at Oxford beneath us, and see the same landmarks and skyline that would still be easily recognised by James Sadler: the hushed college quadrangles, Magdalen Tower, the Radcliffe Camera and Sir Christopher Wren's imposing Tom Tower entrance gate to Christ Church.

As I glance down appreciatively upon Matthew Arnold's famous Dreaming Spires I connect with Sadler's vision; he was the first person ever to see all this from above. Even from this range, I can make out a scholar's bicycle in Merton Street, rattling timelessly across ancient cobbles. Instantly I catch myself pledging that I will never take for granted being on terra firma again, even if that does involve traversing cobble stones on a bike.

Omnipresent is a wash of background noise, and the terrifyingly loud noise of propane being fired. There are two switches, a high and low, to spit propane flames like an angry dragon. Such noises, like dragons' roars, just fertilise my fears. Fellow trippers are laughing. How can anyone laugh at a time like this? They have toasted their flight - which means being pre-lashed. And are looking forward to champagne when we land. I'm looking forward to when we land too. In fact, I want to land now.

Once you reach about 1,000 feet the distracting noises of earth start to leave you behind. The low roar of the ring-road disappears, as do the other tell-tale noises of human endeavour. Suddenly you are afforded a prolonged period of one of the regrettably rarest commodities in our world: silence. Since the balloon moves with the wind, we are literally becoming the wind, blending, intermingling with it. So there is no noise to the breeze, no rustle of anything. Such a dangerous feeling of anxiety, mixed incongruously with a total sense of serenity.

Richard Branson has admitted "I got a tremendous sense of joy from being superbly powerless: human chaff, borne who knows where by the wind." Now I can relate to what he means. Maybe I can risk uncoiling myself from my current foetal position, and take a short peek at the view over the basket's edge?

Then another noisy dragon's breath of propane shoots flames inches from my nose. Finally I dare myself to steal the briefest of glimpses over the basket's side. From this height Oxfordshire resembles a model railway layout. Then my terrified brain orders me to get away from the edge, hooking me back towards the middle of the basket.

"Alright?" asks someone from the Radio 4 production company. "Fine," I lie, badly.

The one aspect that nobody has yet conquered in the modern age is how to steer balloons. Basically a balloonist is rudderless, a passive passenger of currents. The wind direction rather than the pilot always determines the destination. You can see how this would rather clip the appeal of a form of transport. "The train now approaching Platform 4 is for... well, who knows? London hopefully, but if there's a prevailing easterly it could just as easily be Bristol, or Birmingham if the wind changes again."

Today the wind takes us almost exactly on the same route Sadler took on that very first 4 October 1784 ascent. Fittingly I am replicating the exact flight path of the very first Englishman to fly. Now I too am looking down like Sadler on the open countryside to the north of Oxford, spotting the same checkerboard formations of tiny fields shaped in perfect squares that he saw when he passed Otmoor. This is the landscape that would later inspire Lewis Carroll to write his chessboard scenes.

After fifteen minutes we soar alongside a bemused looking red kite clearly thinking "what are humans doing up here?" The earth does look invitingly splendid from above - it's definitely my kind of planet, and I'm discovering at altitude that I am rather keen to see it again and definitely want to spend some more time there. Nervous ain't the word.

Distracting nuggets of info are helpfully dispensed by our pilot who maintains an in-flight commentary. He tells us of a rival balloon company's pilot who once flew over a US air base visible near our current flight path and received the sinister radio message to either land immediately or be shot down. I would have refused to comply - a slow-moving 75-foot giant bright red floating bauble can't be that much of a sitting target for the air force. Oh, hang on...

Our pilot is happy to answer any questions. Balloons have a normal life expectancy of around 500 hours of flying time, as they become progressively porous the older they get. Hence I enquire: "How old is our balloon?" "730 hours," he replies, so it's quite a veteran of the skies. The pilot opens the vent allowing hot air to escape while something similar is happening to my confidence.

Every minute our calm is jolted by the pilot firing twin propane burners. A silver one roars fiercely whenever heat injection is required to add extra propulsive lift. There is also a smaller red burner which is quieter, and used at lower altitudes, particularly when flying over livestock as it is less distressing - to livestock and me.

Reassuringly, the pilot explains the intense training necessary to gain a licence. There are five compulsory examinations. A hydrogen balloon pilot requires a separate licence from that of a hot air balloonist. Hydrogen balloons still need, even in the modern age, several hours of filling time - a timeframe that has not altered significantly since Sadler's pioneering gas ballooning.

It is illegal to fly a balloon without a licence, although in answer to my question, the pilot confirms that there are no police balloons. So there is little chance of being signalled to pull over by a balloon with a flashing blue light flying besides you. ("Excuse me, Sir, would you mind blowing into this tube?" "Why, officer?" "Because we're losing altitude.")

Thinking of owning your own balloon to pop down the shops and seriously confuse head-scratching traffic wardens? "Can I ticket a transportation vehicle without wheels on a double yellow?" Well, all the parking fines you may avoid would be dwarfed by the cost of buying a working balloon. Our balloon has propane fuel tankers costing £2,000. Our burners check out at £8,000, with the handmade basket capable of holding twelve passengers adding another £12,000. The pilot estimates that our balloon costs a total of £36,000.

Then I realise something rather staggering. Not a landmark I've picked out on the ground, but something occurring to me right now in the wicker basket. There is no breeze - at all. I'm told that if you had the reckless tenacity to be flying during a force 8 gale, as of course James and Windham Sadler, being reckless, did, you would not feel any wind on your face. Hold up a flimsy silk scarf, and it would droop limply.

Here comes the science bit: this is due to our velocity and direction being entirely controlled by the air flow, so we are literally moving like the wind. This renders passengers devoid of any sensation of movement. We could be moving at 80mph like Sadler, but he would have felt stationary. Perhaps Sadler was simply unaware of the perils - though I doubt this as he supplied his own navigation charts and cutting-edge scientific instruments.

There is a pervading sense of removed calmness, levitating motionlessness, even though the changing landmarks before signal movement to the brain. If anything, flying in a balloon feels like inverse free-fall i.e. you are actively falling away from earth as it gets tinier and tinier below.

Most balloonists only fly when the ground wind speed is below 10mph. Sadler, of course, would consider this strangely restrictive - although given the bruising experiences he obtained from flying in strong winds, he might as well have complied with the generically adopted practice today.

There are a number of ways that our balloon, and my ballooning experience, is dissimilar to Sadler's. For starters, I didn't design, invent, test and manufacture my own balloon, basket, ropes, stove, netting, and fuel. Nor pilot it. Perhaps the acutest difference is we have a propane burner, relinquishing us of straw shovelling duties.

Other than that, I'm reliant on eighteenth-century technology to raise me over 3,000 feet above, and return safety to, the earth. Apart from a propane gas cylinder and burner, our equipment checklist is unreassuringly identical to Sadler's nearly 250 years ago. As is our flight equipment, landing and navigation procedures (OK, on board computer and radio notwithstanding) as Sadler had no idea where he was going either. That's the wind's decision. Even the clever invention of netting to encase the balloon bag was Sadler's very same equipment choice. Though we are not reliant on ox gut today, which Sadler would likely have deployed to ensure his envelope had an air-tight seal to retain the hot air molecules. Ensuring an air-tight membrane was crucial for silk balloon flyers, particularly with the early adoption of hydrogen, an element with a peculiarly small atom.

Anchored to the ground with guide ropes, our colourful outer membrane is referred to as the envelope. This is confusing, as I want to call it a balloon. An envelope is something different, and it appears to me that the entire plan for flying a balloon can be written on the back of one. This does not reassure me.

Here's the simple truth - and worryingly short if about to entrust your life to such a mechanism - of how a balloon works.

Our balloon is filled with hot air. It is important to anchor the balloon with ropes before starting this procedure, or the anger fits displayed by a small child when losing their balloon will be a good-tempered shrug compared to how the balloon's adult owner will react when informed that you neglected to restrain the balloon when filling it - and it soared away forever.

Firing a burner intermittently jets hot air into the canopy (sorry, envelope - we must use the technical terms). First, though, you must roll out the envelope into a flat design on the ground - and the balloon co-ordinator asks me to help him push it along the grass. "We're pushing the envelope," I remark. Then pretend I was only talking to myself, since no one laughs.

Opening the propane burner heats up the existing air in the balloon, causing it to become lighter as the air molecules thin. In turn, the balloon is now becoming lighter than the surrounding air, so will float upwards. As the air cools, it regains heaviness and accordingly the balloon will begin to sink unless the air molecules are re-heated pronto with blasts from the on-board twin burner. Reassuringly, the mouth of the balloon is not made from standard nylon like the envelope (phew), but an anti-inflammable (what is the opposite of flammable, if inflammable also means flammable?) in-inflammable (that'll do) material known as nomex.

Nomex, a polymer was invented in the 1960s and enables a flame-resistant (could have used that phrase!) fabric to surround the flame at the envelope's bottom. Pioneering balloonists obviously could only use decidedly non-flame-resistant materials such as paper and silk, and results were often terminal. Fatal crashes occurred as the flame was indispensable for ensuring the air in the balloon remained hotter than its surrounding air. This is why balloons are rarely spotted in the midday or early afternoon skyline, as the air is warmer, and thus lighter, than the heavier air offered by dawn or dusk.

The higher the ascent, the thinner the surrounding air: hence higher heat is required for higher altitude. Additional ascension can also be obtained by dispensing ballast, often sandbags attached to a balloon for this purpose in case a sudden lift is required if approaching overhead power wires, church spires or Peter Crouch. A deflation system is reassuringly installed in our balloon, where a cord opens a re-sealable flap. Opening this is known in ballooning parlance as "venting", or "annoying" if you're the only one who wants to use it to land immediately after take-off.

Likewise balloonists will often carry sandbags or even metallic weights as ballast. This is also why so many balloon pilots fly with Richard Branson, although disappointingly no one appears to have needed to lob him out of the basket yet to gain quick altitude.

The mechanism for raising our hot air balloon replicates Sadler's and the Montgolfiers' method from the early 1780s. Like Sadler, our envelope is securely fastened to the basket by cords and netting connected to a tiny hoop at the balloon's crown, as is the case in other forms of balloon which rely upon helium or hydrogen. The latter is the "rarefied air" that Sadler produced himself, and operates upon the principle of having less mass than the surrounding air. Theoretically, a hydrogen balloon, if perfectly sealed, would ascend indefinitely until it reaches even thinner air. Air is thicker, and thus heavier, nearer the earth's crust due to gravity attracting air molecules.

Since indefinite and unending ascent would not be a big selling point in any balloon trip company's brochures, a valve is necessary in both types of balloon to release air. Sadler sensibly ensured these were in his design blueprints, whereas Lunardi blindly rolled the dice of fate by flying without a valve - and thus having little if any say in his landing destiny.

Like Sadler's balloon, we don't have any brakes either. Unlike Sadler's balloon, we turn to propane regularly to provide extra lift.

Rather understandably, it is a definite no-no to throw anything over the basket, but I have a tiny dual-pronged chip fork. With sleight of hand, I furtively manage to drop this over the side without attracting witnesses when we drift over an empty field: it is a direct homage to the moment on Sadler's first manned voyage when he dropped a fork too.

The progressive tide of ever faster travel has swept away the interaction with nature that slower sorts of transport, like walking, gentle biking or ballooning, allow. As if to prove this, another red kite approaches us, coming surprisingly close. Eyeing us with more curiosity than suspicion, he then tilts his wings to the left and swoops away impressively, as if to remind us humans that we're only flying artificially, and not a true natural like him. I lean forward over the edge of the wicker basket for the first time in the flight, keen to see the red kite race away.

Look down and there is a terrifying 3,000-foot drop below. Look upwards and the balloon appears to be on fire with huge blasts of lit orange propane. Neither sight calms my amygdala.

There is a Swede aboard who works as a chef. Wow, this is texting-worthy - only we're not allowed to text in the balloon. I spoke to a real Swedish chef. My smile when he relays the twin information of nationality and profession is greeted by a look that I easily translate as, "I am sick and tired of people saying 'oh, you're a Swedish chef but you don't sound like the Muppets'. That's not even a Swedish accent.'" He says all this, sounding exactly like the Muppets. In order to avoid smiling inappropriately, I stop crouching with knees permanently bent in the basket, and peer right over the side for only the third time in the flight. That has the effect of applying the emergency brakes to my rising smile, and I feel genuinely terrified again.

I start chanting internally, like a mantra, some of the advice imparted by my counsellors: Steve and Claire, the Australian model on the blind date, cerebral phobia expert Dr. Hannah, and many others who kindly helped me on "my journey" to get to the point where I am now: an acute acrophobic 3,000 feet up in a giant wicker hamper. It does help, enormously. For proof that this concerted counselling effort works, see me. Currently 3,000 feet up in that wicker balloon basket.

Then something occurs that I was sincerely not expecting. Half an hour into the flight, I begin to shed the fear. Slowly at first, but then after a few more minutes, large chunks of anxiety begin falling from me. Another five minutes elapse and I'm almost relaxed - not quite, it would be dishonest to say so, but I am immeasurably calmer than the abject emotional arousal in which I'd spent the first forty minutes of the flight. My explanation for this is that my amygdala just got bored with firing "Danger! Danger! Fire! Fire! Panic! Panic!" and thought "well, that's five o'clock, I'm off down the pub." Maybe that's how controlled exposure, or even flooding, techniques work in addressing then nullifying a phobia. Your misfiring amygdala is only prepared to put in so much work on one shift before knocking off for the day.

Once my over-active, hyper-chatty amygdala finally shuts up, I almost begin to enjoy the voyage. A passive acceptance replaces my fears, as if saying "OK demons, you had a chance to do your worst. And you haven't destroyed me yet." After a few more minutes I become even calmer. Then a brand new feeling starts to form. At first it's too far away to identify, like a song in the distance, then I make sense of the new feeling. I am actively determined to appreciate the rareness of the experience. Once relinquished responsibility has been accepted by my rational brain, my irrational brain has gone off shift. For the first time, my brain is soothing me, saying "this is actually going to be OK. Now start to appreciate it before it's over." Then the pilot announces it is time to land. Like a lovely deep sleep that finally arrives at the end of a restless night, where the pillow has never felt softer, the bed never warmer, then the alarm clock rudely goes off. We are about to land, just as I have started to appreciate it.

Like Sadler coming into land, we vent our balloon too. Unlike Sadler, we have to avoid countless overhead - or, rather, "underhead" obstacles given our current view - such as power lines and a busy M40. Therefore a modern balloon pilot has to choose his or her landing spot with even more precision than in Sadler's day, mainly because our environment is either built upon or crisscrossed by high-voltage power wires. From the air it is still possible to appreciate the fine job our countryside is doing in its struggle to keep towns and villages apart. Inevitably, though, this overcrowded isle will eventually merge into one unending giant metropolis called London.

215

Not that landing is an exact science. In fact, purists would argue that balloons never land, only crash. Again, a detail conspicuously absent in most balloon businesses' brochures.

Gently, we drift down to earth. To achieve what aeronauts term "neutral buoyancy" the pilot must ensure the air is only slightly hotter inside than outside the globe. This skilfully achieved, the balloon appears to hover as it commences its gentle touchdown

When our balloon comes into land, we adopt our briefed landing positions - like the emergency landing brace stance demonstrated by stewardesses on planes. (You know the position? You *do* listen to them, don't you? Tut.) Although forewarned that the basket will probably topple over onto its side when landing, our pilot provides the softest of touchdowns - like cotton wool falling onto a haystack.

But there is still much work to be done as soon as we are back on the ground. There are 20-25 tonnes of hot air remaining inside the envelope providing a potentially huge inertia drag factor. This is why you really don't want to be ballooning in windy conditions because a gust of wind now could easily re-launch the envelope like a giant kite, and drag an upturned basket away with it.

This violent lurch can potentially throw the pilot out of the basket, and leave a hapless bunch of passengers without a crew sailing upwards again. This certainly happened several times to Sadler, and at least once to his unfortunate passenger in the flatlands of Lincolnshire between Heckington and Sleaford. That day Sadler was upturned out of the basket only to see his fellow passenger - a man without any aeronautical experience - re-launched by a strong gust. So children, do not attempt to fly a balloon during strong winds. Sadler would almost certainly agree with you, and he did not reach that conclusion by taking the route marked "the easy way".

The air needs to be squeezed out of the balloon as quickly as possible once it is on the deck. Surprisingly, this is accomplished by using a rolling pin, a human rolling pin. Three girls gamely volunteer to act as the required rolling pins and rotate themselves along the balloon surface, compressing air out of the end. One of the rolling pins is a model from the photo-shoot who is wearing a short white summer dress that frequently treats the men present to numerous knickers flashes - probably not the most practical outfit for this job. Though, to be fair, it was hard to predict at the start of the evening the dress requirement to be a human rolling pin. Like Sadler, she is accomplished at both disciplines: ballooning and rolling pastry.

The girls complete the rolling pin job so well that they should definitely move on to pastry next. Once the envelope is flatter than a pancake in Holland, everyone present rolls the balloon into a cylindrical tube shape, and then we pick it up like a giant anaconda. Balloons appear vast when they are laid out on the ground, their sense of proportion distorted when usually viewed in the sky at distance. They really are massive. Next everyone helps funnel the now tubular balloon back into the trailer.

But we're not finished with the basket yet. Unusually, we are told to get back into the wicket basket and re-assume our former flying positions. This is not an easy task, because the balloon basket is now on the back of a trailer. But it's to save us a lengthy walk back to the farmhouse and civilisation - or at least the nearest point that our awaiting minibus can reach on navigable roads.

The farmer whose field we have landed on is given a bottle of champagne - a traditional, and it has to be said, a highly successful, way of ensuring instant friendliness. Some balloon operators I had interviewed told me of bad experiences when encountering the "get orf my land" brigade of old-school load-the-shotgun-first farmers' greetings. Some professional balloon trippers showed me compiled colour-coded maps, marking the friendly, indifferent and troublesome farmers. Knowing where to land without attracting encircling pitch-fork brandishers, and which fields - so that crops aren't damaged, livestock enraged or bulls annoyed - is clearly advantageous.

Here our intrepid pilot continues to multi-task, this time pouring champagne for all. "Does anyone want orange juice instead of champagne?" His question creates the silence it deserves.

Champagne is a traditional conclusion to balloon flights. Anything that includes a free glass of champagne usually enables the function and provider to appear (a) automatically classier than it actually is (b) probably overpriced. Drinking is a long standing ballooning tradition. Sadler never flew without a bottle of brandy on board, sometimes several bottles.

"You deserve a glass of champagne," says a friendly fellow passenger. As one of the tall slim models examines the champagne bottle's label (probably to check how many calories it contains), I wonder if I do deserve any champagne. After all I have managed to overcome "an ordeal" that the man talking to me has just paid over £100 to experience and for which he has driven from Leicester.

Still, phobias are odd things. I've certainly learnt that. And maybe if I have now proven I can overcome my biggest fear, then my other anxieties will become less pungent too. Especially now I've proved that I am the boss of my brain, and I've made a balloon flight in spite of his best efforts to stop me participating. My counselling has helped me engage with the world, yet the knowledge - trusting myself to rational scientific enlightenment - has been the welcome sunlight of a new dawn enabling me to see the route to mental improvement. Just learning about the psychology of anxieties and phobias has helped reduce their potency. I cannot stress how helpful this was as part of the process - and, albeit foolish on my part, I did not expect this to happen.

Before I had cramped my life into the small spaces left where anxiety had not yet infiltrated, like a hoarder forced to live in one small room by the overwhelming clutter of negativity. Now I know that I have overcome my biggest phobia by taking this flight - and guess what? It was OK.

I have ascended above the clouds and yet can now see everything much more clearly. My vision has improved. Sometimes you have to rise above things to see them in perspective, to enable them to make sense. Right, I deserve a pastry. I'm off to the High Street. Anyone recommend a good café in Oxford's High Street?

1 SEPTEMBER 1815: NEWCASTLE

At the age of 62, if James Sadler's bones were not indestructible, then his courage certainly was.

Refusing to be put off by his lifelong catalogue of accumulated crashes, frights and bumpy landings, Sadler senior staged a flight on Tyneside in a titan monster of a balloon described on posters advertising the event as "75 feet in diameter, capable of lifting 72 people". Quite how the last statistic had been worked out remained vague.

The monster globe was certainly impressive. Oddly, it had been commissioned by the King of France two years beforehand. Louis XVIII had placed an order with Sadler to manufacture a huge ornate balloon for his coronation event, though the balloon never reached France. Instead Sadler removed the French symbols and repackaged it as a patriotic British balloon adorned with the Prince of Wales' feathers.

Sadler didn't stop there, pimping up his balloon cart to the edge of excess by adding more stars, gold embroidery, oak wreathes, gold and purple tassels and the twelve signs of the zodiac. Oh, and a few more stars. He then added two carved eagles onto the front and back of the oval-shaped wooden cart. This somewhat meretricious creation, along with the balloon silk, was put on display to the public in the Turk's Head pub in Bigg Market, Newcastle - for the admission charge of one shilling.

A popular Geordie dialect song, *Bob Crank's Account of the Ascent of Mr. Sadler's Balloon*, celebrated Sadler's ascent in the north-east. The press described the Newcastle excursion as his 47th flight. Was there still time for his increasingly brittle bones to accomplish fifty flights?

7 NOVEMBER 1815: EDINBURGH

That rarest of flights in the aeronautical careers of the Sadlers - i.e. one which passed without any life-threatening disasters or even mild perils - occurred when Windham staged a voyage in serenely windless conditions for once, in Norwich on 29 June 1815.

Normal service was resumed in a few months later. Scheduled to make an ascent in the Scottish capital in November, Windham launched his balloon in extremely strong winds. Perhaps because this was insufficiently dangerous, he also conspired to accidentally leave behind his charts and navigational instruments. This prompted an unusual outbreak of common sense from one of the ballooning pioneers, and Sadler used the valve almost immediately to release gas from the globe. After travelling only three miles to the Portobello coastal resort, he landed after spending a mere eight minutes airborne.

2 SEPTEMBER 1816: CORK

James Sadler - most definitely father not son - was still flying aged 63, albeit briefly. Launching in what was described as the very first flight in Cork at 4.40pm one September afternoon in 1816, Sadler senior had safely returned to terra firma by 5.12pm. It is possible that this was his last flight, though that is merely assumption. Stating categorically that this was his 50th flight is where assumption meets speculation, however, as, inconveniently, we do not know where James Sadler took his 50th flight. But a letter in the possession of one the biggest celebrities of the era later confirms that Sadler did reach his half century - as we shall see later.

What we do know is that the Sadlers were about to accomplish an historical aeronautical first in Ireland next summer.

22 JULY 1817: DUBLIN TO HOLYHEAD: RACE TO CROSS THE IRISH SEA

The *London Chronicle* had signed off its report on the Burlington House ascents by prognosticating: "Windham is James Sadler's youngest son and seems to be the most undoubted heir to his father's talents and we may look upon him who has commenced aerial philosophy so early for future experiments which may elicit utility as well as wonder." Almost exactly three years later, Windham lived up to that prophecy when he succeeded in accomplishing a balloon first that had eluded all previous aeronauts including his father.

James Sadler had agreed to loan his balloon to a Mr. Livingstone who, accompanied by the real box office star of proceedings Miss Thompson, took off from Dublin on 20 July 1817. The *Literary Gazette* confirmed that the pair had a safe landing: "After a short excursion they regained solid earth without accident."

This may have provided some income for the Sadlers, as Miss Thompson's latest short fight was the support act to the main event two days later, where Windham Sadler intended his next flight to be both solo and record breaking.

Windham succeeded where Sadler senior had so spectacularly failed five years earlier, and claimed the trophy of being the first person ever to fly across the Irish Sea.

Electing to take the route travelling east - favoured by all previous flyers because of the prevailing wind direction - he commenced his assault on the record by taking off from Portobello Barracks "assisted by his venerable father James Sadler with the balloon's inflation". Using a lightweight wicker basket coated with a leather sheet, Windham had a strategy. He aimed to keep the balloon as low as he could, and chart a straight line trajectory on a south-westerly breeze. Although perhaps fortunate to find such an obliging current, he locked his balloon onto the discovered course. His plan undoubtedly worked, enabling him to clear the Irish coast an hour after take-off when he soared above the Charles II-built Baily Lighthouse at Howth Head.

Maintaining his low trajectory, he calculated his height by regularly dropping eggs into the water. Noting at one stage during the flight that an egg took 29 seconds to produce a splash in the sea, he was able to calculate his altitude. With the Welsh coast now coming into view, the breeze stayed favourable and swept him over Holyhead. Unlike his father a few years earlier, Windham decided to vent the balloon rapidly and land at Anglesey, instead of remaining airborne in an attempt to reach the English mainland.

Upon landing he claimed the record, and noted in his journal with an entitled boast: "The first aeronaut to cross the Irish Channel." It had taken him exactly five hours, almost to the minute. He then returned to Dublin, this time by boat, to attend a celebratory dinner the next day alongside the other guest of honour at the function: his balloon envelope.

30 MAY 1818: SON JAMES DIES

Such good luck for the Sadler's was definitely not hereditary. James Sadler's wife Mary had died in 1791.

Further tragedy occurred, with the *Lancashire Gazette* of 30 May 1818 reporting the sudden death of James Sadler junior: "Captain James Sadler, who was killed in one of the last actions of the East Indies, was the son of the celebrated aeronaut of that same name."

30 JULY 1822: OTHER DANGERS FOR BALLOON PIONEERS

People point out balloons, a ritual unperformed for other transport modes. They

The man who packed a tuxedo: S.A. Andree (Nils Strindberg/Wikimedia Commons)

reserve affection for balloons that other modes of transport rarely enjoy. People don't point to aeroplanes (OK, apart from maybe in Norfolk) or motor cars (perhaps very rural Norfolk).

Balloons even improve landscapes, with photographers happy to click the shapes and colours of balloons soaring across a backdrop of idyllic rural England. Balloons are the welcomed aristocracy of transport, undeniably posh and exclusive yet embraced by the populace. No one looks down on a balloon. Although other transport mechanism have become obsolete balloons survive into their fourth century in good health. People like balloons. That's why they still feel compelled to point them out.

But being a pioneering balloonist is dangerous. Sadler had proven this as categorically as anyone could by 1784. And yet it was a lesson that remained stubbornly unlearnt by his aeronautical successors.

In 1897 a proud Swede S.A. Andree ascended in a hydrogen balloon from Dane's Island located approximately 600 miles south of the North Pole. It was his stated intention to reach the North Pole by air. Whereas the pole had claimed hundreds of lives - some estimates calculate that by the end of the nineteenth century nearly one thousand individuals had perished in attempts to reach the artificial construct that represents the point of the North Pole - Andree's was the very first attempt to reach it in a balloon.

He was so sure of his mission ending in success that he intended to continue flying his hydrogen balloon for another several thousand miles afterwards until he reached San Francisco for a pre-planned landing in the sunny Californian city. Additional hubris was added by the detail that he even reportedly packed a tuxedo in the balloon basket in order to attend the formal dinner thrown in his honour at San Francisco Town Hall. Needless to say, the caterers only got their deposit for the function.

After taking off he and his two companions literally disappeared into increasingly thin air as they drifted away on a strong northwards breeze. They were not seen again until over thirty years later when a Norwegian boat discovered their bodies - and some photographs - in a remote Arctic region. It was a reminder, a hundred years after Sadler's pioneer flights, how dangerous the occupation continued to be.

Even during Sadler's lifetime, there were other inherent perils. In Cheltenham, Gloucestershire - the Georgian spa town which had earlier suffered a lengthy bout of balloonomania when Sadler ascended there - witnessed a malicious problem on 6 August 1822. The *Strabane Morning Post* continues the story:

> It is said that Mr. Green, the aeronaut, before he ascended with his balloon from Cheltenham, expressed his opinion to his companion that the cord had been cut by 'black legs' from London, as not less than £20,000 was betted on the event at Cheltenham, besides great sums in London. The severed cord appeared to be cut by some instrument as sharp as a razor, and the operation must have been effected with great dexterity, to avoid notice in the presence of such numbers.

This is an early reference to celebrated balloonist Charles Green who nearly perished in a sabotaged flight. Significant sums had been wagered on the balloon not flying further than Cheltenham, an outcome that "blacklegs" were determined to provide, even if that included nobbling the aeronaut with his balloon. Green and his passenger suffered severe injuries, and were close to being killed. The *Cheltenham Chronicle* was at the scene, and in the balloon basket itself, as it was the newspaper's owner who accompanied Green as his co-pilot on the flight. He filed this report in his own newspaper in a piece headlined "The Descent of Mr. Green's Balloon at Ecton":

> On Tuesday, July 30, 1822, about four o'clock in the afternoon, Mr. Green, accompanied by Mr. S. V. Griffith, proprietor of the *Cheltenham Chronicle*, ascended from Cheltenham; the balloon went up in a most beautiful style, to the admiration of an immense assemblage of persons; it was visible for 25 minutes, and took a south-east direction. The Balloon descended near North Leach, but on touching the ground the aeronauts could not immediately extricate themselves: the balloon

reascended, and the netting, being partly cut, gave way when about 30 feet from the earth, and Messrs. Green and Griffith were precipitated with great violence to the ground. Mr. Green received a serious contusion on the left side of the chest, and Mr. Griffith a severe injury of the spine.

The balloon was secured about six o'clock the same evening, having fallen in a wheat field of Mr. Wright at Ecton Lodge, apparently without the least injury.

As if the Sadlers hadn't enough stalking dangers from weather, altitude and gas to contend with, they now also had to add murderous betting syndicates to their list of potential fatal concerns.

12 AUGUST 1823: WORLD'S MOST MAGNIFICENT AND LARGEST BALLOON

Father and son act the Sadlers were not lone operatives in the world of exhibition ballooning. They would often pop up supporting other aeronauts, though most probably for an agreed fee. On one occasion, their names appeared on handbills advertising - not in an understated way it has to be said - "THE WORLD'S MOST MAGNIFICENT AND LARGEST BALLOON". In case that description risked being too modest, the owner got his own trumpet out of its case and proceeded to give it another long and loud blow: "My balloon far exceeds in magnitude and splendour any aerostation machine hitherto made or exhibited in any part of the entire world." They were partial to an overstatement, were the Georgians.

A Mr. Graham of London was responsible for this monster globe, and monster boast. He claimed the envelope was built with sufficient capacity for 250,000 gallons of gas, "which on this occasion will be supplied by the Imperial Gas Company". His listed dimensions are relatively puny, being sixty by forty feet, so one suspects he was helping himself to a considerable amount of free Imperial gas for other reasons.

Yet the balloon was exhibited at an Oxford Street drapers, where shoppers could see it after first parting with a shilling for the privilege. A further 3s 6d was required to be present at the launch site in the gardens of White Conduit House in Pentonville, "where Mr Graham will be assisted in inflation and ascent by the well-known and celebrated aeronauts Messrs Sadler".

Even by 1823, almost forty years since Sadler's historic first flight, his was still the name to put on the poster if you wanted to attract punters to a ballooning event.

12-13 SEPTEMBER 1823: SHEFFIELD

Before undertaking the immensely dangerous York flight, where gales meant that landing was a dice throw with fate, the Sadlers had been experimenting with coal gas for ballooning.

Although they were still called "fire balloons" in popular parlance, hydrogen had replaced hot air ballooning decades earlier. Now a third type of flying was available, an alternative to hydrogen: coal gas. Initially, however, coal gas seemed unlikely to replace hydrogen as the aeronaut's lighter-than-air gas of choice.

Windham now chalked up two uncharacteristic failures. Twice in Sheffield in September 1823 he had sold tickets for an advertised coal gas flight, but failed to ascend on both days when he was unable to raise the balloon even though the globe was visibly brimming with gas. He later attributed these two rare failures to "the density of the coal gas with which it was to be inflated and the humidity of the atmosphere".

This appears to have been an unusual double setback for Windham, as he tried on both the Friday and Saturday to launch to no avail. According to the *Worcester Journal*, he returned five days later with a hydrogen balloon, and this time was able to become airborne, travelling a distance of "17 miles in perfect safety".

SEPTEMBER 1823: YORK

Surprisingly, Windham Sadler returned to coal gas for his next escapade in late September 1823 when he ascended from York - but only just. The transition from hydrogen was not always straightforward, as the latter of two ascents in York that month proved. He was not helped by yet another gale.

Battered against the ancient city walls by a violent and persistent wind, Sadler was - not for the first time, it should be noted - reported as being fortunate to survive. Quite how delusional the Sadlers were in considering themselves immortal is surely open to psychological debate.

Choosing to launch at Toft End near Micklegate, a single booming detonation from a signal gun at 11.30am indicated that the inflation process had begun. Not many locals were in attendance - in noticeable contrast to the huge crowds drawn from dawn at similar ascents. This was most likely for the very sensible reason that a storm was brewing.

The First Royal Dragoons marching band then appeared, parading alongside the city walls. "About an hour before the ascent took place, a very heavy gale of wind came upon, accompanied with rain."

Worse was to be discovered. The gale had knocked the partially inflated balloon over and an inexpertly packed grappling iron with prongs facing upwards

224

punctured the globe. Delayed by several hours, the car was finally fixed to the repaired balloon at 4.30pm, with the storm still raging.

"Notwithstanding, Mr Sadler threw out ballast immediately. He had great difficulty in clearing the walls. Indeed the car was bashed with considerable force against them. But Mr Sadler cast himself down, guarding against the considerable shock and violence."

Having buffeted York's city walls like a medieval invader, he finally rose clear. At which point he stood upright in the basket for the first time "to convince his anxious friends he was uninjured".

"The wind during the journey was very turbulent." At one point, heading towards Selby, the balloon cart sliced through the tops of several elm trees "offering no obstacle to his progress, such was the violence of the winds". Knocking him around the basket like a human pinball, the gale was disinclined to decrease in ferocity. Crashing through the tops of another wooden glade, Sadler squatted in the basket "to avoid being torn to pieces".

His earlier entanglement with the city walls had caused life-threatening damage to the balloon, as it has snapped the venting rope. This rendered Sadler unable to control the balloon's deflation. He was thus left with only one landing option - optimistically throwing out the grappling irons when low enough to reach treetops.

This he did, though at an impractically fast speed caused by the fully inflated balloon coupled with gale force winds. Several of the prongs snapped off due to the pressure, until his final grappling iron made contact with a willow tree. The stretching chain soon broke, but it had the fortuitous effect of slowing down the balloon.

Seizing his chance, Sadler ejected himself from the balloon cart. After an aborted attempt to rupture his balloon by splitting it along a seam, he had decided to make a jump for the ground while he was close enough to earth to have a reasonable chance of survival. The gale then buffeted the globe onto a tree branch, lancing the balloon so thoroughly that it deflated instantaneously, crashing to the earth almost beside him.

At 5.10pm he had landed - or, rather, ejected - at Snaith, six miles south of Selby.

Although inevitably dazed, Sadler incurred remarkably few injuries. He was taken to Selby where his conditioned was described as "fatigued, but uninjured except for his hands".

He was certainly injured financially. Only £105 was taken in ticket sales, an amount which one local newspaper rued "would almost certainly not cover the cost of the inflation alone". While hardly any locals were prepared to buy a ticket in the gale, "an immense crowd was collected in the adjacent streets". Sadler described his flight into the angry face of a gale as a "tremendous experience", which is further evidence that the Sadlers were born devoid of an anxiety gene.

Presumably at some point over the next two hundred years balloonists had compiled enough experience to decide, "maybe we shouldn't fly in gales as it's really, really dangerous." This was not a lesson any of the Sadlers learnt in their lifetime - with ultimately tragic consequences

OCTOBER 1823: LIVERPOOL GAS

Windham Sadler had by now been appointed as the manager of the Liverpool Gas Light Company, a commercial operation co-founded by his father in 1817. Sadler the elder had presumably persuaded the company's board to appoint Windham as manager in spite of his son's age and inexperience. Windham was only twenty years old at the time. Alongside his father, he was chiefly responsible for providing Liverpool with a coal gas works, predominately designed by the Sadler family. Cheap and readily manufactured coal gas was therefore only a turn of the tap away, which is probably why Windham continued moonlighting as a professional aeronaut, significantly making several flights in the north-west and utilising this local, and most probably free, gas resource.

Windham used his locally sourced coal gas for a home town flight in Liverpool that was widely described as being his twentieth ascent.

Coal gas was being used for ballooning from around 1821. The celebrated aeronaut Charles Green, who assisted Windham Sandler with a flight from Leeds in 1823, is usually credited as being the very first flyer to use coal gas for manned balloon flights, when he took off from London's Green Park on 19 July 1821.

13 OCTOBER 1823: BIRMINGHAM

Forty-nine years after his father's debut, balloonomania continued unabated - proven by a huge Birmingham crowd present for several hours before take-off to see Windham Sadler launch from the canal side area The Crescent. This time local schoolboys were entrusted with the responsibility of holding the ropes until the balloon was fully inflated.

Tickets for the inner sanctum of the launch site exchanged hands for a comparatively modest 3s 6d each, revealing that the cost of a balloon spectator's ticket had markedly declined. As had the asking price for a seat in Sadler's balloon itself. Whereas over a decade previously a balloon ride could be secured for 100 guineas, now only 20 guineas was being asked.

A Mr. James Busby had parted with 20 guineas to be Windham's co-pilot. Busby had chosen a good day to fly, as the weather was calm and the flight, uncharacteristically for Sadler involvement, was free of any incident. Flying for only 25 minutes, the pair were reunited with land four miles due west of Stourbridge after completing their journey of 17 miles.

3 APRIL 1824: PIMLICO TRAGEDY

Tragedy stuck Sadler again. His second wife Martha (née Hancock) Sadler died in Pimlico on 3 April 1824, leaving her son Windham and husband James. Almost counterbalancing his continued fortuitous survival, Sadler had now suffered the devastation of seeing two wives die.

3 MAY 1824: ROCHDALE

By 1824 the burgeoning industrial town of Rochdale required a second gas works to meet expanding demand. Hence the Rochdale Gas Light and Coke Company opened a new gasworks, built in the classically Doric architectural style, in Dane Street. For this they booked a celebrity and his balloon: step forward and into the basket, one Mr. Sadler.

Reports of the age illustrate a typically encountered research problem; we do not know which Sadler flew at Rochdale. It was almost certainly James' son Windham - after all, though James Sadler was a contender for Britain's most courageous man, even he is unlikely to have been flying again at the age of seventy-one. Even so, as with several much earlier flights in the second decade of the nineteenth century it is unclear as to whether it was father or son - Sadler senior or junior - piloting the balloon that took off at 2.30pm in serene conditions.

The balloon was supplied by the new gas company. "At nearly half-past two, Mr. Sadler and companion stepped into the car, and after receiving the flags from Lady of the High Sheriff of the county. The balloon ascended slowly from the ground, amidst the cheers of well wishers giving them every success. After continuing in sight for thirty-five minutes, the voyagers descended having travelled only eight miles. Sadler and his friend arrived again in Rochdale that afternoon, to receive the acclamations of the people."

By the 1820s the press were beginning to include occasional quotes from the main protagonists of stories, although this was still decades away from becoming the mainstream practice associated with journalism today. Windham Sadler was quoted as saying: "Everything being properly so, a [large] quantity of ballast as to allow the slow power of ascent. The balloon rose, with a slow and steady ruction of North by West as the sun shone." Another development was Sadler junior's adoption of a more cautious approach to ballooning - his father would have quite probably gone more than eight miles in 35 minutes and shed the ballast before the launch.

It is a portentous final statement from Windham Sadler, as the sun was not to shine on Sadler's son for much longer. Windham Sadler died in anything but cautious circumstances a few months later, fatally crashing into a chimney.

29 SEPTEMBER 1824: FATAL CRASH

Making what was described as his 31st ascent by newspapers and obituarists, Windham Sadler took off from Bolton in the late summer of 1824. He was piloting the balloon with his manservant James Donnelly also aboard. Again, Sadler had opted to take off in conditions described as "high wind, rain and a dense and cloudy atmosphere being most unfavourable". Similar conditions a few weeks earlier had resulted in him being repeatedly clattered against the city walls at York, before crashing violently into tree tops near Selby. Whereas in the past Windham had always got away with such obtuse recklessness, fortune was finally to turn against him.

After the restraining ropes were released, Windham's balloon rose at a disturbing pace due to a combination of high winds and likely over-inflation. Using coal gas again, he over-cautiously added more gas than was required, presumably in an attempt to avoid the problems encountered at his Sheffield and York flights.

After being airborne for quarter of an hour, visibility was so poor in the driving rain that he decided to attempt a landing. Unable to control the balloon in violent winds, he struck a chimney stack so robustly that it was knocked down. Flying over Foxhill Bank, located between Blackburn and Accrington, Windham had thrown out a grappling hook. Connecting with a tree, the sudden force of the rope caused by the balloon's velocity in the gale yanked Sadler out of the cart. He was left dangling upside down, clinging to the edge of the basket, before the constant buffeting of the car against the chimney's remaining masonry caused him to lose his grip and fall. Eyewitnesses told a Blackburn newspaper that "he fell thirty yards into a meadow".

His servant Donnelly remained in the car and was blown for a further three miles by the strong gale, until he managed to jump out with the aid of the broken grappling iron. The balloon was later discovered on the other side of the country, floating off the coast near Bridlington.

Although his servant Donnelly survived, Sadler died the next morning from injuries sustained in the crash - almost certainly without regaining consciousness. Donnelly was reported as having "injuries of a most serious kind".

Pronounced dead on 30 September 1824 in a room at an inn near the crash site where he had been taken to recuperate, he left a widow Elizabeth pregnant with his unborn daughter Catharine. At her birth she was subsequently given the middle name Windham in her late father's honour. Tragedy struck the family again, when she died in Great Crosby aged only eighteen, and was buried in the same graveyard as her father.

While a resident in Hanover Street, Liverpool, Windham had opened, along with his wife Catherine, a medicated bathing house specialising in warm vapours on the street where they lived. The successful business was maintained by his widow after Windham's untimely death.

Windham was buried, with six other members of the Sadler family including his 21-month-old son George (died in 1816) in nearby Christ Church graveyard in Hunter Street, Liverpool - a city he had helped shed light upon. His wife Catherine died in 1832.

27 MARCH 1828: DEATH AND GRUDGES

Outliving his sons Windham by eighteen months and John by ten years, James Sadler died in 1828. His second wife Martha Hancock had predeceased him in 1824. For all his reckless escapades, death cheating balloon crashes and failures to turn up for his appointments with the Grim Reaper, it was a noticeable paradox that he died peacefully in his bed at the advanced age of seventy-five. "Our little lives are ended with a sleep," as Shakespeare says.

His death was bizarrely recorded by the *Oxford University Herald* three days later in the briefest of mentions, when the newspaper baldly stated: "Mr James Sadler, elder brother of Mr Sadler of Rose Hill, Oxford has died." Not a jot about his internationally famous career as a world-changing aeronaut and inventor. James Sadler's death made the front pages in France, but not in his own town. Sadler's brother Thomas, star of the one line Oxford University official obituary, died a year later in 1829.

It seems that Oxford University was not prepared to end the grudge with Sadler just because he had died. In spite of being one of Britain's brightest stars, Sadler only received one long paragraph for his obituary in *Jackson's Oxford Journal*. Sadler had somehow made a powerful enemy, with Oxford University culpable in attempting to downgrade his achievements, though ultimately unsuccessful in its campaign to airbrush him out of history.

His epitaph had been uttered during his lifetime, when Sir John Coxe Hippisley noted in 1812 that Sadler "has been harshly used. There is not a better chemist or mechanic in the Universe, yet he can hardly speak a word of Grammar."

Dr. John Fisher, writing a letter to his friend the celebrated painter John Constable on 31 May 1824, had earlier revealed the whereabouts of a retired Sadler. The letter rather drips with contempt for Sadler's circumstances as a pensioner in an alms-house lodging. And yet he offsets this somewhat by mentioning his noble achievements. So much for being afforded National Treasure status. The letter the celebrated *Hay Wain* painter received informed him:

> Sadler the aeronaut is a pensioner at the Charterhouse. How scheming,
> beggars a man. He was a pastry cook in good business in Oxford. He
> drank tea at the Lodge the other day, being an old crony of my father.
> He says he used all his powers of persuasion with Harris to abandon
> the voyage, for he knew him to be ignorant of the management of a
> balloon. Sadler has made fifty voyages.

The letter confirms one of Sadler's last known whereabouts, and crowns him as
the achiever of fifty flights.

Lieutenant Thomas Harris, whom Sadler apparently attempted to dissuade
from aeronautical adventure, had been killed on 25 May 1824 when falling
out of his balloon basket after hitting an oak tree near Carshalton in Surrey.
Courageously, Harris' uncle immediately announced his intention to fly in the
same balloon that had cost his nephew his life, in order to raise funds to support
Harris' widow, who had also been in the balloon basket at the time of the fatal
crash, yet survived with serious injuries. The *Morning Chronicle* reported a few
days later that the fundraising flight had been a success and crucially not claimed
any more lives.

Charterhouse in Smithfield, London, still provides the same function today,
housing forty "brothers" who require financial assistance in alms houses. Daniel
Defoe, credited with inventing the novel, was moved to observe obsequiously
in 1722: "Charterhouse is the greatest and noblest gift that was ever given for
charity, by any one man public or private in this nation." Nice try, Defoe, but
clearly not obsequious enough as he wasn't offered a place.

Sadler was conferred as a Brother of Charterhouse by none other than
reigning monarch King George IV, and was also given a civil pension allowance
to match. He lived here from 1824 until the winter of 1827, when he returned
to Oxford. The need for state charity revealed his abject lack of wealth in spite of
being a household celebrity for over half a century.

Indeed, Sadler died in penniless obscurity, admired in his lifetime but
destined to be uncrowned by future generations. The ODNB merely confirms:
"Wealth at death: very little." Yet had Sadler even begun to collect the fortunes
in admission fees owed to him from his exhibition flights, and placed proper
patents for his cannons, steam engines, rifles and naval inventions, then he
would have been a wealthy man.

Sadler's name ought to be remembered as long as there is an England.
Unfortunately that appears unlikely to happen. The winds of fashion change
course. And although Sadler was successful at finding the wind direction he
wanted in his lifetime, his subsequent fame has encountered fluctuating

conditions. Over two hundred years later, that wind is perhaps changing direction again. Sadler's reputation may yet rise into the jetstream of not only aeronautical history, but British history too.

Fittingly, Sadler's great-great-nephew was Professor Herbert Charles Sadler. He certainly inherited the family genes, being employed by the US Department of Naval Architecture and Marine Engineering. Moreover, he was instrumental in pioneering flight - this time in glider designing. He took part in exhibition flights with the Wright Brothers and other pioneering aviators of the age in Boston, Massachusetts. Bet he baked a mean pastry too.

But as Sadler knew, no one can control the direction the wind blows in - and that is true of the winds of fashion. Just as no historical biography these days could possibly open with its subject's date and place of birth and conclude chronologically with details of their death.

James Sadler died in George Lane (now George Street), Oxford on 27 March 1828.

EPILOGUE: THE BEGINNING? KING OF THE CASTLE AT LAST

Fully forty years since my last visit I am back at Tattersall Castle. This is my Everest.

I set up base camp in the Castle's seating area, munching on posh crisps bought from the shop, while strategising my ascent. To conquer Everest mountaineers endure exhaustion, thinning oxygen, extreme cold and vertiginous altitude, but not the menace that I have to beat if I am to reach the summit of Tattersall Castle's battements: people persuading you to join the National Trust.

They are very persuasive. Join today and you get your first heritage building admission refunded - like a drug dealer keen to give you your first gram of smack for free. Maybe a lot fewer castles would have been breached in history if, instead of battlements and moats, defenders had placed National Trust salesmen to repel invaders. "If you are planning to invade and ransack only two more castles in the next twelve months, then you are definitely better off joining today."

Somehow I make it inside by paying only the entrance fee. Inside, other visitors give me a "how did you manage to do that?" look. A couple are visiting from Russia, the only time they've been to the UK, and somehow they got suckered into the annual membership. No one leaves the National Trust. You think you can, but you can't.

Drink, crisps and a reasonably priced sandwich from the castle's shop downed in the tea room (thankfully they no longer sell Cresta), I head straight for the steps. No distractions. Yes, there is a room with an impressively large fire place and some tapestries, but I am here for a set purpose, a mission. It's time to complete the task I so spectacularly failed forty years ago.

The stairs are still intimidating. They really are. A seemingly endless spiral staircase, with a red brick wall constantly circling away to my left, steps fanning out from a central stone pole. There is dust on the steps. Instinctively I head to the extreme left, utilising the widest part of each step. My heart is pumping. My brain is anything but calm. I clutch the stone handrail set back into the wall. But only briefly, as I want to increase my pace.

Already I know I can do this. I am not enjoying the experience, but that doesn't matter. What matters is my confidence that I will succeed. I know I can. Just keep going.

I attempt to radio-jam the anxiety signals my brain is transmitting by getting another part of my conflicting mind to emit CBT mantras. "The danger is imagined not real." Determined, I keep going. My pace picks up. I think about

Miss Harrison. I guess where my tears would have fallen, where I froze and could not continue. Back then I was physically incapable of moving my healthy legs. If anything, today my legs are moving too fast. I am rushing to accomplish this. Snatching not taking the opportunity. Yes, I want the ordeal to be over. As quickly as possible. But I make myself slow down. That will make striding up the stairs easier. And safer.

Remembering the breathing techniques Claire and Steve taught me, I think of their shared determination that I can do this. I recollect the advice the Aussie model gave me, how that posh schoolgirl spotted so easily my bathmophobia affliction, and that time I was stuck in fear on church tower steps with my first girlfriend. I recall the perceptive insights Dr. Hannah gave me, rolling back my ignorance to reveal how a phobia works. Once you understand how the circuitry works, you can start tampering with it. I am the captain of my brain ship. I'm the one at the wheel of HMS *Richard's Brain*. And she's steering a course full steam ahead.

I climb the 149th step out of the 150 on the spiral. I pause. This time voluntarily. Raise my head high and take a big final stride towards the daylight.

What, no raining ticker-tape? No knightly trumpeted fanfare?

My reward is the view from the roof. No, I am not ready yet to approach the edge. Or go anywhere near it. I am not yet completely rehabilitated. But there are fine 360-degree views of the Lincolnshire flatlands. Rows of cabbages in a nearby field are lined up in military precision like soldiers awaiting inspection, planning to attack the castle's defences.

My other reward, bigger than an admittedly splendid view, is the accomplishment. I am as proud of my helpers as I am of myself. A bathmophobe who is finally king of the castle, even if forty years late. If I can do this, then there is hope for others whose lives are restricted by phobias. A glossophobe can address a room of people. A lifelong arachnophobe can pick a spider out of the bath, even one of those spiders that are so big they probably change TV channels whenever you vacate a room. A crocodyliphobe can... hang on, having a debilitating fear of crocodiles is not irrational - in fact it comes highly recommended.

I can now go upstairs on a bus. In fact, most staircases no longer bother me, to the extent that I would no longer consider myself bathmophobic - more of an ex-bathmophobe. It is surprisingly how quickly the new norm replaces the old normal. Although I still do not willingly embrace heights, I can now tolerate them enough for acrophobia to stop being a barrier excluding me from life experiences.

However, I am unlikely to sit on a girder eating my packed lunch alongside those workers who built the Manhattan skyline, as depicted in that iconic photograph.

That's for two reasons: 1. I'm not an idiot. OK, make that three reasons. 2. I am only partially rehabilitated 3. Though I'm crucially free of the restrictions I previously placed on myself by avoiding stairs and heights, I cannot manage unnecessary exposure to extremely dangerous heights.

But here's the thing. The Big Thing. I never expected to be cured. This is why my counsellors disqualified the term "cure" from being used in our sessions. Instead, I have crucially learnt to manage, and thereby control, my anxieties and phobias. And from there I expect them to recede naturally, not grow exponentially as they did when remaining unaddressed for decades. It is as if trained engineers, counsellors and educators have begun rewiring my brain, altering my neuro plasticity, allowing me to begin viewing the future with an unrepentant optimism.

ABOUT THE AUTHOR

My publisher requires a list of my achievements for an 'About the Author' section. Hence, here is a list:

1. I'm rubbish at compiling lists.

3. And even worse at counting.

2. Told you.

4. I co-wrote the UK screenplay for the 2014 movie *The Unbeatables* starring Rupert Grint and Rob Brydon directed by Best Foreign Picture Oscar-winner Juan José Campanella.

5. Hugh Dennis said my 2013 book documenting the world's stupidest criminals, *As Thick As Thieves*, made him "regret not taking up a life of crime". It was an Amazon no. 1 Bestseller.

6. I write for BBC Radio 4's *The News Quiz* and *The Now Show*. Yes, that's how I met Hugh Dennis.

7. I wrote a book about *Britain's Most Eccentric Sports*. It was described by Dr. Phil Hammond as "very, very funny!" German comic Henning Wehn said, "it's better than all 26 days of a cricket match."

8. Before that I wrote *Oxford Student Pranks: a History of Mischief & Mayhem*, TV's Dr. Lucy Worsley said, "I was expecting it to be a jape-filled jamboree of jollity, but it turned out to be full of sex and violence as well."

9. I also write for BBC2's *Dara O'Briain's Science Club*.

10. Somehow I once won the National Football Writer of the Year Award and am a Chortle comedy award winner.

11. I pen a monthly Oxfordshire Limited Edition column for *The Oxford Times*.

13. Unluckily, my counting has not improved.

ACKNOWLEDGEMENTS

Enormous thanks to top archivist and librarian Scott McLachlan. Without Scott's research skills this book would not have been accomplished. He helped me track down the myriad contemporary newspaper sources, as well as the later specialist aerostation literature, which help form the recognisable narrative of Sadler's strange life.

Thanks to: Sophie Clarke, Kim Curran, Mark Davies, Hugh Dennis, Jennifer Elliott, James Ferguson, Matthew Ledbury, Oliver Ledbury, David Raymond, Dr. Hannah Stratford, Martha Tilston, Catherine Wolfe-Smith, Lucy Porter, Dr. Lucy Worsley, Adventure Balloons Company, St. Edmund Hall Oxford and all my counsellors, especially the real Steve and Claire.

Special thanks to biographer extraordinaire Frances Wilson for confirming that this book was a Very Good Idea and boldly encouraging me to write it.

If you have been affected by any topics raised in this book, then further information is available from:

Cognitive Behaviour Therapy:
http://www.babcp.com/Default.aspx

Comedy books:
http://www.amazon.co.uk/Richard-O.-Smith/e/B005FXQP1A/ref=ntt_athr_dp_pel_1